THOMAS MATTHEWS'S WELSH RECORDS IN PARIS

Great Seal of Owain Glyndŵr.
Frontispiece to *Welsh Records in Paris* (1910)

Thomas Matthews's Welsh Records in Paris

A Study in Selected Welsh Medieval Records

Dylan Rees
J. Gwynfor Jones

UNIVERSITY OF WALES PRESS
CARDIFF

www.uwp.co.uk

British Library CIP Data
A catalogue record for this book is available from the British Library.

ISBN 978-0-7083-2301-4
e-ISBN 978-0-7083-2302-1

Printed in Great Britain by CPI Antony Rowe, Chippenham, Wiltshire.

CONTENTS

List of Illustrations

Preface

Thomas Matthews, whose native language was Welsh, has been described among other things as an '*arloeswr*' – a pioneer. Such a description, while fully merited, does not do full justice to the scale and scope of his interests. In the decades following his death in 1916 his contribution to Welsh culture was slowly, almost imperceptibly overlooked, neglected and ultimately largely forgotten. His numerous books were never republished and there was hardly any interest, scholarly or otherwise, in his life and work. The one exception was *Welsh Records in Paris* (1910) with its collection of documents, translations and commentaries, especially those relating to Owain Glyndŵr. This work ensured that at least the small number of historians, who made use of his sources, were to some extent aware of him, if they knew very little regarding his background. Starting in the 1990s there emerged a renewed interest in Matthews' and he is cited in a number of Welsh language works, mostly relating to art history. This interest has been largely sustained into the present century. The centenary of the publication of *Welsh Records in Paris* is therefore an appropriate time to examine and evaluate Thomas Matthews's contribution to Welsh literature, history and the arts.

This book has a number of aims. Firstly, to provide an overview of Matthews's life and examine the breadth and range of his work and interests in the context of a Wales experiencing rapid industrial and social change. Secondly, to consider the role of Matthews as a medieval historian and carefully to re-examine his judgements and place in Welsh historiography. Our third aim is once again to make available the complete unabridged 1910 text of *Welsh Records in Paris*, so that its sources, translations and facsimiles can be accessed more easily by anyone interested in Welsh medieval history, and particularly the life of Owain Glyndŵr.

Matthews expressed the hope that *Welsh Records in Paris* would 'in some way be of service to students of the History of Wales'. We fully endorse his original aim, and would like to add our own hope that the present work will also prove to be of use to those interested in Welsh literature and the arts during the early years of the twentieth century.

Acknowledgements

I have solicited many favours and incurred numerous debts while researching the life and work of Tom Matthews. Particular thanks are due to the following, for whom no request was too great and whose patience and courtesy appeared at times limitless: the various staffs at the National Library of Wales in Aberystwyth, Swansea Central Library, Carmarthen Library and Carmarthenshire County Record Office. Valuable information was provided by the following: Professor Huw Pryce, Brian Hopkins, Iwan Jones (who kindly allowed me access to his papers), Marc Ward of the National Art Library and Jean Rose, archivist for the Random House Group, and Philip Sutton RA, for allowing his work to be reproduced for the dust jacket. Particular thanks to the following colleagues at Gorseinon College who acceded without demur to every request for help which I made of them: Andrew Gardiner, Jarrod Waldie and Neris Morris. I gratefully acknowledge the generous research grant provided by Carmarthenshire Antiquarian Society, which greatly facilitated my work. The University of Wales Press, and Sarah Lewis in particular, have guided me through the various stages of publication and kept faith with the project over a number of years, and I am enormously grateful to them for their help and encouragement. I wish to pay particular thanks to Professor J. Gwynfor Jones, who agreed without hesitation to join me in producing this volume, and whose unstinting support has been most welcome. My final debt is to my family, Claire, Carys and Morgan who willingly accepted the lengthy absences incurred in working on this book, which is dedicated to them.

Dylan Rees

It has been my privilege to co-operate with Mr Dylan Rees in the preparation and publication of this volume which contains *Welsh Records in Paris* by Thomas Matthews, a pioneer among Welsh historians in the early twentieth century. I wish to thank Dylan for his full support and for allowing me to examine copies of some of Matthews's correspondence deposited at the National Library of Wales, Aberystwyth.

J. Gwynfor Jones

I Claire, Carys a Morgan
Gyda chariad a diolch am eu cymorth a'u hysbrydoliaeth

An Introduction to Thomas Matthews: The Man in his Time

With the centenary of the publication of *Welsh Records in Paris* (1910), it is fitting that this important work, which has never been reprinted but which is routinely used by historians researching into medieval Wales, is once again available to those who share Thomas Matthews's interest in this aspect of our nation's past. Copies of the original are nowadays rarely seen on the open market and when available are usually secured through the antiquarian book trade where they can command premium prices. They can still be accessed, however, in our more established reference and university libraries.[1] If at times the book can appear elusive, what of its author? Sadly, his fate is rather less satisfactory than the book with which he is usually most readily identified. Thomas Matthews died on 6 September 1916 at his beloved home, Eryl, in Kings Road, Llandybïe, Carmarthenshire. His death was in many ways overshadowed by the far greater tragedy unfolding that autumn, on the battlefields of the Somme in north–eastern France, one of the bloodiest chapters in our country's history. This was reflected in the local press where his passing was recorded in a respectful yet rather brief notice.[2] While Matthews's death was mourned by those who knew him well, it was but one among thousands that summer and autumn across Wales. Those from the village who made the ultimate sacrifice in the service of their country were appropriately honoured in the parish church. There is, however, no such memorial to Matthews in the church or anywhere else in the village.[3]

Posterity has not looked favourably on the reputation and contribution of Thomas Matthews to the cultural life of Wales. There is no reference to him in the *Dictionary of Welsh Biography* or J. E. Lloyd's monumental *History of Carmarthenshire* (vol. II, 1939). Even highly acclaimed works published in the recent past by John Davies and K. O. Morgan pass over his career and work.[4] Yet there are tantalizing fragments strewn across several books that offer glimpses of what he achieved in a comparatively short but intense period of activity spanning little more than the half-dozen years preceding his death (1910–16). The first substantive trace appeared appropriately in Gomer M. Roberts's acclaimed *Hanes Plwyf Llandybïe* (1939). Roberts knew Matthews well and devoted a section in his summation of the literary tradition of the parish to his friend.[5] In the decades following the Second World War Matthews all but vanished without trace from our cultural vista. It was almost as if he had never existed. Yet exist he most certainly did, and few of his generation lit the intellectual sky as brightly and brilliantly in his day as Tom Matthews. He has left in published and unpublished form a considerable corpus of material in both Welsh and English on a broad range of different topics reflecting his own interests and the causes which he embraced with such vigour and passion during his lifetime. In more recent years there has been a perceptibly slow and rather disparate recognition of some aspects of his work. The more numerous references which can be identified relate to his passion for visual culture in general and art in particular.[6] It is hoped that this short introduction will offer an insight into the range of work which Matthews produced and the causes which he championed, while at the same time setting him in the context of his age.

South Wales during the last quarter of the nineteenth century experienced widespread economic change. Industrialization was gathering pace, particularly in the mining and metallurgical industries. The insatiable demand for labour resulted in a rapidly expanding population as inward migration patterns took advantage of an improving railway network to facilitate the relocation of people from rural counties on both sides of the Welsh border into the Valleys running through the south Wales coalfield and into the adjacent coastal towns.[7] In marked contrast to the boom conditions experienced in the industrial areas of south Wales was the poverty of the countryside as agriculture, the bedrock of rural economies, slipped into a deep and prolonged depression.[8] As the populations of rural villages and parishes stagnated and then declined, those of the new communities which grew around coal mines, tinplate, copper and steel works expanded rapidly. The wide range of opportunities in these industrial towns and villages for wealth creation contributed to the emergence of a new indigenous urban bourgeoisie with its own aspirations for social and political advancement and also a range of cultural needs.

Many of the new migrants into the south Wales coalfield came from the surrounding rural counties of Cardiganshire, Pembrokeshire and north Carmarthenshire. They brought with them two features which in no small measure helped shape the cultural dynamic of this new society, namely the Welsh language and their Nonconformist religion. In some ways the two were synonymous as the Welsh language was the dominant medium in the new chapels.[9] Around the chapels, a flourishing culture emerged based on singing, reciting poetry, powerful preaching and the study of the Scriptures. The chapels helped sustain and nurture Wales's unique cultural identity centred around the various local and national eisteddfodau.[10] It would be misleading to suggest that the whole of the newly- emerging urban community was upright and sober, and attended chapel on a regular basis. Equally popular as alternative sources of entertainment and pleasure were the public houses, rugby, football and a myriad other pursuits and pastimes.[11] But Nonconformity was sufficiently embedded in the national consciousness to help shape many of the traits associated with late Victorian Wales. Among the foremost of these was a passionate belief in the value of education as a means of providing opportunities for those of humble birth and modest means to escape from the urban and social deprivation that were the worst features of rapid industrialization. The Education Act of 1870 established a network of elementary school boards in those areas which had no access to the provision made by the Anglican Church's National Society, or the Nonconformist British and Foreign Schools Society. Although tensions between the state and the Nonconformists over payments to support the new system would simmer, and ultimately boil over in the opening decade of the twentieth century into the 'Welsh Revolt', large numbers of Welsh children took full advantage of these opportunities to gain a firm grounding in the three Rs.[12] The Welsh Intermediate Schools Act 1889 offered the tantalizing prospect of secondary education for able working-class children if they succeeded in gaining a scholarship to pay for their fees to the new County Schools. By 1903 there were ninety-five County Schools across Wales educating a total of 8,789 pupils.[13]

The rapid industrialization that was occurring, particularly in south Wales, was generating enormous wealth, which in turn helped bring about profound and lasting social change. In essence this added up to 'a kind of national renaissance'.[14] Wales had acquired its first University College in 1872 when Aberystwyth opened its doors to undergraduates. Following the recommendations of the Aberdare Report of 1881 two more colleges were established at Cardiff (1883) and Bangor (1884). The three colleges joined together to form the federal University of Wales which came into existence in 1896. This was almost the first distinctively Welsh institution since the abolition of the Court of Great Sessions in 1830. Other important national institutions would follow in the new century. In 1905 approval was given for the establishment of a National Library at Aberystwyth. A Royal Charter was granted in 1907 to incorporate a National Museum which was to be based in Cardiff, the recently designated capital city of Wales (1905).[15] Among the most powerful of stimuli to the cultural renaissance which was also taking place was the National Eisteddfod, an annual festival of the arts which traversed Wales from north to south in alternate years. The focus of this annual festival was essentially literature and music, with the highlights being the crowning and chairing of the bards. Arts and crafts were viewed very much as the poor relation of the spoken, sung and written word. Wales was not considered to have any visual culture worth merit. It was not until the Aberdare eisteddfod of 1861 that a serious attempt was made to incorporate arts and crafts into the competitive part of the eisteddfod.[16] It would take the vision of T. H. Thomas (Arlunydd Penygarn) to bring arts and crafts fully into the main body of the festival.

An equally important aspect of this cultural renaissance, particularly in helping to create a sense of identity was the renewed interest in the history of Wales. For many outside Wales the Principality was nothing more than an appendage of England, notoriously summed up in the reference in the index of the *Encyclopaedia Britannica* '– for Wales – see England'. While numerous eisteddfodau offered prizes for the submission of local histories, often of variable quality, interpreting the past of Wales was very much the preserve of professional historians.[17] Foremost among these was J. E. Lloyd, whose seminal work, published in 1913, was a two-volume history of Wales before the Edwardian conquest – a perceived golden period when Wales was free from the Saxon yoke. He would later produce a study of that most iconic of Welsh historical figures Owain Glyndŵr. To counter the rather elitist and erudite work produced by Lloyd there was a need for a more populist approach. This was provided by another of the great figures in this cultural renaissance, Owen M. Edwards, 'perhaps the most powerful single personal influence upon the generation up to 1914'.[18] Occupying a pivotal role in the educational and cultural life of Wales, Edwards founded a number of periodicals aimed at various groups from children to adults interested in cultural issues and on to more serious academics. In 1891 he launched one of his most influential magazines, the monthly *Cymru*, which covered a range of literary and artistic themes in an accessible and engaging way aimed at educating and entertaining the more culturally aware of the Welsh working and middle classes.[19] The society in which Tom Matthews lived, worked and socialized was both vibrant and dynamic, yet appeared slightly unsure about the direction it was taking.

In the political world, socialism was becoming firmly rooted in the south Wales Valleys and was challenging the hegemony established by Liberalism and its Nonconformist allies. Matthews in his own way contributed to providing Welsh society with a sense of identity and in opening up for wider audiences a range of interests which had previously been the preserve of the rich, the privileged and the well educated. Through his writing, research and connections he emerged as a staunch nationalist and champion of the riches buried deep in Welsh culture.

Tom Matthews was born on 3 September 1874 in Glangwendraeth in the parish of Llannon, Carmarthenshire. He was the eldest of eight children of Robert and Elizabeth Matthews. Robert Matthews came from Clydach in the neighbouring county of Glamorgan, and was employed as a schoolmaster in the Gwendraeth Valley at the time of his eldest son's birth. Tom's mother Elizabeth was a native of Carmarthenshire, having been born and brought up in Llangyndeyrn. Before Tom was two years old, his father moved the family to Llandybïe in January 1876 when he was appointed headmaster of the village's National School, a position he would retain until his retirement in 1917.[20] At Llandybïe the Matthews household expanded rapidly and seven other children were born, although only four would survive beyond infancy.[21] In seeking to explain what helped nurture and forment Tom Matthews' interests his background is a rather obvious initial point of reference. By all accounts it was a loving and caring household which provided a stimulating environment for the children to develop and refine their intellects. Robert Matthews occupied a position of considerable status and responsibility in the village, and during his spare time was a keen naturalist and fisherman, a talented musician and a witty and engaging companion. Very much a pillar of his local community, he served as chairman of the Llandeilo Board of Guardians in 1916.[22] Some doubt was cast on this rather idyllic and cultured upbringing in which Tom Matthews grew up, in an obituary published in the pages of *Cymru* in November 1916. The writer suggested that Matthews's schooldays, in the charge of his father, were fairly aimless and uninspiring, and that his knowledge of Welsh was in effect rather rudimentary.[23] The article went on to claim that the defining moment in the young Matthews's formative years occurred when he chanced upon the bright red cover of the first copy of the periodical *Cymru* in a local newsagent. Inspired by what he read, he bought as many of the subsequent copies as he could and voraciously consumed their content. These issues of *Cymru*, we are told, opened his eyes to the history of Wales, broadened his understanding of Welsh literature and in essence redirected the trajectory of his life. He was a young man transformed, who from that day forth became an avid reader, thoroughly immersing himself in Welsh culture. Whether the self-congratulatory tone of the obituary in taking credit for helping to launch the young Matthews on the road to literary and cultural success is in any way accurate is difficult to discern.[24] What is clear is that his home environment, under the care of Robert and Elizabeth Matthews, was steeped in Welsh culture. Robert was a gifted and talented teacher who was clearly an inspirational figure and later mentor to his son. In the Matthews household Welsh was certainly the language of the hearth and it is difficult to imagine that the children would have flourished so well had life at home been in any way arid and sterile.[25]

In 1880 Tom Matthews entered the village school in Llandybïe to undertake his elementary education. The village and parish of Llandybïe in which the young Mathews grew up and was educated were situated right on the margins of the south Wales coalfield. It was a village with a very distinct character, embracing as it did both the traditions of a typical Welsh country village and those allied with the newly emerging industrial communities. The anthracite coal seams which traversed the central portion of the parish were under laid by the carboniferous limestone measures which marked the northern boundary of the coalfield. Colliers in the village referred to the limestone outcrops as the farewell rock beyond which there was no more coal. Mining and limestone quarrying coexisted comfortably with arable and dairy farming and more traditional rural crafts and trades such as coopers, blacksmiths, corn milling, hat making, and woollen weaving. The industrial developments in the parish were mirrored in its demographic changes, which over the course of Thomas Matthews's life saw significant population growth.[26] One way in which this growth impacted itself directly upon Robert Matthews was the pressure on accommodation in the village school. A log book entry for 2 November 1877, records: 'the School is crowded to such an extent that we find great difficulty in doing ordinary work.' At the annual examination held at the end of that month it was noted that 'the greater part of the Third Standard had to do their exercises kneeling'.[27] Yet, despite these changes, the village did in many ways manage to retain its character and distinctiveness. Llandybïe with its surrounding area was more than blessed with its fair share of legends, folk traditions and a wide variety of pastimes, local festivals and pursuits. Among the more distinctive of these were those relating to sin eating, mock mayors, *priodas geffylau* and the *gwylnos*. There were also well-known local legends linked with Owain Lawgoch and the Dinas limestone outcrop just outside the village, and the lake of Llyn Llech Owain near Gorslas.[28] The parish's thirst for Welsh arts was quenched annually at a well-established local eisteddfod offering a range of prizes in various musical, choral and literary competitions.[29] This would also be accompanied by a carnival, concerts and competitions in quoits and timbering.

At the age of fourteen, Tom Matthews in 1888 completed his elementary education. It was quite usual in the late nineteenth century for able pupils to stay on in an elementary school beyond the age of eleven, to develop their education further, if there was no opportunity to progress on to a secondary school. The nearest school to Llandybïe which offered secondary education was Llandovery College a fee-paying public school beyond the means of a humble schoolmaster with an expanding family. Although county schools were established in the vicinity of Llandybïe in the near future the opportunity to attend these came too late for Matthews to benefit.[30] It is likely that, at the behest of his father, the next stage in Matthews's education would help set him on the path to the profession which he would ultimately embrace with such conviction. Matthews became articled to his father as a pupil teacher – a trainee who would shadow a more experienced practitioner with a view to qualifying into the profession after a six-year period. Although details of the terms of his employment are unknown, they are unlikely to differ in any significant way from those offered to his sister Bessie, who was accepted as a pupil- teacher in 1894 at an annual salary of £7 for the first year, with an increase of £1 a year in each subsequent year of the agreement.[31] One of Matthews's contemporaries who started as a pupil teacher at the same time recalls their training:

> Tom Matthews and I sat our annual secular examinations at Llanelly (on Saturdays), our Scripture examinations at Llandeilo, Science and Art at Hendy and the Queens Scholarship at Carmarthen Training College. Tom and I picked up many a half-crown by slipping up to the Church during playtime to ring the bells after weddings. We were well in with Mari Bowen the Caretaker.[32]

Having successfully completed his training in 1894 he worked for a term in a neighbouring school. The following year he applied for and was successful in gaining an award which allowed him to study for the Board of Education's elementary education certificate at the University College of Wales in Cardiff. After gaining this qualification he enrolled as a full-time student in the faculty of arts to study a course in English and graduated with a third-class honours degree in 1899. Following his graduation and already having savoured the joys of working with children, it was a relatively easy decision for Tom Matthews to embark on a teaching career. As a graduate his employment prospects were considerably enhanced and he was able to apply for work in the more prestigious and better paid county or intermediate schools. During the next decade he worked in a number of intermediate schools in various parts of Wales: the County School Pwllheli, 1900–1; Ynys-fach (Resolven) Vale of Neath Pupil Teacher Centre, 1901–5; and the County School, Fishguard. While at Fishguard he joined the local lodge of Freemasons and progressed up the Order becoming ultimately a grand master.

The general revival of interest in Welsh culture during the Edwardian period clearly struck a chord with Matthews. In his spare time he was becoming increasingly interested in a range of literary and cultural issues. During this period he decided to resume his studies by researching for a higher degree at the University College in Cardiff. As a graduate in English he returned to this area for his research, and in 1908 was awarded an MA for a dissertation on 'The History and Significance of Early Elizabethan Drama'.[33]

During this time Matthews became a regular figure at the Annual National Eisteddfod and forged a number of lasting friendships with several literary and artistic figures. At the 1906 National Eisteddfod held in Caernarfon he was admitted into the *Gorsedd* of bards. He would remain passionately committed to the eisteddfod's ideals of both preserving and showcasing the very best of Welsh culture and the arts at its annual festival. As a single man with few commitments, a regular salary and lengthy vacations, he was also able to travel. His first of many foreign excursions was in 1901 when he boarded a coal ship out of one of the south Wales ports bound for Brittany. He spent several weeks travelling and absorbing the culture of a kindred Celtic nation, and retained until his death a great love and affection for the Breton people, and especially their language.[34] According to one of his friends, R. W. Jones, it was during his time at Fishguard that a fire kindled in his breast which burned fiercely for the rest of his life to study the literature and history of his country.[35] Matthews left Fishguard County School in 1908 to devote more time to a number of research projects he had embarked on and wished to guide through to publication. Some of these including *Welsh Records in Paris*, would require travelling abroad. He moved back to stay with his parents in Llandybïe and when an opportunity occurred he provided cover for a term at Ysgol y Gwynfryn in Ammanford during Gwili's absence. Following the publication of his first two books, Matthews sought to return to full-time teaching and looked around for a suitable position. In April 1911 he was successful in gaining a post as the first specialist Welsh teacher at one of the most prestigious schools in south Wales – Lewis Boys' School in Pengam, described by some as the Eton of the Valleys.[36]

It is not an easy task to apply an appropriate appellation to the life and work of Tom Matthews. The varied and multifaceted nature of his sometimes eclectic interests defies simple categorization and moreover contain a number of inherent contradictions. He did not study history in any formal way while at university, yet he displayed a keen interest in the subject throughout his life and made a singular bequest in this field. His degree was in English, yet Welsh was the language in which many of his most significant contributions to Welsh culture were made. Although without any formal training in art criticism, he immersed himself deeply in the visual culture of Wales and sought to popularize art for a mass audience. Yet the art which he championed, eschewed the avant-garde and cutting edge of his day, even among contemporary Welsh artists, in favour of those ploughing a more traditional and formal, academic furrow. In broad terms, the essence of his legacy to the intellectual and cultural life of Wales rests on three quite distinct areas, namely Welsh history and folklore; language literature and national identity; and the role of visual culture in Wales.

Welsh History and Folklore

The renewed interest in Welsh history was one of the driving forces behind the formation of the Carmarthenshire Antiquarian Society in 1905. Although Tom Matthews was not a founder member, he joined shortly afterwards in 1907 and remained committed to the society and its ideals and was proud of his association with it. He became very friendly with the second president of the society and one of its key figures, Alan Stepney-Gulston of Derwydd. Although Matthews and Stepney-Gulston lived in the same parish the contrast between their life styles was vast. While Matthews came from a comparatively modest background, Stepney-Gulston was one of the county's largest landowners and possessor of an ancient lineage stretching back hundreds of years. What they had in common was a shared love of Welsh history in all its guises – people, events, traditions, artefacts and records.[37] It was in the pages of the society's periodical, the *Transactions*, that Matthews published his first article on Welsh history, a short item on the Carmarthen election of 1796. It was little more than a narrative account of the event accompanied by very little analysis, and suggested no real hint of any particular flair in this field.[38] Much more interesting and suggestive of his future interests was a series of linked articles on Owain Lawgoch and the local legend associated with Llyn Llech Owain, which he began in May 1910.[39] In these articles Matthews displayed a rare talent for combining local tradition and folklore, relating to Owain's supposed final resting place at Ogof Cilyrychen, part of the Dinas limestone outcrop near Llandybïe, with an almost forensic contextual analysis of a range of medieval sources from Geoffrey of Monmouth to the Harleian MS. In a further article exploring the origin of the 'Cath' place-names, it is clear that working closely with primary sources was kindling an interest in philology and that he was willing to engage in debate with others on the accuracy of his interpretations.[40] His awareness of the richness and variety of popular traditions and culture took on a tangible form when he donated an item from Llandybïe, used in New Year celebrations to the recently formed National Museum. A number of years later he and a group of friends proposed forming a Welsh Folk Society, although nothing appears to have resulted from the suggestion[41] Matthews's curiosity and passion for Welsh history was undoubtedly fired as a result of working on so many original manuscripts. His expanding interest coincided with a renewed interest in Welsh culture in general and a curiosity about the origins and essential features of the nation's past. It may well have been the many hours spent researching historical documents which led him to decide to embark on a project to try and locate, identify, transcribe, catalogue and publish those Welsh records secreted away in foreign libraries.

During one of his visits to Brittany Matthews had struck up a close friendship with a young Breton academic, Paul Diverrès. The two shared a range of interests in cultural and historical themes and resolved to help one another as far as possible in carrying out their respective researches.[42] A detailed correspondence ensued in which Matthews helped Diverrès with his research into the Arthurian legend. He also offered to translate for him, part of the *Mabinogion* into Breton.[43] In return Matthews asked his friend if he could locate and transcribe for him some manuscript sources relating to Wales in the École des Chartes and the Bibliothèque Nationale in Paris. Matthews was also proposing to 'prepare for School purposes a book of Celtic tales'.[44] As it turned out, nothing came of this project or of a number of others he aired, but the search for records relating to Wales would be developed further.[45] In the course of 1908 Matthews took the decision to resign his position at the County School in Fishguard and devote his energies to full-time research. The focus of his attention was clearly medieval Welsh history, particularly the study of any surviving manuscripts from the period. He was continuing to support the work of his friend and agreed to prepare for him a translation with notes, of one of the great treasures of Welsh literature, *The Black Book of Carmarthen*. Matthews's own thoughts appear to have crystallized into a plan to locate and transcribe all surviving documents relating to Wales in foreign libraries and archives. This was an ambitious project, and he hoped to use his contacts with friends in Brittany to support his work. By late 1908 Paul Diverrès and another Breton friend, Yves Berthou (Grand Druid of Brittany) were both living in Paris and able to provide him with accommodation during his stay in the city.

The challenge which Matthews had set himself of tracking down and producing a catalogue of all manuscript sources relating to Wales was not in essence original. Edward Owen had already embarked on a similar project to identify Welsh records held in the British Museum.[46] Matthews hoped his work would complement Owen's by casting the net wider to encompass the major European libraries and archives. Given his contacts in Paris, the Archives Nationales was the obvious starting-point for his project. He left Llandybïe on 26 December 1908, taking the cheaper route to Paris via Le Havre.[47] Matthews stayed a little over a fortnight in the city and clearly worked very quickly, visiting a number of locations and transcribing and arranging for photographic copies to be made of the small number of manuscripts which he identified. The speed of his work laid him open to the charge of carelessness and oversight.[48] During the months following his return from Paris he was engaged in sometimes lengthy discussions over the quality of these photographic reproductions of some of the original documents to be included in the book which he planned to publish. The result of his tireless efforts was the work which more than any other cements his place in the historiography of his nation, *Welsh Records in Paris*, which in its day was a piece of unique research and transcription relating to important sources of medieval Welsh history in foreign archives. In the preface, which he wrote in 1909, he noted that it was at the suggestion of Stepney-Gulston that 'the whole of the known documents issued by Owen Glyn Dŵr are included'.[49] The reason why he agreed to this suggestion was the approach of the quincentenary in 1916 of Owain Glyndŵr's death, and the hope that the inclusion of the documents might stimulate a renewed interest in his life and more importantly his nationalist aspirations for Wales, and perhaps be a national tribute to Owen's greatness'.[50] The book was published by the well-established firm of Carmarthen printers W. Spurrell and Son. The illustrations of some of the main documents, the quality of which had so exercised Matthews during the spring of 1909, were clear and handsomely produced.[51] *Welsh Records in Paris* was very well received, prompting one reviewer to note that Matthews 'has rendered excellent service to all students of Welsh history'.[52]

Having completed the writing and revising of *Welsh Records in Paris*, Mathews next set off, towards the end of 1909 with his sights firmly set on exploring the libraries and archives of Rome, especially those of the Catholic Church in the Vatican. With fewer contacts in the Eternal City and limited funds at his disposal, Matthews sought accommodation according to his means in a more modest part of the city. During his stay he contracted malaria, and although he recovered from it, its effects periodically blighted his health for the remainder of his life.[53] Armed with a letter of introduction from Bishop

Hedley to his excellency Cardinal Merry del Val, he hoped to repeat in the papal archives the search for documents directly relating to Wales he had successfully undertaken in Paris. This promised to be far more fruitful, given the centralised nature of the Catholic Church and the large number of documents likely to have been sent by Welsh sees and scholars to Rome in the pre-Reformation period. He was able to examine directly Gerald of Wales's autograph manuscript, presented to Pope Innocent III in his abortive attempt to secure the see of St David's in 1176. He returned from Rome with photographs of pages from *Llyfr Gogannau a'r Pyniau Moesol*, and was the first in modern times to view 'The Mirror of the Church' which had for centuries been considered lost, and the 'Book of Invectives' containing the replies Gerald drew up to rebut the accusations of his enemies. An insight into the reasons underpinning Matthews's quest was offered by him in a paper delivered to the Archaeological Section of the Cardiff Naturalists Society on 11 November 1910 when he argued:

> The search should proceed until all manuscripts bearing upon Welsh literature and history are known and catalogued. . . I make this suggestion with one object alone, and that is that Wales be able to show a corpus of documents of the sources of its history comparable with those of any country.[54]

As a keen nationalist Matthews was fully aware of the role history could play in giving national identity real credibility through highlighting its heroes and establishing its legitimacy as an independent entity in the distant past. Moreover this might also establish Wales's historical credentials in the international community. Although no book appeared as a result of his research in Rome his paper to the Cardiff Naturalists was published and included a number of illustrations of the documents he had examined.[55]

Possibly the most unusual and unexpected historical activity in which Tom Matthews was involved was the organization of a pageant to recreate an incident in the life of one of Carmarthenshire's most important historical figures. Sir Rhys ap Thomas was one of the key supporters of Henry Tudor's successful attempt to seize the English throne at Bosworth in 1485. In 1507 he was invested as a Knight of the Garter, and this was celebrated by a large tournament at Carew Castle. Matthews and his fellow organizers hoped to recreate the spectacle of this tournament as part of the festivities linked to the National Eisteddfod held in Abergavenny in 1913. The cast list for the pageant included several vicars, a brace of doctors, assorted members of the gentry and even a chief constable. All the participants appeared in full period costume, the highlight of which was a jousting competition. The local paper declared: 'The unqualified success of the meeting was due in large measure to that brilliant scholar Mr. Thomas Matthews.'[56]

Language, Literature and National Identity

Tom Matthews, whose first language was Welsh, was always interested in its linguistic structure and antecedents. His love of Welsh spread and overlapped into an interest in other Celtic languages, particularly Breton. What drew his initial interest to Brittany is unclear – possibly a desire to explore a language with shared common roots to Welsh, or simply experiencing directly during his first foreign visit in 1901 how a fellow Celtic nation was managing to retain its distinct national identity in the shadow of its much more assertive and dominant French neighbour.[57] Whatever the reasons, Breton culture became one of the areas which he cherished most during his life. Establishing close ties with Brittany appealed to his sense of forging pan-Celtic solidarity as a means of trying to preserve these ancient European languages. He strove to achieve this by establishing closer cultural ties between the two nations, mainly under the auspices of the National Eisteddfod. Following his first visit in 1901 he returned several times to prepare the groundwork for much closer co-operation between the two small Celtic nations. With typical zeal Matthews thoroughly immersed himself in the Breton language, becoming completely fluent in it. He was present at the Celtic festival at Saint-Brieuc and was a member of the eisteddfod committee which welcomed a delegation from Brittany to the 1907 National Eisteddfod held in Swansea. Matthews worked tirelessly as an unofficial ambassador between the bards of Wales and their Breton counterparts, and was responsible for selecting topics for members of the *Gorseddau* in both countries. In evaluating Matthews's contribution in bringing Wales and Brittany closer together, Diverrès noted: 'Not only did Matthews have a good understanding of our language, he also knew the worth of everyone in the Breton movement and was not distracted by external influences.'[58] In 1908 and 1910 he led the Welsh delegations to the Celtic festivals in Brest and Nantes. His passion for Brittany was deep, profound and typically practical. Wherever possible he tried to provide as much encouragement and support as he could to help speakers of the language seal in print their literary heritage. He did this in many ways: by writing a number of stories in French, notably 'Tristan and Esyllt' which were published in *Clocher Breton (Kloc'hdi Breiz)*, supporting F. Valle and Loeiz Herrieu in drawing up a *Geirlechres* – a grammar in French, Breton and Welsh which ran in the same periodical from 1906–7 until 1914. He also acted as a facilitator for the publication of articles by Breton writers such as Yves Berthou in *Cymru*.[59] Shortly before his death, he mooted in the winter of

1915 the idea of setting up a new pan-Celtic magazine which would provide writers in Welsh, Breton and Gaelic with an outlet for their work. Indisputably his 'interest and knowledge of Celtic affairs were profound'.[60] After his death, Diverrès revealed that Matthews had left a number of unpublished works relating to Brittany, including an introductory chapter to a book on Celtic drama. The most important by far of these works was a grammar in the Breton language. He also devised a series of introductory lessons for Welsh-speakers interested in learning Breton. In this area alone Matthews's interests were broad in scope and prodigious in effort.[61]

Matthews reserved a particular fondness for the literature of Wales. His various teaching appointments afforded him ample opportunity to study directly a number of micro-cultures and to access a rich vein of raw material on which to base several short articles. Matthews was keenly aware that Anglicization was eroding the hold of the Welsh language in many parts of the country, particularly in the mining villages of south Wales, and that he had a real opportunity to collect and preserve local works for posterity. He gathered and produced collections of previously unpublished poems and stories, for which he provided a brief commentary. Among the last of these was a collection of poetry drawn from the community of Glyncorrwg.[62] Not only was he keen to record local works and bring them to a wider audience; he was also as a teacher keen to inspire his pupils to produce their own poems and prose. While at Pengam he initiated and oversaw a number of projects which led to the publication of collections of various literary items by his students. Such works are rare enough in contemporary Wales; in the years before the Great War they are virtually unique and went some way to further enhancing the reputation of the school. Shortly after his appointment at Lewis School, he encouraged his pupils to collect from the community examples of the area's local literature. These were published in 1912 as *Llên Gwerin Blaenau Rhymni*.[63] In his foreword Matthews expressed the hope that the pupils would write creatively and with originality, and that their efforts would serve as an expression of the life of ordinary people in *Yr Ardd Ganol* ('the Middle Garden', as the area around Pengam was known locally). In an era when children were not encouraged to be vocal, analytical or critical, the collaborative approach required to research, write and produce such a work as *Llên Gwerin* was certainly ground-breaking.[64] He edited two other works: the first, *Barddoniaeth ar Gyfer Ysgol Lewis Pengam* (1915), was an anthology of poetry for his students, which he carefully selected to meet what he perceived to be of interest to their maturing intellects. Some of the choices in the anthology were well known while others were drawn from the locality and reflected the traditions of the community. The second work,

Dail y Gwanwyn (1916), appeared shortly before his death, and was considered 'a gem with the romance of spring coursing through every page'.[65] Matthews took great care in the presentation and layout of the book, which was well illustrated and contained carefully designed capitals preceding each item, the inclusion of which offered more than a hint of a future project. All profits from the sale of the book, which amounted to £28, were donated to Netley hospital.[66]

During the course of 1913–14 Matthews, under the patronage of Owen M. Edwards, embarked on a new venture which in some ways dovetailed neatly with the research he had already undertaken for *Welsh Records in Paris*, particularly those aspects relating to the life and times of Owain Glyndŵr. He was invited by Edwards to produce two short works for the Cyfres y Fil series.[67] The books covered the life and work of two little-known fourteenth-century poets, Siôn Cent (*c.*1367–1430) and Iolo Goch (*c.*1320–*c.*1398), both of whom were roughly contemporaneous with Owain Glyndŵr. Each book provided a brief introduction to the life of the poet, with the main focus on the selected examples of his work accompanied by a number of illustrations. Edwards also hoped that the two books would fit in with the renewed interest the five hundredth anniversary commemorations of Owain's death would bring to this period of Welsh history and literature.[68]

Thomas Matthews's own literary output fused his considerable knowledge of medieval Welsh history and literature, with an ability to create plausible scenarios and characters as a means of providing insight for his audience into some of the key events of European history. Evolving his empathetic skills, he produced a series of fictional Letters from Rome written by eminent Welshmen who visited the city over the centuries, drawing extensively on his own thorough knowledge of its topography, art and architecture. The series, which was written for *Cymru*, began in 1911 and continued through to 1916 with the posthumous publication of the tenth and last letter – from Dafydd ab Sion to Gwenllian the daughter of Siancyn ab Owen of Derwydd in Iscennen (Carmarthenshire). This final letter explored the theme of religion during the period before the Protestant Reformation. The imaginary letter was not a genre that was widely used in Welsh literature at that time and remains fairly uncommon to this day. In evaluating the series Owen M. Edwards said:

> Thomas Matthews broke new ground in many different fields of literature. He was one of the first to explore the relationship between the art and literature of our country. He also showed how to write historical stories – a branch of literature our young boys and girls should embrace with relish.[69]

Visual Culture

When everything is taken into consideration regarding Tom Matthews's contribution to the intellectual life of Wales, the one area where he stands head and shoulders above his contemporaries is in the field of visual culture Despite having no formal training in art history or appreciation, he emerged as a trenchant and articulate champion of the visual arts in Wales during the Edwardian period, and single-handedly set out to inform Welsh-language readers of their indigenous visual heritage and tradition. Although his contribution is now largely unknown, the scale and scope of his achievement merits recounting.[70] It is unclear when exactly Matthews became interested in art, but it was probably while conducting his researches in Paris and Rome.[71] During his stay in these centres of art and learning he took the opportunity to visit the Louvre and the Vatican and experience for himself the wonderful paintings and sculptures in their collections. He was particularly taken by the works of the masters of the Renaissance. Enthused and enraptured by this experience, he sought out on his return to Wales evidence of a domestic visual culture. His disappointment with what he discovered was palpable, and he decided to devote as much time and energy as his other commitments would permit to researching and promoting visual culture in Wales. Matthews's efforts to promote art in Wales encompassed several strategies – publishing books and articles to inform and enlighten his fellow countrymen about the artistic achievements of their compatriots, championing the cause wherever possible of those contemporary artists whom he admired, writing critical works and finally ensuring that the seeds of art appreciation were planted in the next generation through his visionary promotion of art education in the nation's schools.

The first book on art which Matthews wrote was a biography of the well-known Welsh-born sculptor, John Gibson RA (1790–1866), which was published in 1911. Gibson had lived and worked in Rome for most of his life and Matthews came across examples of his work while staying in the city. When he died, Gibson left a vast correspondence between himself and Mrs Margaret Sandbach, the grand daughter of William Roscoe, his first patron, spanning the years 1839 until her death in 1852. During 1849 the tone of the letters became distinctly more autobiographical, possibly in the hope that Mrs Sandbach would use them as the basis of a memoir of the sculptor. Her death in 1852 removed this possibility. It is possible that T. H. Thomas, who had known Gibson in Rome, drew Matthews's attention to the correspondence and encouraged him to produce the book.[72] Colonel Sandbach of Hafodunos near Abergele allowed Matthews free access to his family's private papers relating to Gibson. Although the book is described as a biography, this label, as Matthews himself freely admits in the opening sentence of the preface, is somewhat misleading: 'This biography of John Gibson is largely an autobiography.'[73] Consequently, the text is for the most part written in the first person, having been drawn almost entirely from Gibson's own notes and letters, with the author's role reduced to some selective editing, a discussion of the location of Gibson's birthplace, and compilation of a catalogue raisonné of his work.[74] This is not to minimize Matthews's achievement but it helps to explain how he was able to embark on this project and see it through to publication so soon after the appearance of *Welsh Records in Paris*.[75] The book, which was well illustrated, was one of the earliest to focus on the life and work of a prominent Welsh-born artist. Matthews undoubtedly hoped that the romance of the story of a poor boy from Conwy, blessed with a rare talent, who overcame enormous obstacles to achieve fame and fortune, would resonate with his fellow countrymen and help inspire others.[76]

As a committed *eisteddfodwr* Matthews would have been familiar with the work of T. H. Thomas (Arlunydd Penygarn, 1839–1915) – before he undertook his researches on Gibson. Thomas was one of the last surviving members of the sculptor's circle of Welsh friends in Rome and was able to provide Matthews with 'much guidance and information'.[77] In addition to being a prominent artist, Thomas was one of the driving forces behind attempts to raise both the profile and the standard of the National Eisteddfod's annual arts and crafts exhibition.[78] Another important member of this circle was Penry Williams (1800–85), the Merthyr-born artist. Both of these men in different ways would provide Matthews with the inspiration to continue researching and writing about Welsh artists, with the aim of bringing their works to the attention of a much wider audience, especially those who considered Welsh to be their first language.[79] In 1912 he embarked on a series of fifteen articles in *Cymru* tracing the life and work of Penry Williams. These examined critically his artistic contribution, and were for the time profusely illustrated with examples of his work, enabling readers to reach their own judgements as to its merits.[80] Matthews was keen to use his emerging reputation as a writer and critic to introduce to as wide an audience as possible the work of new artists, or those who he considered required retrospective evaluations. His selections were highly personal and ignored many who are nowadays much more familiar. Among those he publicized in one way or another were the painters Margaret Lindsay Williams and Edgar H. Thomas and the sculptor David Davies.[81] In his final article on art, Matthews berated the civic fathers of Merthyr for neglecting to purchase and display in his home town any work by David Davies.

Of the many artists Matthews encountered and studied, he reserved a particular fondness and admiration for Christopher Williams. From a point where he once declared of art in Wales, that 'the work at present is not of a very high order in this part of the world', as his understanding grew so did his belief that there was indeed a great deal which was worthy of praise in the nation's visual culture.[82] It is unclear when the two first met, but it is likely to have been through the close connections both had with the National Eisteddfod. Williams who lived and worked in London was gaining a considerable reputation as a portrait painter but retained close family links with Wales and particularly Carmarthenshire.[83] Their shared interests in promoting Welsh art became the basis of a firm and lasting friendship, and also led them to take a number of foreign visits together. Matthews emerged as the staunchest champion of Williams's work and clearly identified him as a leading figure in any future revival of the visual arts in Wales. Williams's was inspired by early Celtic myths and tales from a more heroic period of Welsh history before the Edwardian conquest. A number of his works drew on themes contained in the *Mabinogion*. Matthews identified Williams as an innovator who, in turning to Welsh themes, was liberating his inherent Celtic gifts and was signalling a reawakening of a dormant Welsh tradition in art. At the time of his death Matthews left a draft copy of a Welsh-language biography of Christopher Williams. Had it been published it would have been the first such work on a living Welsh artist in Welsh.[84] In 1911 Williams completed one of his most important works, the allegorical *Deffroad Cymru*, which Matthews considered to be a seminal work and a visual statement of the re-emergence of Wales as a nation.[85] Following the death of his friend, Williams wrote:

> We have lost one of the best, and genuine nationalists. I feel the loss of Tom Matthews keenly. Perhaps I knew him as few did. He always had an enthusiasm for Wales. When we were in Morocco (1914) or Holland (1912), it was the contrast of those countries and peoples to Wales and the Welsh that interested him – the similarities or differences of their manners and customs, their poetry and art and music, and he always attempted to get what he thought was good out of there, and see it was possible that Wales should have it too.[86]

Matthews was determined to use his position as a commentator on the contemporary art scene and writer of art history along with his close links to the eisteddfod not only to argue for a vision of Welsh art but to identify and promote a specific Welsh school of art. According to Peter Lord, Matthews's pioneering articles on art in the pages of *Cymru* 'created a new critical language'.[87] He synthesized his ideas and views in an important work published in 1914 – *Celf yng Nghymru*. The catalyst for the essay was an exhibition held in Cardiff the previous year, to explore and celebrate the contribution made by past and contemporary Welsh-born artists. Matthews's sometimes extravagant prose was lavished on the event which he signalled as 'the beginning of a new period, because here can be seen work by Welsh artists of enormous vision who have succeeded in reaching the highest level of Artistic achievement, and who are in the vanguard of Art not only in Wales but in the world'.[88] By highlighting the achievements of selected individuals such as Richard Wilson, Matthews hoped to dispel the notion that Wales had no artistic tradition, and therefore no worthwhile Welsh paintings. His aim in a wider aesthetic context was simple, not art for art's sake but art to elevate life.

Not all the schemes and projects which Matthews proposed were successful. One that failed to materialize was a vision he had of publishing high-quality numbered limited-edition volumes on hand-made Japanese vellum paper, illustrated with specially commissioned calligraphy inspired by the distinctive beauty of medieval Welsh illuminated manuscripts.[90] The genesis of the plan may well have been his interest in the life and work of Sulien and his son Rhigyfarch.[91] Matthews had examined the small number of surviving manuscripts from Llanbadarn which were linked to Sulien. During 1910–11, he travelled to Ireland to continue his research on Rhigyfarch and to examine any other related manuscripts. While in Dublin he visited Trinity College to view the Book of Kells, and was clearly enthralled by one of the greatest surviving treasures from the Celtic era.[92] The appeal for subscribers to back what would be an expensive venture failed to secure sufficient interest, and the proposal was abandoned. Nothing also came of his suggestion that a School of Welsh Script be created. Despite the failure of the publishing venture it is possible to detect the legacy of his interest in calligraphy and printing in *Dail y Gwanwyn* (1916), and *The Tournament at Carew Castle* (1914) where ornate initial letters and borders were freely used throughout the text.[93]

Towards the end of his life Matthews was working on a book which he hoped would help embed art firmly into the mainstream of elementary education in Wales. *Perthynas y Cain a'r Ysgol*, his last book, appeared in the spring of 1916, and was in many ways a pioneering work. In it he outlined his vision of the contribution he believed art could make to education, particularly when examples were displayed in schools. Matthews's concern was that the power and beauty of art to enhance the aesthetic quality of pupils' lives, while at the same time providing them with a moral and intellectual compass, be recognized across the educational sector in Wales. A central aspect of the work was the provision of practical advice and guidance to teachers on where to obtain high-quality reproductions of paintings and how these could be displayed to their best advantage. Notwithstanding Matthews's 'florid and sanguine rhetoric', this work was important and forward-looking in the focus he placed on the learning environment itself – the classroom, an arena he was intimately acquainted with as a practising teacher.[94] His declared aim was essentially simple: 'These notes and suggestions and the lists which follow have been published in the hope that they will provide some guidance to the growing number of teachers and others committed to bringing beauty into children's lives.'[95] The book was very well received. *Welsh Outlook* declared it 'a small volume whose like has never yet been published in Wales', a work that if its suggestions were strictly applied would 'revolutionise the appearance of the educational buildings of our land'.[96] While it is difficult not to admire the essential humanity and hope, expressed by Matthews in his book, this is not the case with the lists of paintings he recommends for display in Welsh classrooms. These works reflect the author's own tastes and predilections, favouring as they do Old Master and Pre-Raphaelite paintings. As noteworthy as those which are included are those artists Matthews chose to omit. Not one of the French Impressionists (Manet, Monet, Degas, etc.) is recommended. Equally selective is his list of Welsh artists, where no place is found for those in the vanguard of modernism – Augustus and Gwen John or J. D. Innes. The omission of John in particular is curious as Matthews himself had declared him to be 'one of the most important in the contemporary art world'.[97] Notwithstanding any criticisms which could be levelled against Matthews's highly personal selections, the *raison d'être* of the book is as valid and appropriate now as in his day.

The breadth and scope of Tom Matthews's interests and research is very impressive. His efforts were nothing short of Herculean, as he crammed a vast amount into a comparatively short life. Between 1910 and 1916 he either wrote or edited a dozen books, with a further three in draft form, in addition to the numerous articles he published (see Appendix). It has been suggested that his fame as an author might have been greater had he taken more care in the preparation of his books and articles.[99] The speed with which he worked placed a considerable strain on his rather weak constitution. He provided an insight into the pressure he was under in a letter to a friend:

> I have been especially busy the last three months. I hope the work will lighten shortly. It is too heavy now. I had to travel to keep appointments in addition to extra and my usual work – over eight hundred miles last week, and fell asleep over my work Thursday, through fatigue.[100]

An additional burden which Matthews was acutely aware of was financial. Even though he was a single man with few family commitments, working in a respected profession, he was by no means financially secure. He hoped to make a profit of £40–£50 from sales of *Welsh Records in Paris*, which would then fund further research in Rome.[101] Publishing the biography of Gibson placed a considerable strain on his limited financial resources.[102] The punishing schedule which drove him to organize, research, write, travel and hold down a teaching post, began to take its toll after the outbreak of war in 1914. There were several bouts of illness, possibly linked to the malaria he had contracted while in Italy, before his death at his parents' home in Llandybïe in 1916. Those who knew him well felt his loss deeply. As his close friend D. Rhys Phillips wrote: 'His harp was broken early, he went to his grave before contributing half the work he had available.'[103]

In summing up the contribution of Thomas Matthews to Welsh learning, two words can with some certainty be appended to him – pioneer and visionary. His researches in foreign archives and the stance he adopted on the benefits of promoting art education in Welsh schools clearly broke new ground. The championing of the visual culture of Wales and the new critical language he used in his Welsh-medium articles and books were ahead of their time. While there can be no dispute regarding his enormous drive, great energy and limitless passion for his country and its culture, there remain some concerns about the sheer volume of his output over a comparatively small span of time, which may have compromised the quality of his work. It was argued that his work revealed too much the hand of the apprentice rather than that of the master, and that it would have been better received had he taken more time and greater care over the preparation of his books and articles. Another view is that his fear of his own mortality drove him incessantly to cram as much as he could into the limited time he believed he had available.[104] Whatever the final analysis, his work merits study. Given the range and scope of what he was attempting, perhaps the most fitting epithet for Thomas Matthews is *Athraw i Athrawon*,[105] the teacher's teacher.

Thomas Matthews the Historian

The closing years of the nineteenth and early twentieth centuries saw the dawn of a new age in the literary and historical development of the Welsh nation.[1] It revealed the emergence of a new generation of scholars intent on strengthening a sense of Welsh national conciousness, which led to the establishment of national institutions such as the University of Wales (1893) and the National Library (1907) which promoted historical scholarship in Wales, most of it devoted to the nation's medieval past. It was an exciting period when Welsh literature, antiquity and history formed an essential part of a rich cultural revival.[2] In the historical field notable scholars became prominent intent on reviewing and reviving Welsh medieval history with a view to publicizing in print the significance of the nation's cultural past. The Dafydd ap Gwilym Society at Jesus College, Oxford, for example, was regarded as a breeding ground for a virile group of academics including historians such as Sir John Rhys, Sir John Edward Lloyd and Sir O. M. Edwards.[3] Welsh history was newly interpreted and made to reflect Welsh nationalism in the Liberal traditions of the age. Sir John Edward Lloyd, the most eminent scholar of his day in the field of medieval Welsh history, in his famous two-volume *History of Wales from the Earliest Times to the Edwardian Conquest*, published in 1911, became one of the pioneers of the scientific interpretation of history, presenting a narrative account of the nation's development down to 1282 to a wider reading audience.[4] He rejected the idealistic interpretations of the past and based his research on the historical sources that were available in his day. His intentions were clarified by him in an article published in the *Transactions of the Royal National Eisteddfod of Wales* held at Liverpool in 1884, in which he asserted that he intended to write a history of a nation, and not a state, because it was a subject worthy of being recounted in the most rigorous scholastic manner.[5] 'Lloyd', Huw Pryce asserts, 'presented a picture that chimed comfortingly with the progressive, evolutionary assumptions of the later nineteenth century by depicting the Welsh of the present as a marked improvement on their ancestors.'[6]

In order that this aim might be pursued further a call was made for serious scholarly research into medieval records deposited in the Public Record Office, the British Museum and other repositories and libraries on the continent. Henry Owen, the Pembrokeshire lawyer, in his introduction to George Owen's *Description of Penbrokshire*, published in 1892 by the Honourable Society of Cymmrodorion in its Record Series established in that year,[7] declared the need for the publication of existing historical sources relating to Wales, and considered that his work would initiate a process that had already developed in England:

> I trust that this series will be long continued. . . There are numerous Welsh manuscripts scattered up and down the land whose publication would be of value and interest, and might tend to divert the lately revived national feeling away from the wearisome wrangles of the hustings and the pulpit to the more reasonable study of the national history and literature.[8]

Owen pioneered the way to the publication of a number of medieval sources in the Cymmrodorion Record Series such as *The Court Rolls of the Lordship of Ruthin or Dyffryn Clwyd of the Reign of Edward the First* (1893), *The Black Book of St David's* (1902) *and The Episcopal Registers of the Diocese of St David's, 1397 to 1518* (1917).

Historical method and scholarship were soundly based on authentic sources and demanded palaeographical and other archival skills. In Wales this created a more scientific approach to the study of Welsh medieval history since it led to a new historiographical legitimization of 'the historical roots of Welsh nationality'.[9] It was featured in such works as *The Welsh People* (1900) by John Rhys and D. Brynmor Jones, *The Welsh Wars of Edward I* (1901) by J. E. Morris, *The Council in the Marches of Wales* (1904) by Caroline Skeel and *The Mediaeval Boroughs of Snowdonia* (1912) by E. A. Lewis. Edward Owen's *Catalogue of MSS relating to Wales in the British Museum* (1898–1903), another publication in four volumes in the *Cymmrodorion Record Series*, and Ivor Bowen's *The Statutes of Wales* (1908), together with the increasing number of sources relating to English history, such as the Rolls Series and State Papers, became indispensable tools to conduct serious historical research. Such activity eventually encouraged Welsh scholars to publish pioneering articles in *Y Cymmrodor* (1877 onwards), the *Bulletin of the Board of Celtic Studies* (first published in 1921) among other scholarly journals.[10]

In view of this new historical environment and the emergence of new historical techniques, what can be said about Thomas Matthews's status as a medieval historian? He had not had the experience or benefit of an Oxford education but had obtained an honours and MA degree in English at the University College of South Wales and Monmouthshire. He had become well acquainted with the cultural and artistic traditions of the nation[11] and was well aware of the new academic spirit, noted above, which burgeoned in Wales in his day, promoting the advancement of scholarship and learning. In the preface to one of his books written in Welsh he stated:

> Ni all neb ameu fod rhyw ysbryd newydd yn treiddio drwy'r wlad y dyddiau hyn. Rhyw ysbrydoliaeth dwys newydd na phrofodd y genedl er ys dros ganrif. Heddyw teimlwn fod cynnwrf yng ngwersyll delfrydau dyn. Mae'r hen ddelfrydau yn dadfeilio; y mae'r hen amcanion fel pe baent yn myned yn ofer; y mae'r hen ddyheadau fel pe baent wedi colli eu nerth. Y mae delfrydau newydd o'r hyn ydyw gwir wladgarwch yn cael eu datblygu. Y mae'r genedl i'w hail-eni. Y mae gwewyr esgor uchel amcanion y genedl newydd gerllaw.[12]
>
> No one can doubt that there is some new spirit penetrating through the country these days. Some new inspiration which the nation has not experienced over a century. Today we feel that there is a stir in the camp of man's ideals. The old ideals are decaying; the old aims are as if they have lost their strength. New ideals of what is true patriotism are being developed. The nation is being newly born. The anguish of the birth of the new nation's high aims is at hand.

Although he was referring at the time to the reawakening of the fine arts in schools, a subject in which he was extremely interested, one cannot but consider it also to be a statement which refers to the broader span of literature, language and history. Matthews was determined to seek original sources which related to the history of medieval Wales, and it is altogether surprising that a person who suffered bouts of ill health achieved so much during his comparatively short life. His enthusiastic approach to the publication of his *Welsh Records in Paris* drew the attention of other historians to the wealth of sources which he discovered assisted by friends, librarians and scholars who enabled him to fulfil his ambition.[13] During his visits to libraries on the Continent, such as the Archives Nationales in Paris and the Vatican Library in Rome, he became aware of the need to catalogue, preserve and print documents relating to Wales consulted by him. He considered this practice to be necessary, and in a learned talk given by him to the Cardiff Naturalists' Society on 11 November 1910 he spoke his mind clearly when referring to the non-existence of 'class lists' and lists of British 'special collections' in foreign libraries.[14] He believed that steps should be taken so that 'Wales may be able to show a corpus of documents of the sources and illustrative of its history comparable with those of any country'. Until that had been accomplished, he stated further, the good reputation of the University of Wales and other public bodies in Wales would be undermined.[15]

Thomas Matthews left Fishguard County School in 1908 to research more thoroughly the history and literature of Wales at the Archives Nationales, and he was assisted, among others, by Sir E. Maunde Thompson, M. Henri Petit, curator of the Archives de la Haute-Vienne at Limoges, M. Paul Diverrès, director of the Sorbonne, Ifano Jones, of the Welsh Section of the Reference Department of Cardiff Free Library, John Fisher, librarian of St Asaph Cathedral Library, and D. Rhys Phillips, Welsh librarian at Swansea Free Library.[16] Doubtless many of the official sources used in *Welsh Records in Paris* were those recommended to him by these scholars whose reputation was widely acknowledged in academic circles.

Matthews took much interest in Celtic studies, and his correspondence reveals his constant inquiries into all aspects of the subject relating to the early Welsh language and literature as well as other Celtic cultures. He was made an honorary member of the Gorsedd of Bards in the Royal National Eisteddfod held at Caernarfon in 1906, which assisted him in making useful contacts with other Celtic scholars and antiquaries.[17] He was associated with the Cardiff Cymrodorion Society, which had a wide reputation as a centre of Welsh culture in the city, and befriended Edward Thomas (Cochfarf), one of its founders who shared similar interests in Breton traditions and culture and who ardently promoted an awareness of Welsh citizenship at a time when Anglicization was rapidly increasing in Cardiff.[18] Such was his enthusiasm for these causes that his correspondence with Paul Diverrès led to a working partnership between them to ensure that *Welsh Records in Paris* was published.[19] A group of ten letters written to Diverrès contains comments on a variety of cultural matters together with queries and requests concerning original sources to be included in his book. It was Diverrès who contacted Berthaud Frères, Paris printers, and a Mr Gaudier, who was employed to copy some of the original sources for him. It is evident that Matthews wanted his book to be published as soon as possible, and his correspondence with Diverrès made that clear. 'I want the book to be published as quickly as possible,' he wrote in a letter to him in 1909, and on several occasions he urged him to attend to his many requests. The reason for this urgency is not easily explained, but it is evident that Matthews considered it necessary to publish his research, possibly to satisfy his need to share his discoveries with others. He was well aware that the five-hundredth anniversary of Owain Glyndŵr's death was to be commemorated in 1916, a fact made clear in his preface. 'In a few years', he stated, 'the quincentenary of Owen Glyndwr's death will remind us of the close of his struggle, and it may not be inappropriate here to express the hope that that anniversary will see a national tribute to Owen's greatness.' Matthews, however, was never to see the end of that year for he died on 6 September.

Originally Matthews had no intention of publishing his transcripts but, on his own admission, was urged to do so by Alan Stepney-Gulston of Derwydd, Llandybïe, landowner and first president of the Carmarthenshire Antiquarian Society, who urged him to prepare them for publication and gave him full support.[20] It was probably a mistake on his part to have yielded to this pressure, in view of the fact that he was aware of the need for further research and revision. The volume *Welsh Records in Paris*, which appeared in 1910, was printed by the famous Spurrell Company of Carmarthen. It was a private venture because a large number of distinguished individuals and organisations subscribed to it. Among them were Henry Campbell Bruce, second Lord Aberdare, Edward Anwyl, J. W. Willis Bund, J. H. Davies, David Lloyd George, J. E. Lloyd, W. Llewelyn Williams and J. Gwenogvryn Evans. At the end of the volume a total number of 125 subscribers and fifteen public libraries were added, including Cambridge University Library, the John Rylands Library, Manchester, Trinity College Library, Dublin, and the Meyricke Library, Jesus College, Oxford. This response must have heartened the author, his modest aim being to 'be of service to students of the history of Wales'.[21] He did not expect to make a large profit from the venture, but that seems not to have caused him any concern.

It is surprising, however, that in subsequent years some historians writing on Owain Glyndŵr and his rebellion made no mention of his work at all in their lists of source citations, such as J. D. Griffith Davies and more recent scholars such as Ian Jack, who did not refer at all to *Welsh Records in Paris* in his survey of medieval Welsh sources in 1972.[22] In his *Owen Glendower* (1931), J. E. Lloyd, however, made ample use of the published letters transcribed by Matthews, and so did R. R. Davies, in his authoritative study *The Revolt of Owain Glyn Dŵr* (1995). What is evident is that Matthews had it in mind to publish original documents with translations and relevant commentary on their background and content based primarily on the context relating, in Glyndŵr's case, to the more illustrious years of the revolt. He had no further ambition than to aid researchers who examined the revolt, a historical theme which, in the past, had been over-romanticized.

The content and structure of the volume were designed by Matthews as groups of transcripts in the original Latin, excepting one written in French. Two of them are thirteeenth-century documents, namely Llywelyn ap Iorwerth's alliance with Philip Augustus, king of France (1212) (pp. 3–4) and a series of five papal bulls issued by Pope Urban IV to Richard de Carew, bishop of St David's, with a view to organizing another Crusade in 1263–4 (pp. 7–20). These are followed by four letters regarding Owain Glyndŵr's close diplomatic ties with Charles VI of France (1404–6) (pp. 23–54), which are followed by an appendix of six items (pp.103–10), including a short Treasurer's Journal, the other five of which are copied from texts printed in other published works, and are translated by Matthews. These are followed by descriptions of the seals of Llywelyn ap Iorwerth, Owain Glyndŵr and Gruffudd Yonge, Glyndŵr's Chancellor (pp. 119–21), a short lineage chart in Latin of Alice Scudamore (p.122), one of Glyndŵr's daughters who had married John Scudamore (Skidmore) of Kentchurch, his firm supporter and member of a notable Border family, followed by general notes on some individuals and other references in the texts (pp.123–31), an index and list of subscribers (pp. 139–43).

The historical texts command the central part of the volume. The Latin transcripts and translations are correct for the most part but do contain some misprints and mistranslations. R. F. Treharne, a thirteenth-century scholar, drew attention to some transcriptional errors in his article on the Franco-Welsh treaty of 1212, a contribution which takes a critical view of Matthews's interpretation and conclusions regarding the letter, the first printed in the volume, sent by Llywelyn ap Iorwerth to Philip Augustus.[23] In a comparatively short introductory survey to the letter's context he proceeds to explain the political background and the reason why the alliance was formed. Since the document is undated, Matthews presents the arguments for 1212 and 1216 as probable dates, and wrongly decides on the latter. He admitted that it was no easy task, and although arguments could support 1212, on balance he chose 1216. In fact, in a letter to Paul Diverrès in March 1910, he referred to his uncertainty as to the dating, regarding the source as a 'disputed document' because Edward Owen had dated it after the 1280s, basing his opinion on the script alone.[24] 'I shall have some fun over this document,' he jokingly added at the end of his letter!

The background to this document by Llywelyn ap Iorwerth relates to the conflict between King John, the papacy and France. In 1212, because of the Interdict imposed on the king, Pope Innocent III urged Philip Augustus to declare war on him and subject him to the ecclesiastical control of Rome.

Native Welsh rulers were absolved from submitting themselves to King John and the Interdict was removed. Y Berfeddwlad, an extensive region in north-east Wales, had been repossessed by Llywelyn in July 1212, which may have been followed by the alliance with Philip Augustus later in the year. Matthews, however, found difficulty in deciding on the date of this agreement. The Welsh *Chronicle of the Princes* (*Brut y Tywysogion*) referred to the five-year truce between King John and Philip Augustus after the battle of Bouvines (27 July 1214) between Lille and Tournai in northern France, where John was heavily defeated. When that truce was made between King John and Philip no reference is made in the *Brut* to an agreement between Llywelyn and the French king, and no Council of Welsh lords at Aberdyfi is mentioned before 1216 (which Matthews wrongly believes to have been held in 1215). When Louis the Dauphin brought his armies to England on 7 January 1216 Matthews interpreted this as an indication of Llywelyn's support for France based on an agreement reached in the Aberdyfi Council of 1215 (*sic*). Philip, however, owing to changed relations between him and King John and Pope Innocent III, paid little attention to that invasion, which occurred at the time when Llywelyn's power was in the ascendancy. According to this alliance in 1215 (*sic*) Llywelyn and Philip agreed that they would not make peace with England, thus supporting and respecting each other's honour. Matthews concludes that since there was no Council before 1215 and no agreement between Llywelyn and Philip before 1217, the year after the invasion of England, he finally decided, clearly on rather flimsy evidence, as he himself admitted, that 1216 was the more likely date for the alliance.[25]

In his article published in the *Bulletin of the Board of Celtic Studies* in 1958,[26] which adds the text of the alliance in an appendix, R. F. Traherne re-examined the probable dating of this alliance and concluded that Matthews was incorrect. He referred to errors in his examination and interpretation of the subject matter and proceeded further to recount the circumstances in 1212. On that basis he concluded that Llywelyn, despite his success in regaining Y Berfeddwlad, still needed Philip's support, since he could not allow France to come to terms with King John. Philip himself was keen to maintain Llywelyn's support because John intended to invade Normandy and other territories acquired by France in 1204. It appears, therefore, according to Treharne, that the alliance was formed in May or June 1212, after Llywelyn had regained his lost territory and before his hostages were hanged by the king on 14 August in the same year. At the time the triumphant Llywelyn still feared that King John's armies might attack his territories again from Chester. Matthews rejected 1212 as the most likely date since there was no mention of an alliance with Philip Augustus in the Chronicle, and no reference to one when recording the seven-year truce between Philip and King John in 1214. Moreover, there was no reference to Llywelyn counselling with his fellow rulers in 1216 – the Aberdyfi Council – wrongly dated by Matthews, as noted above. Other arguments are added by Treharne, and he states that there was no evidence that the Aberdyfi Council initiated a Franco-Welsh alliance. Since King John had submitted to the Papacy on 15 May 1213 and had assumed the Cross, Llywelyn came to terms with the king on 3 June of that year, agreeing a truce which lasted until 1215 In that case, any alliance between Llywelyn and Philip could not have been concluded after that date or before August 1212. Treharne's interpretation is more penetrative and lends more credence to a greater range of sources than Matthews's.[27]

The second group of documents relate to five papal bulls, three issued by Pope Urban IV (1261–4) to Richard de Carew, bishop of St David's, a well-known theologian and philosopher, and two to Welsh prelates and higher clergy.[28] In a letter to Diverrès in February 1909 Matthews requested that M. Gaudier proceed to copy the bulls immediately since they were full, unlike those supplied by Diverrès himself, which were made from the catalogue and were merely extracts.[29] The background formed part of an attempt to organize another Crusade against the infidel, and the pope's desire to maintain the conflict between Christians and Saracens in Palestine. Urban wished to defeat Baibars Bundukdārī, a Kitchak Turk, the leader of the Mamaluke mercenaries of Egyptian sultans.[30] He had led a force against St Louis IX of France in the First Crusade, and in 1262 set up the Latin kingdom of Palestine, thus urging the pope to appeal for help to defeat him in the Holy Land, which explains why the bulls were deposited in Paris. Matthews, having discovered the five bulls, had them printed and translated, thus revealing Bishop Carew's appeal to the diocese of St David's and possibly reflecting the prominence given to that diocese in such a critical situation, a matter which became evident in Owain Glyndŵr's Pennal letter of 1406.

The demands were laid out in Wales in similar fashion that they were to be sent to other sees. An annual tax was to be levied over a period of five years of a hundreth part of the increase of all income of Welsh clergy. Ten horsemen and fifteen well-equipped soldiers were to be provided, their expenses to be paid by the bishop, and people were urged to volunteer to join the Crusade. Those who joined were to be fully pardoned and granted indulgences.

It appears that the diocese of St David's was regarded by the pope as the prime diocese in Wales since its bishop, formerly canon of the diocese, is personally approached as the Welsh Church's representative. He was a descendant of Nest, daughter of Rhys ap Tewdwr and, despite Henry II's opposition to his election, was granted the diocese by Pope Alexander IV in 1256. This was a practice that Innocent III had initiated using his *plenitudo potestatis*.[31] Such documents are essential evidence of the attempt by the Papacy to generate support for yet another Crusade which did not materialise. They also reveal the importance attached to St David's as the metropolitan church in Wales and to the persistent attempt by Louis IX of France, despite previous failures, to conduct a campaign against the Arabs in the Holy Land. In this series of bulls Matthews brought to light a small but significant group of documents, not dissimilar in content to letters sent to other bishops of the realm, highlighting the role of the Welsh Church in Crusading activity. As Matthews himself commented, the documents were interesting also in view of Gerald of Wales's efforts, earlier in 1199, to ensure that St David's was recognized as the metropolitan church of Wales.[32]

The eleven documents in the last group (including the appendix) have attracted historians more than the others, chiefly because they relate to the peak period in Owain Glyndŵr's career. They are concerned with his close relations with Charles VI of France and the alliance concluded between them against the Lancastrian king Henry IV who usurped the English throne in 1399. Matthews supplies a detailed factual background to these letters and draws attention to some central features which highlighted Glyndŵr's foreign policy in 1404–6 and which were very productive. In fact, the letters deal with the most dynamic and practical policy projected by the self-designated Prince of Wales. Matthews's introduction extends to eighteen pages (pp.xxi–xxxix), detailing Glyndŵr's negotiations with France and other allies of his. The first transcript is a commission granted to Gruffydd Yonge, Doctor of Canon Law and Glyndŵr's chancellor, and Sir John Hanmer, Glyndŵr's brother-in-law, his sister Margaret having married the Welsh leader. The Hanmers were among Glyndŵr's staunchest supporters, John Hanmer's father, Sir David Hanmer, being a well-known lawyer in north-east Wales.[33] When the opportunity arose after the Anglo-French truce (1289), by then completely worthless because of the ongoing conflict between the two countries, Glyndŵr took positive action to gain French support. On 10 May 1404 Gruffudd Yonge and John Hanmer were sent to the French court to seek an alliance with Charles VI, and that treaty was concluded on 14 July 1404 against Henry IV, their common enemy.[34] Its importance lies in the fact that, within four years of rebellion breaking out, Owain Glyndŵr was officially recognized by the French king as Prince of Wales.

Matthews's commentary on the background to the Glyndŵr letter refers chiefly to the immediate events leading to the revolt on 16 September 1400 and to subsequent good relations with France. Following that, the author refers to the parliament summoned at Dolgellau on 10 May 1404, which may have led to the decision to send the two ambassadors to Paris. The treaty, contained in a huge document, was ratified by Owain at Llanbadarn castle on 12 January (pp. 25–39), and Charles VI produced his own ratification on 14 June whereupon Glyndŵr acted in his role as Prince of Wales.[35]

The second document is a letter addressed to Charles VI dated at Pennal on the southern coast of Merioneth on 31 March 1406 acknowledging his support for the rival Pope Benedict XIII at Avignon, in which he declared: 'I recognize him as the true Vicar of Christ on my own behalf, and on behalf of my subjects' (p. 83).[36] The third document is Owain's famous 'policy', dated again on 31 March 1406 (pp. 42–54), in which he confidently used his right as prince, and formally declared again that be recognized Benedict 'as the true Vicar of Christ in our lands, by us and our subjects'.[37] In an age of papal schism and political insecurity, however, this declaration proved itself eventually not to be of any political benefit to Glyndŵr. The letter to Charles VI is better known as the document which contains the famous 'Pennal' policy which signified a major political breakthrough for Glyndŵr.[38] Its main contents are well known, principally that Charles should seek papal support for bold proposals submitted by Owain: firstly, that ecclesiastical censures should be removed and that the Papacy was to confirm official acts of the clergy. Then followed the proposal to instate St David's formally as the metropolitan church in Wales with the other Welsh bishops, together with the bishops of Exeter, Bath, Hereford, Worcester, Coventry and Lichfield, as suffragans. This section of the agreement ran as follows:

> . . . that the Church of St David's shall be restored to its original dignity, which from the time of St David, archbishop and confessor, was a metropolitan church. . . For being crushed by the fury of the barbarous Saxons, who usurped to themselves the land of Wales, they trampled upon the aforesaid church of St David's and made her a handmaid to the church of Canterbury.[39]

This was indeed a remarkable manifestation of the true significance of St David's as a metropolitan church, the position it claimed, fully supported by Gerald of Wales two hundred years earlier. The Welsh language was declared official in the Church and no clergy were to be appointed unless they spoke it. Appropriations of English colleges or monasteries were to be revoked and annulled, and two university colleges were to be established, one in north and the other in south Wales. This last proposal was a remarkably enlightened one which was to be realised almost 500 years later. No detailed analysis is offered by Matthews of the document's content. It is rather left as a memorial to the alliance with France and strong links with the breakaway Papacy at Avignon. In his major work *The Welsh Church from Conquest to Reformation* (1962) Sir Glanmor Williams examines this Pennal document in much greater depth, and sees it, not primarily a religious policy, but rather a political one to strengthen Glyndŵr's Principality. It was intended to enhance the prestige of the Welsh Church in an age of serious exploitation, to reinforce papal support against the English government and to establish an independent Church as an 'inescapable pre-requisite' of the Principality which Glyndŵr envisaged. As Sir Glanmor Williams says,

> The 'Pennal policy', then, ought not to be thought of as a project for disinterested ecclesiastical and educational reform adduced by starry-eyed idealists born long before their time. It is a utilitarian political assessment of the practical needs of a would-be independent government of the fifteenth century.[40]

There is none of this thinking in the author's introduction and, bearing in mind the generation in which he wrote, that probably would not have been expected.

In the appendix to the volume Matthews adds Owain Glyndŵr's letters to the king of Scotland and the Lords of Ireland in 1401–4 (pp. 103–5). Although dates are not attached to the letters themselves, he sought their support in the revolt against Henry IV.[41] He appealed to the Scottish king Robert III (1390–1406) for men-at-arms to aid him in his campaigns. He drew attention to the union between them through Brutus, 'the first crowned king who dwelt in this realm of England, which of old times, was called Great Britain'.[42] The same appeal was made to the Lords of Ireland, but the need for horsemen and footmen was added in that letter.[43] The Scottish letter failed to reach its destination, and the appeal to the Irish was, not unexpectedly, unsuccessful. The purport of the letter to Henry Don (Dwnn) of Cydweli is similar (pp. 105–6), seeking his assistance in stressful times against the English 'who, for a long time elapsed, had oppressed us and our ancestors'.[44] Henry Don, a prominent landowner and chief steward of the lordship of Cydweli, was the son of Gruffudd Dwnn of Croesallgwn in the parish of Llangyndeyrn, Carmarthenshire, and one of Glyndŵr's staunchest military supporters. He had joined Glyndŵr by 1403 and was highly regarded by him in view of his ancestral connections with a powerful Carmarthenshire family.[45]

The main link between these three letters is the prominent references made to prophecy and the myth that a leader would arrive to liberate the true Britons from the yoke of their Saxon oppressors. Prophecy, or vaticination, has a long history extending back to the traditions regarding Merlin and Taliesin. In *c.* AD 930 the famous prophetic poem *Armes Prydein Vawr* and, more significantly, Geoffrey of Monmouth's *Historia Regum Britanniae* (*c.*1136), together with other subsequent vaticinatory outbursts in prose and poetry, highlighted its principal features in the Middle Ages.[46] This prophecy was clearly manifested in these three letters, especially that to the king of Scotland, which formed a central part of Glyndŵr's political propaganda. The central figure was Brutus of Troy, traditionally regarded as the first crowned king of Britain. In this letter Glyndŵr recounted that Brutus had three sons, Albanactus, Locrinus and Camber, and he informed Robert III that he was descended from Albanactus. The descendants of Camber were the Welsh, tracing their descent from Cadwaladr Fendigaid, the last crowned king of the Britons, who died in AD 664. In the prophetic poetry of later centuries the return of Cadwaladr to lead the Welsh against the English had become a common theme. Following Cadwaladr's death legend has it that the Welsh and the Scots were continuously oppressed by the Saxons. Prophecy, however, maintained that liberation was still at hand and that it 'shall be delivered by the aid and succour of your royal majesty [i.e. Robert III]'.[47] In the opening sections of the Irish letter Glyndŵr also stated that 'a great discord or war hath arisen between us and our and your deadly foes, the Saxons'.[48] He addressed Henry Don confidently seeking his assistance again

> to deliver the Welsh race from the captivity of our English enemies . . . And you may know from your own perception that, now, their time draws to a close and [as] according to the ordinance of God from the beginning, success turns towards us, no one need doubt a good issue will result, unless it be lost through sloth or strife.[49]

Prophetic potency, fired by professional poets intent on inspiring a strong national feeling among rising Welsh gentry, gave Glyndŵr and his supporters added support to continue the struggle against the Lancastrian dynasty, and it reached its highest point in the Tripartite Indenture or treaty drawn up at Aberdaron, the home of David Daron, dean of Bangor, on 28 February 1405 – not 1406, as printed by Matthews (pp. 108–10).[50] This 'Indenture' was an agreement between Owain Glyndŵr, Edmund Mortimer (brother of the deceased Sir Roger Mortimer, fourth Earl of March and legal claimant to the throne), Glyndŵr's son-in-law, and Henry Percy, Earl of Northumberland, father of Henry Hotspur, killed in battle at Shrewsbury in 1403. This was a defensive agreement, fragile in its structure, which proposed to divide England and Wales between them to defend each other against the English crown.

Their main object was to protect their own interests and, in Glyndŵr's case, to promote his national aspirations. According to the treaty Northumberland was territorially to receive the lion's share, namely twelve counties in the North and Midlands of England, excluding Cumberland and Durham. Mortimer was to obtain England south of the area extending eastwards from Worcester to Warwickshire and Norfolk. It was Glyndŵr's portion, however, which was the most interesting, namely an area which formed an extended Principality covering large tracts of western England and the Marches from the Severn estuary to Worcester, north to Bridgnorth and the source of the river Trent; then further north to the source of the river Mersey in the Pennines, and from there westward to the coast, thereby following the historic division between Mercia and Northumbria. The extent of such a region was remarkable, and to achieve it would have been a completely impossible task. It was doubtless an exercise in political propaganda based on historical ideology and prophecy. According to Glyndŵr's plan, however, the Indenture appeared to be moving positively towards realizing his dream of establishing a consolidated Welsh Principality. His inheritance in northern Powys and Deheubarth, and his firm alliance with France, had added significantly to his prestige. His power by then was based on his claim to the Principality of Gwynedd. He had adopted the arms and title of the princes of that kingdom, had established the trappings of princely government including the great and privy seals, and had strengthened his hold over large sections of Wales, the marches and sections of English Border territory.[51]

In an age of prophetic claims this plan seemed real to Glyndŵr if not to others of his contemporaries. The extension of his Principality into the western parts of the English Border signified to him a reconquest of areas lost to the English. Names mentioned in the 'Indenture', the Ash Tree (Onennau Meigion) and Kinvar bore significant connections with ancient prophecies. This was an imaginative and visionary plan aimed at achieving an ambition which was totally unrealistic. Its strength for Glyndŵr, however, lay essentially in its historic associations, its 'nationalistic' aspirations and its role in promoting his cause.[52]

Matthews prints the text of the Tripartite Indenture with translation from Henry Ellis's *Letters Illustrative of English History*.[53] In error he took 1406 and not 1405 as the year when it was drafted. His introductory section is too short and descriptive, and fails to examine the full implications of Glyndŵr's main ambitions and the strong prophetic influences upon him. To comment merely that 'Owen and his heirs were to have Wales, that is modern Wales, together with the portions of the counties of Gloucester, Worcester and Stafford and the counties of Monmouth, Hereford, Salop and Chester'[54] is far too general and inadequate a statement when evaluating the true significance of the territory apportioned to him. Matthews seemed not to have fully appreciated Glyndŵr's position at the time, and his note on 'prophecy' (pp. 126–7) fails to convince the reader of its essential features and dominance, especially in relation to his policy. Little is said of Glyndŵr's long-term legacy in Wales excepting a brief and vague reference to the establishment of the University of Wales (p. xxxix) when commenting on the Pennal policy. The misattribution and misquotation at the very end of Matthews's survey is unfortunate. It was not Iolo Goch but Gruffudd Llwyd, another poet patronized by Glyndŵr, who composed the couplets, not in an elegy, since no elegy to Glyndŵr has survived, if one was ever composed, but in a *cywydd moliant* (ode of praise) in his honour.[55]

The French letter transcribed (pp. 106–8) refers to the forty ships which Henry III, king of Castile and León, had agreed to send to Charles VI to assist him in his invasion of England via the Welsh coast. The letter, dated 7 July 1404, was written at a time when the Count of la Marche was preparing to move with his forces into Wales from Brittany with 1,000 lancers and 500 crossbowmen (pp. 106–7).[56] Glyndŵr by then was at the height of his power, believing that French reinforcements would strengthen his military advance into England. Indeed, sixty ships did set sail from Harfleur, leading to three landings by French and Bretons, but they were easily driven back on the south coast of England, which spelt disaster for Glyndŵr at a time when few good opportunities might have come his way during his ambitious campaign.[57]

The last document (p. 118) is part of a French treasurer's journal relating to the term commencing 1 January 1414, in which is recorded in a letter patent that the royal chancellery of France was to pay expenses to the Welsh ambassadors Gruffudd Yonge, bishop of Bangor at the time, and Philip Hanmer, to the tune of 100 livres, valued at £80 Parisian currency. This is a very short administrative entry which Matthews discovered when searching the French archives.

Following descriptions of the seals of Llywelyn ap Iorwerth, Owain Glyndŵr and Gruffydd Yonge, general notes are added on ten items, most of which are short biographies of prominent individuals named in the text, namely Richard de Carew, Gruffydd Yonge, Owain Glyndŵr and Henry Don. Although aimed at explaining further references in that text, the comments are unequal in value as explanatory notes, often vague and uninformative with little direct references to the texts. The descent of Alice, Owain Glyndŵr's daughter, who married Sir John Scudamore, taken from BL Harleian MS 807, in fact adds very little to what Matthews transcribed in his volume (p. 122).[58]

Four clearly reproduced facsimiles are included in the volume, namely the great seal of Owain Glyndŵr (frontispiece), the treaty between Llywelyn ap Iorwerth and Philip Augustus (1212), Glyndŵr's commission to Gruffydd Yonge and John Hanmer (1404) and Owain's autograph letter to Charles VI of France (1406).

How, then, is the historian to assess Thomas Matthews's contribution to the history of Wales as reflected in this volume of sources? The letters which he used to compile his introduction were those available among printed sources of his own day including, in the Rolls Series, *Brut y Tywysogion* (1890), F. C. Hingeston's edition of *Royal and Historical Letters during the Reign of Henry IV* (1860), *Registrum Epistolarum Fratris Johannis Peckham, Eulogium Historiarum*, edited by C. T. Haydon (1858–63) and Giraldus Cambrensis' works (1861–9). Among Welsh sources he used the Historical Manuscripts Commission, *Reports on Manuscripts in the Welsh Language*, edited by J. Gwenogvryn Evans (1898–1910), *Gweithiau Iolo Goch*, edited by Charles Ashton (1896) and *A Catalogue of Manuscripts relating to Wales in the British Museum* (1900–22). He also consulted a number of French and Latin chronicles relating to Scotland and France, as well as Sir Henry Ellis's editions of *Original Letters Illustrative of English History, Chronicon Adae de Usk*, J. H. Wylie's *History of England under Henry IV* (1884–98), N. H. Nicolas's edition of *Proceedings and Ordinances of the Privy Council of England*, (1834–7) and *Rotuli Parliamentorum* (1783–1832), published by the Record Commission, together with some French printed sources. Doubtless Matthews based his survey of the Franco-Welsh treaty of 1212 and Glyndŵr's diplomatic policies on reputable historical sources, sparse though they are. It is surprising, however, that he made no reference to A. G. Bradley's *Owen Glyndŵr and the Last Struggle for Welsh Independence* (1901) which, despite its shortcomings, might well have added to his narrative commentary. Compared to the more extensive bibliography used by J. E. Lloyd in his volume on Glyndŵr (1931), based principally on official sources, Matthews was disadvantaged, but his commentary on transcripts was quite remarkable, in view of the small number of critical studies he could consult. This accounted for his confined interpretation of the historical background and printed texts.

Doubtless Thomas Matthews was a historian of his generation, and it would be altogether inappropriate to dismiss out of hand what in fact he did achieve. It is evident that the volume's structure lacks unity, the commentary falls short of modern historical analysis, and the textual notes are haphazardly organized. His conclusions regarding Llywelyn ap Iorwerth's letter to Philip

Augustus, are based on very thin evidence, and his examination of the Church's role during the 1260s is at best undeveloped, adding no explanatory annotations. However, regardless of some errors in transcription and translation and inadequate attention given to the structure of references, Matthews's versions have been consistently used by some modern historians as essential sources for studying the most important phase in Glyndŵr's career.

It appears that Thomas Matthews's major weakness in publishing this volume of sources and commentaries is that, in the first instance, he had not organized it with sufficient precision. It has been called the work of an apprentice not yet fully able to use his tools sufficiently well. The testimony revealed in a letter written by G. Hartwell Jones, the learned rector of Nutfield, on the occasion of Matthews's death drew attention to what he considered to be his main weakness: 'Gwnaeth wasanaeth da i Gymru, ac yr oedd ynddo addewid am bethau mwy; feallai iddo gyrraedd at ormod o waith ar yr un pryd, a thrwy hynny fyrhau ei ddyddiau' ('He served Wales well, and had promise of greater things to come; it may have been that he accomplished too much work at the same time, thus shortening his days').[59] Although he examined and published documents relating to the practical politics of Owain Glyndŵr's bid to establish his independent Principality, there is still an over-indulgent romantic touch in his section on the Welsh leader's ascendancy, similar to his treatment of the poet Iolo Goch in his edition of his work in *Cyfres y Fil*. The early section refers to the poet's poetry as signifying a new era in Welsh national consciousness:

> Y mae yr agwedd genedlaethol yn fwy grymus heddyw nag y bu erioed. Cawn yn ei gywyddau gân gwawr deffroad cenedlaethol i ryddid – rhyddid i weithio allan ei hiachawdwriaeth ei hun, heb i sythfryd un gelyn nag estron lethu ei datblygiad.[60]
>
> (The national aspect is more powerful today than it ever has been. We find in his odes the dawn-song of a national awakening to freedom – freedom to forge its own salvation without the arrogance of any enemy or foreigner to weaken its development.)

Doubtless an exaggerated viewpoint which reflected 'nationalistic' tendencies of the age shared by Matthews. Despite this criticism, however, Roger W. Jones, headmaster of Lewis School, Pengam, where Matthews was employed as a teacher, proceeded to defend him against his critics:

> Y mae gwaith arloeswyr – pioneers – yn wastad yn agored i feirniadaeth lem gan rai a eisteddant yn gysurus ar eu haelwydydd gartref, a dilys gennym

fod rhai pethau yn y llyfr hwn heb fod uwchlaw beirniadaeth. Tebyg ei fod yn dangos llaw y prentis yn rhy eglur, ond cofier mai ei brentiswaith oedd, a dylid ei werthfawrogi am y gwaith da sydd ynddo, gwaith ym marn un sydd yn alluog i farnu, 'nas gall yr un efrydydd o hanes Cymru ei adael heb ei chwilio'. Diau y buasai yn well, er mwyn clod yr awdwr, pe buasai yn cymryd mwy o amser ym mharatoad ei lyfrau a'i erthyglau, ond nid ei les ei hun, na'i glod ei hun, oedd mewn golwg ganddo, ond lles ei genedl, ac mor fuan ag yr enillai unrhyw ysglyfaeth byddai am rannu'r ysbail gyda'i frodyr.[61]

(The work of pioneers is continually open to severe criticism by those who sit comfortably at home, and it true that some things in this book are not above criticism. It seems that he show the apprentice's hand too clearly, but remember that it was his apprenticeship, and he should be appreciated for the good work which is in it, work, in the opinion of one able to judge, 'no student of Welsh history can leave without examining it'. Doubtless it would have been better, for the author's sake, if he had taken more time preparing the volume, but it was not his own benefit, nor his own fame, that was in his sight, but the benefit of his nation, and as soon as he gained any prey he would share the spoils with his brothers.)

The closing section of his lecture on Welsh records in foreign libraries, delivered before the *Cardiff Naturalists' Society* in 1910, explains clearly what he considered essential to advance the history of Wales, namely the accumulation and cataloguing of historical documents which would enable historians to conduct their research in a scientific manner. He himself endeavoured to accomplish in *Welsh Records in Paris* what be desired Welsh historians to undertake for the good of the nation:

The search should proceed until all MSS bearing upon Welsh literature and history are known and catalogued. Then will come the 'making of books' which is not possible at present, owing to the inadequate nature of our data. Then will also follow an issue (a definite one) of the sources of our history, well printed and well edited. So long as this is not done so long will it be a reflection on the university and upon public bodies in Wales . . . I would suggest the formation of a Society at Cardiff. . . especially to print some of the MSS stored at the City Library. But all in all, I make this suggestion with one object alone, and that is, that Wales may be able to show a corpus of documents of the sources and illustration of its history comparable with those of any country.[62]

Thomas Matthews partly contributed to achieving that aim.

Notes

An Introduction to Thomas Matthews: The man in his time

1 Two of the many works which cite *Welsh Records* as sources are R. R. Davies *The Revolt of Owain Glyn Dŵr* (Oxford 1995), which contains many references to Matthews's work in its footnotes although curiously overlooks the work in the bibliography, and more recently Huw Pryce (ed.), *The Acts of Welsh Rulers 1120–1283* (Cardiff, 2005).

2 *Amman Valley Chronicle and East Carmarthenshire News*, 14 September 1916. Two brief notices recorded his death one in Welsh of just over eighty words and a rather longer version in English.

3 I am indebted to Mr Brian Hopkins of Llandybïe, a fellow member of the Carmarthenshire Antiquarian Society, for trying to locate Thomas Matthews's grave and to Kathy Thatcher who finally pointed me in the right direction.

4 This oversight has continued with the omission of any reference in the *Encyclopaedia of Wales* (Cardiff, 2008) to Matthews's life.

5 Gomer M. Roberts, *Hanes Plwyf Llandybïe* (Cardiff, 1939), pp. 243–4. What made this such an important work in the field of local history was the professional approach which the author applied to his task. Roberts provided a bibliography along with detailed notes and references to each chapter outlining rigorously his sources, unlike other contemporary local historians who allowed little scope for further research.

6 See for example Eric Rowan, *Art in Wales* (Cardiff, 1985), p. 185, Peter Lord, *The Visual Culture of Wales: Industrial Society* (Cardiff, 1999), pp. 60,180, 183 and Ivor Davies and Ceridwen Lloyd-Morgan (eds), *Darganfod Celf Cymru* (Caerdydd, 1999), pp. 95, 96, 98, 103.

7 As a direct consequence of industrialization the population of Glamorgan increased from 397,859 in 1871 to 1,252,451 by 1921. While the figures for Carmarthenshire were less dramatic they do show an increase over the same period from 115,710 in 1871 to 175,073 by 1921. See Russell Davies *Secret Sins: Sex, Violence and Society in Carmarthenshire 1870–1920* (Cardiff, 1996), pp. 14–20 for a detailed account of the changing population trends in Carmarthenshire in the last quarter of the nineteenth century – both causes and impact.

8 The great depression in British agriculture of the last quarter of the nineteenth century was brought about by a combination of factors, notably years of under-investment in new methods and machinery which placed the industry in a poor position to meet the

increased competition from emerging producers in other parts of the world Some products were resilient, and the market for dairy produce in particular was able to survive and expand. Menyn Sir Gar was sold in great quantities in markets on the coalfield.

9 The first census to provide data on the Welsh language was that of 1891. It showed that 898,000 adults, 54.4 per cent of the population in Wales and Monmouthshire, were able to speak Welsh. The percentage of Welsh speakers in Carmarthenshire was much higher at 90 per cent.

10 For a detailed account of the emergence of Nonconformity and its various denominations see Russell Davies, *Hope and Heartbreak: A Social History of Wales and the Welsh 1776–1871* (Cardiff, 2005), pp. 324–41. In 1891 the great Liberal prime minister, William Ewart Gladstone declared: 'The Nonconformists of Wales are the people of Wales', an assertion all the more striking as Gladstone was a High Church Anglican.

11 For an introduction to the variety of sports available see Martin Johnes, *A History of Sport in Wales* (Cardiff, 2005), pp.1–22.

12 The new schools were secular and were supported from the local rates and administered by elected and accountable school boards. These were abolished by the Education Act of 1902, and county councils were made responsible for maintaining the schools out of local rates. Nonconformists objected to these payments and a number of local authorities refused to implement the Act. See K. O. Morgan, *Wales in British Politics 1868–1922* (Cardiff, 1991), pp. 182–98.

13 Ibid., p. 182. The population of Wales according to the 1901 census was 2,033,287.

14 K.O.Morgan *Rebirth of a Nation: Wales 1880–1980* (Oxford, 1981), p. 94.

15 *Amgueddfa Cymru; National Museum of Wales Celebrating the First 100 Years* (Cardiff, 2007), p. 4.

16 Peter Lord, *Y Chwaer-Dduwies Celf: Crefft a'r Eisteddfod* (Llandysul, 1992) p. 29.

17 One exception was Daniel E. Jones, *Hanes Plwyfi Llangeler a Phenboyr* (Llandyssul, 1899), which was submitted to the Drefach-Felindre Eisteddfod of 1897.

18 Morgan, *Rebirth of a Nation.*, p. 103.

19 *The Dictionary of Welsh Biography down to 1940* (London, 1958), pp. 192–3.

20 *Y Genhinen* (1917), 109. Much of the biographical detail relating to Matthews is drawn from this two-part article written by his close friend D. Rhys Phillips, the Welsh Librarian at Swansea Central Library. Phillips was himself an important historian who produced a study of the Neath Valley.

21 Carmarthenshire Records Office, Carmarthen (CROC). The 1901 census return for the parish of Llandybïe records four children being present in the Matthews household of Sunny Hill on census night. Tom's seven brothers and sisters were Benjamin, Jane, David, Bessie, Margaret, John and Robert. I am indebted to Mr Brian Hopkins for this information.

22 *Y Genhinen* (1917), 109.

23 *Cymru* (November 1916), 203.

24 Another view suggests that 'it was Watcyn Wyn who was his primary inspiration'. See T. H. Lewis and Gomer M. Roberts, *Yr Eisteddfod a Bywyd Bro* (Llandybïe, 1944), p. 45. Matthews taught for a short time in Ysgol Gwynfryn.

25 Tom's sister Bessie became an assistant mistress in an elementary school, and his brother David went on to gain a degree. Robert Matthews's resourcefulness and ingenuity are recalled in Bryn Thomas, *Days of Old: Llandybïe Notes and Memories* (Carmarthen, 1975), p. 23: to allow his pupils to view an eclipse of the sun safely he blackened pieces of glass over a candle.

26 The population of the parish according to the 1871 census was 3,171, and it had grown to 8,019 by 1921, an increase of 153 per cent. Between the 1851 census and 1861 there had been a slight fall in the parish's population from 2,885 to 2,821.

[27] T. H. Lewis, *A Short History of Llandebïe National School 1851–1951* (Ammanford, 1951), p. 22.

[28] T. H. Lewis, 'Some Llandybïe Novels, *The Carmarthenshire Antiquary*, V (1964–9), 25–8; also Roberts, *Hanes Plwyf Llandybïe*, pp. 247–89 and Thomas, *Days of Old*, pp. 81–8.

[29] Matthews was one of the two guest judges for the carnival which accompanied the Eisteddfod in 1910; Thomas, *Days of Old*, p. 85. A detailed account of the parish's rich literary tradition is given in Lewis and Roberts, *Yr Eisteddfod*.

[30] Dylan Rees, *Carmarthenshire: The Concise History* (Cardiff, 2006), p. 103. County Schools would open in Llandeilo in 1894 and Ammanford in 1914.

[31] CROC, Minute Book of the National School Llandybïe 1892–1912 (Llandybïe CPR 8/10).

[32] Lewis, *A Short History*, p. 25, the recollections of Mr David Thomas, a retired headmaster living in Maesteg.

[33] I am indebted to Professor. J. G. Jones for checking the University of Wales calendar regarding this reference.

[34] *Y Genhinen* (1917). 109.

[35] R. W. Jones, *Cymru*, LII, 307 (February 1917), 60.

[36] See Arthur Wright, *The History of Lewis School Pengam* (Newtown, 1929).

[37] *The Carmarthenshire Antiquary*, XLI (2005): Terrence James, 'A Brief History', pp. 7–12 for an account of the origins of the society; Dominic Conway, 'First and second presidents', pp. 37–40 for a profile of Alan Stepney-Gulston.

[38] *Transactions of the Carmarthenshire Antiquarian Society*, IV, 67.

[39] Ibid., VI, 9–16.

[40] Ibid., 60–3; his debate was with Timothy Lewis MA.

[41] National Library of Wales (NLW), D.Rhys Phillips Collection 3195, T. Matthews to D. Rhys Phillips, 20 August 1913. The item which Matthews donated was a paper decoration in the shape of a candle, a '*perllan*'.

[42] NLW, Paul Diverrès Collection 190 (MS 123C), T. Matthews to Paul Diverrès, 8 October 1906.

[43] Ibid., T. Matthews to Paul Diverrès, 12 February 1907.

[44] Ibid., T. Matthews to Paul Diverrès, 11 October 1907.

[45] Nothing came of his proposal to assemble a collection of Breton books and works on Celtic drama, and present them ultimately to the recently formed National Library of Wales.

[46] E. Owen (ed.) *A Catalogue of the Manuscripts relating to Wales in the British Museum*, 4 vols (Cymmrodorion Record Series, 1900–22).

[47] NLW, Paul Diverrès Collection 190 (MS 123C), T. Matthews to Paul Diverrès, 20 December 1908.

[48] See Huw Pryce (ed.), *The Acts of Welsh Rulers 1120–1283* (Cardiff, 2005), p. 251 for a charter relating to Cwmhir Abbey 1212 in the *Bibliothèque Nationale*, which Matthews overlooked.

[49] T. Matthews, *Welsh Records in Paris* (Carmarthen, 1910), p. xi.

[50] Ibid., p. xi.

[51] Matthews commissioned the company of Berthaud Frères in Paris to undertake the production of the illustrations and these were supplied to the printers in Carmarthen.

[52] *Archaeologia Cambrensis*, X (1910), 404–6. The reviewer also added that all students of Welsh history will be 'doubly grateful to Mr. Stepney-Gulson for his suggestion that the whole of the known documents on Owen Glyndwr be included'.

[53] R. W. Jones, *Cymru*, LII, 307, (February) 1917, 61.

[54] *Transactions of the Cardiff Naturalists Society*, XLIII (1910), 31.

[55] NLW, Paul Diverrès Collection 190 (MS 123C), T. Matthews to Paul Diverrès, 23 November 1909; this letter has attached to it a cutting of an article by Arthur Mee taken from the *Western Mail*. Mee expresses the hope that the documents will be published: 'it is surely to be hoped that Wales will see to it that Mr. Matthews is enabled to complete the task in which he has already acquitted himself with such signal credit and distinction.' The reason why nothing appeared may well have been financial, as he undoubtedly needed the support of either a patron or a major publisher in order to realize his objective.

[56] *Monmouth Guardian*, 8 August 1913.

[57] There were very close ties between the village of Llandybïe and Brittany through the onion trade.

[58] *Y Genhinen* (1917), 110.

[59] *Cymru* (1913): Yves Berthou, 'Erthyglau ar Landreger'.

[60] *Carmarthen Journal*, 22 September 1916.

[61] NLW, Paul Diverrès Collection 84 (MS 139B), Gwersi Llydaweg. In the foreword Matthews expresses the hope that the lessons will allow anyone interested an opportunity to study at first hand the literature of a fellow Celtic nation.

[62] *Cymru* (January 1916), 31.

[63] *Llên Gwerin Blaenau Rhymnei, o gasgliad Bechgyn Ysgol Lewis Pengam* (Rhymni, 1912). This provides a very good indication of the nature of Welsh culture in an area which is now very much Anglicized.

[64] I am indebted to the late Mr Iwan Jones for allowing me to consult his lecture notes on Tom Matthews.

[65] *Y Genhinen* (1917), 112.

[66] Wright, *The History of Lewis School*, p. 124.

[67] The *Cyfres Y Fil* series was launched in 1901 by Edwards with a view to making accessible to ordinary people, at an affordable price, important works of Welsh literature. The two works produced by Matthews were, according to Edwards, a new departure since they were focusing on less well known figures from the medieval period.

[68] T. Matthews, *Gwaith Siôn Cent* (Llanuwchllyn, 1914); Owen M. Edwards's foreword, p. 4, and *Gwaith Iolo Goch* (Llanuwchllyn, 1915).

[69] *Cymru* (November 1916), 229.

[70] Peter Lord, *Imagining the Nation* (Cardiff, 2000). Lord provides a careful analysis of the emergence of an artistic tradition in Wales during the second half of the nineteenth century. He goes some way to evaluating the contribution of Thomas Matthews in helping to promote Welsh art during this period.

[71] This is certainly the opinion of his friend and former headmaster at Lewis School, R. W. Jones, *Cymru* (February 1917), 61.

[72] *Y Genhinen* (1917), 111.

[73] T. Matthews, *The Biography of John Gibson, RA, Rome* (London, 1911), p. v.

[74] Ibid., Appendix II, pp. 249–52.

[75] The contract with William Heinemann was signed on 27 January 1911 and the book published later that year on 5 October, priced 10s. 6d. Matthews did not receive any advance and agreed a royalty of 10 per cent. A review in *The Studio*, 55, 223 (March 1912), 164, was rather less than complimentary of the subject, noting that Gibson's letters which 'form the bulk of Mr Matthews' book are considerably marred by the egotism of their author'.

[76] *Cymru* (February 1917), 61.

[77] T. Matthews, *The Biography of John Gibson*, p. viii.

[78] Lord, *Y Chwaer Dduwies*, p. 49 Pennod V. Diwygwyr y De – Cenhedlaeth T. H. Thomas.

[79] Public art galleries were a comparatively new development in Wales during this period. Progress was slow, The Mostyn Art Gallery opened in Llandudno in 1902, but it was not until 1911 that the Glynn Vivian Art Gallery in Swansea opened its doors. Although the National Museum and Gallery was not completed until 1927 a small gallery and museum was attached to Cardiff Free Library from 1882, while temporary exhibitions arranged by the National Museum were mounted in Cardiff City Hall in 1913–14.

[80] *Cymru* (1912–13). The articles started in January 1912 and appeared almost continuously (no items in November and December) through to May 1913 when 'Y Cyfnod Olaf' completed the series. For Margaret Lindsay Williams see *Cymru*, (November 1914), 216.

[81] T. Matthews, *Arluniaeth Edgar H. Thomas* (1914). This is a curious work, over half of which deals with the author's views on art rather than the declared subject. For David Davies, Y Cerflunydd, see *Cymru* (February 1916).

[82] NLW, Paul Diverrès Collection 190 (MS 123C), T. Matthews to Paul Diverrès, 11 May 1908.

[83] See Dylan Rees, 'Christopher Williams and Carmarthenshire' Heather James and Patricia Moore (eds), in *Carmarthenshire & Beyond: Studies in History and Archaeology in Memory of Terry James* (Llandybïe, 2009).

[84] NLW, MS 16331D, a corrected proof copy of an unpublished biography of Christopher Williams, from the Liverpool printers Hugh Evans and Sons. The final chapter – chapter 5 – is in manuscript form.

[85] Matthews used *Deffroad Cymru* as the frontispiece to his last published work in 1916.

[86] *Cymru* (1916), 247, letter dated September 1916.

[87] Davies and Lloyd-Morgan, *Darganfod Celf Cymru*, p. 103.

[88] T. Matthews, *Celf yng Nghymru* (Caernarfon,1914), reproduced from *Cymru*, 6.

[89] Ibid., 22.

[90] NLW, Paul Diverrès Collection 83 contains a draft MS of the first work Matthews hoped to publish, *Calon ar Galon: Can y Caniadau*, September 1912 – a collection of five love letters which he planned to print in an initial run of 200 copies (later amended to 300).

[91] Sulien (1011–91), who was born in Llanbadarn-fawr, became bishop of St David's in 1072. Rhigyfarch (1056–91), was his eldest son and author of a life of St David.

[92] Matthews published a short work, *Celf Addurn Ysgol Sulien* (1914) on the bishop and his circle.

[93] A privately printed edition of sixty-one copies of *The Tournament at Carew Castle: A Pageant* (Pengam, 1914) is the closest Matthews got to achieving his ideal. Ornate capitals are also very evident in his unpublished biography of Christopher Williams.

[94] NLW, ex1148: Ruth Richards, 'The Reawakening of Wales: Painting Ideology and National Culture in Early Twentieth Century Wales' (unpublished MA thesis, University of Sussex, 1989), p.14.

[95] T. Matthews, *Perthynas Y Cain a'r Ysgol* (Caerdydd, 1916), p. 60.

[96] *The Welsh Outlook* (April 1916), 134–5.

[97] Matthews, *Celf yng Nghymru*, p. 16. John at this time was establishing an international reputation for himself, having exhibited twenty-seven works at the 1913 Armory Show in New York. Matthews himself admired the integrity and truth which he sought to convey in his work.

[98] See *Picturing America* (Montebello, 2008) published by the National Endowment for the Humanities in an attempt to identify forty core works as representative of the best in American art with which all school students should be familiar.

[99] R. W. Jones in *Cymru* (February 1917), 60.

[100] NLW, Paul Diverrès Collection 190 (MS 123C), T. Matthews to Paul Diverrès, 20 December 1908.

[101] Ibid., T. Matthews to Paul Diverrès, 28 March 1909.
[102] NLW, D. Rhys Phillips Papers 3201, 2 November 1915, 'Bu cyheoddu y llyfr yn golled i mi. Ni chafodd werthiant werth son amdano yng Nghymru. Dau aeth i Gaerdydd!'
[103] *Y Genhinen* (1917), 109.
[104] Iwan Jones, 'Thomas Matthews: Arloeswr yr Ardd Ganol', *Taliesin*, 124 (Spring 2005), 113.
[105] *Cymru* (February 1917), 63.

Thomas Matthews the Historian

[1] K. O. Morgan, *Rebirth of a Nation: Wales 1880–1980* (Oxford and Cardiff, 1980), pp. xxx; J. G. Edwards, 'Hanesyddiaeth Gymreig yn yr ugeinfed ganrif', *Transactions of the Honourable Society of Cymmrodorion* (1953), 21–31; N. Evans, 'Finding a new story: the search for a usable past in Wales, 1869–1930', *Trans. Cymmr. Soc.*, N. S. 10 (2004), 144–62.
[2] D. Johnston, 'The literary revival', in *idem* (ed.), *A Guide to Welsh Literature c.1900–1996* (Cardiff, 1998), pp. 1–21.
[3] D. Ellis Evans and R. Brinley Jones (eds), *Cofio'r Dafydd: Cymdeithas Dafydd ap Gwilym 1886–1986* (Swansea, 1987), chs 1 and 2 (by J. E. Caerwyn Williams and J. Tudno Williams), pp. 21–114; J. E. Caerwyn Williams, 'Cyfraniad Cymdeithas Dafydd ap Gwilym: y blynyddoedd cynnar', *Y Traethodydd*, CXXXVIII (1983), 184–98.
[4] H. Pryce 'Modern nationality and the medieval past: the Wales of John Edward Lloyd', in R. R. Davies and Geraint H. Jenkins (eds), *From Medieval to Modern Wales: Historical Essays in Honour of Kenneth O. Morgan and Ralph A. Griffiths* (Cardiff, 2004), pp.14–29; J. G. Edwards, 'Sir John Edward Lloyd', *Proceedings of the British Academy*, 41 (1955), 319–47; R. T. Jenkins, 'Syr John Edward Lloyd', *Y Llenor*, 26 (1947), 77–87; *Oxford Dictionary of National Biography* (Oxford, 2004), 34, pp. 141–2; *Dictionary of Welsh Biography, 1941–1970* (London, 2001), pp.172–3; J. E. Caerwyn Williams, 'Cenedlaetholdeb haneswyr Cymru gynnar Rhydychen', in Geraint H. Jenkins (ed.), *Cof Cenedl: Ysgrifau ar Hanes Cymru*, XIII (1998), pp. 14–28.
[5] J. E. Lloyd, 'History of Wales', *Transactions of the Royal National Eisteddfod of Wales, Liverpool 1884* (Liverpool, 1885), 341–2.
[6] Pryce, 'Modern nationality and the medieval past', p. 25.
[7] R. T. Jenkins and Helen M. Ramage, *A History of the Honourable Society of Cymmrodorion (1751–1951)* (London, 1951), p. 186.
[8] Henry Owen (ed.), *The Description of Penbrokshire* (London,1892), p. xxviii.
[9] Pryce, 'Modern nationality and the medieval past', p. 29.
[10] N. Evans, 'Finding a new story', 160.
[11] Iwan Jones, 'Thomas Matthews: arloeswr yr ardd ganol', *Taliesin*, 124 (Spring 2005), 103–15; Dylan Rees, 'Thomas Matthews, M.A. (1874–1916), Llandybïe: historian, writer and art critic', *The Carmarthenshire Antiquary*, XL (2004), 129–38.
[12] T. Matthews, *Perthynas y Cain a'r Ysgol* (Undeb Cymdeithasau Cymraeg, 1916), p. 11.
[13] Rees, 'Thomas Matthews', 133; D. Rhys Phillips, 'Thomas Matthews, M.A.', *Y Geninen*, XXXV (1917), 207.
[14] T. Matthews, 'Welsh records in foreign libraries', *Cardiff Naturalists' Society: Report and Transactions*, XLIII (1910), 20–1.
[15] Ibid., 31.
[16] Matthews, *Welsh Records in Paris*, preface, xi–xii.
[17] D. Rhys Phillips, 'Thomas Matthews', 109.
[18] For the Cardiff Cymrodorion Society see J. G, Jones, *Y Ganrif Gyntaf: Hanes Cymrodorion Caerdydd 1885–1985* (Cardiff, 1987); and for Cochfarf *idem*, 'Edward Thomas (Cochfarf):

dinesydd, dyngarwr a gwladgarwr', *Trafodion Cymdeithas Hanes Bedyddwyr Cymru* (1987), 26–45.

19 NLW Paul Diverrès Collection 190 MS 123c (Letters 1906–16). Some of the letters written to Diverrès between February 1909 and March 1910 contain references to his preparation to publish *Welsh Records in Paris*. It is altogether surprising that Matthews gave Diverrès but a slight acknowledgement in his preface. He did, however, add his name to the list of subscribers and informed him that a complimentary copy of the book would be given him.

20 Matthews, *Welsh Records in Paris*, p. xi.

21 Ibid., pp. 139–43.

22 R. I. Jack, *Medieval Wales: The Sources of History. Studies in the Uses of Historical Evidence* (London, 1972).

23 R. F. Treharne, 'The Franco-Welsh treaty of alliance in 1212', *Bulletin of the Board of Celtic Studies*, 18 (1958), 60–75 (here 61–2 (n. i), 75 (nn.d and f)).

24 Paul Diverrès Collection, letter dated 12 March 1910.

25 Treharne, 'The Franco-Welsh treaty of alliance in 1212', 74–5. See also H. Pryce, *The Acts of Welsh Rulers 1120–1283* (Cardiff, 2005), no. 235, pp. 392–3; H. Rothwell (ed.), *English Historical Documents, 1189–1327* (London, 1975 edn.), pp. 306–7.

26 Matthews, *Welsh Records in Paris*, xvii; Treharne, 'The Franco-Welsh treaty of alliance in 1212', 67–74.

27 Ibid. See also I. W. Rowlands, 'King John and Wales', in S. D. Church (ed.), *King John: New Interpretations* (London, 1999), pp. 283–4. The author argues that the treaty may have been negotiated in May or June 1212 and not July or early August, as Treharne states.

28 Matthews, *Welsh Records in Paris*, pp. 7–20.

29 It is not at all clear whether Gaudier did, in fact, carry out the task.

30 S. Runciman, *A History of the Crusades*, Vol. III: *The Kingdom of Acre* (Cambridge, 1975 edn.), pp. 315–17.

31 A. W. Haddan and W. Stubbs (eds), *Councils and Ecclesiastical Documents relating to Great Britain and Ireland*, 3 vols (London, 1869–78), I, pp. 481–4; Matthews, *Welsh Records in Paris*, p. 123; Glanmor Williams, *The Welsh Church from Conquest to Reformation* (Cardiff, 1962), p. 23; Thomas Jones (ed.), *Brut y Tywysogion or The Chronicle of the Princes (Red Book of Hergest Version)* (Cardiff, 1955), pp. 248–9; *Fasti Ecclesiae Anglicanae*, ed. J. le Neve, 3 vols (Oxford, 1854), I, p. 29.

32 Williams, *Welsh Church*, p. 31.

33 Ibid., pp. 215–16; Matthews, *Welsh Records in Paris*, p. xx; R. R. Davies, *The Age of Conquest: Wales 1063–1415* (Oxford, 1987), pp. 190–1.

34 J. E. Lloyd, *Owen Glendower: Owen Glyn Dŵr* (Oxford, 1931), pp. 84–5.

35 Matthews, *Welsh Records in Paris*, pp. 82–4; R. R. Davies, *The Revolt of Owain Glyn Dŵr* (Oxford, 1997 edn.), pp. 116–17 ff.

36 Matthews, *Welsh Records in Paris*, pp. 32–9.

37 Ibid., p. 97.

38 For the background to this document see Lloyd, *Owen Glendower*, pp. 119–21; Davies, *The Revolt of Owain Glyn Dŵr*, pp. 169–73; Williams, *Welsh Church*, pp. 223–5.

39 Matthews, *Welsh Records in Paris*, pp. 97–8.

40 Williams, *Welsh Church*, pp. 223–4.

41 Matthews, *Welsh Records in Paris*, pp. 111–13; *Chronicon Adae de Usk A.D. 1377–1421*, ed. E. Maunde Thompson (2nd edn, 1904), pp. 72–4. See also *The Chronicle of Adam Usk 1377–1421*, ed. C. Given-Wilson (Oxford, 1997), pp. 148–52.

42 Williams, *Welsh Church*, pp. 213–14; Matthews, *Welsh Records in Paris*, p. 111.

[43] Matthews, *Welsh Records in Paris*, p. 112; Davies, *The Revolt of Owain Glyn Dŵr*, pp. 188–90.

[44] Ibid, p.113. This letter was copied by Matthews from H. Owen and J. B. Blakeway, *A History of Shrewsbury*, 2 vols (London, 1825), I, pp. 181–2. He has, in error, mis-spelt 'Blakeway' as 'Blakeney'.

[45] G. H. Hughes, 'Y Dwniaid', *Trans. Cymm. Soc.* (1941), 115–16; T. W. Newton Dunn, 'The Dwn family', ibid. (1946–7), 273–4; Davies, *The Revolt of Owain Glyn Dŵr*, pp. 200–1.

[46] For more background on the prophetic tradition see Glanmor Williams, 'Prophecy, poetry and politics in medieval and Tudor Wales', in *idem, Religion, Language, and Nationality in Wales* (Cardiff, 1979), pp. 71–86; Lloyd, *Owen Glendower*, p. 95; Davies, *The Revolt of Owain Glyn Dŵr*, pp. 159–61, 167–9; E. R. Henken, *National Redeemer: Owain Dŵr in Welsh Tradition* (Cardiff, 1966); A. D. Carr, *Owen of Wales: The End of the House of Gwynedd* (Cardiff, 1991), pp. 87–98.

[47] Matthews, *Welsh Records in Paris*, p. 111.

[48] Ibid., p. 112.

[49] Ibid., p. 113.

[50] H. Ellis (ed.), *Original Letters Illustrative of English History* (2nd series London,1827), I, pp. 27–8.

[51] Davies, *The Revolt of Owain Glyn Dŵr*, pp. 161–2. Matthews omits the following short preface to the agreement printed by Ellis; '*Hoc anno Comes Northumbriae fecit legiam, et confederationem, et amicitiam cum Owino Glendor et Edmundo de Mortuo mari, filio quondam Edmundi Comitis Marchiae, in certis articulis continentibus formam quae sequitur et tenorem.*'

[52] Davies, *The Revolt of Owain Glyn Dŵr*, pp. 167–9.

[53] Matthews, *Welsh Records in Paris*, pp. 108–10.

[54] Ibid., p. xxxvii.

[55] See Charles Ashton (ed.), *Gweithiau Iolo Goch* (London, 1896), p. 223; H. Lewis, T. Roberts and I. Williams (eds), *Cywyddau Iolo Goch ac Eraill* (Cardiff, 1972), pp. xli,124. Matthews, misled again by Ashton, wrongly attributes to Iolo Goch two couplets in a prophetic strict-metre poem whose author is unknown, but possibly Lewys Glyn Cothi later in the fifteenth century, in praise of Owain ap Gruffudd ap Nicolas of Dinefwr. See p. xxi (n. i) and Ashton, XII. I. Williams, 'Llyma fyd rhag sythfryd Sais', *Y Llenor*, I (1922), 62–70; H. Lewis, 'Rhai cywyddau brud' and 'Cywyddau brud', *Bulletin of the Board of Celtic Studies*, I (1922–3: Parts 3–4), 254, 307; G. A. Williams, *Owain y Beirdd* (Aberystwyth, 1998), pp. 11–12.

[56] Matthews, *Welsh Records in Paris*, pp. 114–15.

[57] Davies, *The Revolt of Owain Glyn Dŵr*, pp. 192–3; Lloyd, *Owen Glendower*, p. 88; F. Lehoux, *Jean de France, duc de Berri, sa vie, son action politique (1340–1416)* (Paris, 1966–8), III, p. 21 (n. 4); *Chronique du religieux de Saint-Denys*, ed. L. Bellaguet (Paris, 1839–52), III, pp. 222–4.

[58] British Library Harleian MS 807,94b; H. Owen (ed.), *A Catalogue of the Manuscripts Relating to Wales in the British Museum*, 4 vols (London, 1903), II, p. 212.

[59] D. Rhys Phillips, 'Thomas Matthews', 111.

[60] T. Matthews, (ed.) *Gwaith Iolo Goch* (Llanuwchllyn, 1915), p. 3; Dafydd Johnston, *Iolo Goch* (Caernarfon, 1989), p. 8.

[61] R. W. Jones, 'Thomas Matthews', *Cymru*, 53, 307 (February 1917), 60, freely quoted in Iwan Jones, 'Thomas Matthews: arloeswr yr ardd ganol', p. 109.

[62] T. Matthews, 'Welsh records in foreign libraries', 31.

Thomas Matthews (1874–1916)

Thomas Matthews (standing left) with colleagues at
Lewis School, Pengam, 1914; R. W. Jones (headmaster), seated right.

Thomas Matthews (far right), Crwys (third from left) and
Samuel Maurice Jones (second from right) at the
1910 National Eisteddfod, Colwyn Bay.

Front cover of *Dail y Gwanwyn*, published in 1916.

Goleuni y Gwanwyn by Christopher Williams R. B. A.
from *Dail y Gwanwyn*.

Selection of capitals used in *The Tournament at Carew Castle: A Pageant* (Pengam, 1914)

Woodcut from *Dail y Gwanwyn*, 1916, where the Three Feathers of the Prince of Wales are reinterpreted from a nationalist perspective.

Appendix: List of Thomas Matthews's Published and Unpublished Works

Published Works

Welsh Records in Paris (Carmarthen, 1910)
The Biography of John Gibson, R.A., Sculptor, Rome (London, 1911)
Llen Gwerin Blaenau Rhymni (ed.) (1912)
Gwaith Siôn Cent (ed.), (Llanuwchllyn, 1914)
Celf yng Nghymru (Caenarfon, 1914)
Celf Addurn Ysgol Sulien (Caernarfon, 1914)
Arluniaeth Edgar H. Thomas (Caernafon, 1914)
The Tournament at Carew Castle: A Pageant (jointly with Ada L. Forestier-Walker) (Pengam, 1914)
Gwaith Iolo Goch (ed.). Llanuwchllyn, 1915)
Barddoniaeth ar gyfer Ysgol Pengam (ed.) (Pengam, 1915)
Dail y Gwanwyn. Barddoniaeth, Llen-gwerin a Straeon gan Fechgyn Ysgol Lewis Pengam (ed.) (Pengam, 1916)
Perthynas y Cain a'r Ysgol (Caerdydd, 1916)

Unpublished Works

Gwersi Llydaweg
Calon ac Galon. Can y Caniadau – a series o five love letters to be printed privately dated 3 September 1912
Celf Christopher Williams – corrected proof pages of the first five chapters and a draft manuscript copy of the last chapter, given to the NLW by the printer Meistri Hugh Evans a'i Feibion Lerpwl in 1939 and 1946

Welsh Records in Paris

EDITED

With an Introduction, &c.

BY

T. MATTHEWS, M.A.

University College of South Wales, Cardiff; Member of the Carmarthenshire Antiquarian Society

CARMARTHEN: W. SPURRELL AND SON

1910

INTRODUCTION.

WELSH RECORDS IN PARIS.

CONTENTS.

TO

ALAN STEPNEY-GULSTON, ESQ., J.P.

Y DERWYDD, LLANDEBIE

FIRST PRESIDENT

OF THE

CARMARTHENSHIRE ANTIQUARIAN SOCIETY

THIS BOOK IS DEDICATED

IN APPRECIATION

OF HIS INTEREST IN THE

HISTORY AND LITERATURE OF WALES.

PREFACE.

IT was after considerable hesitation that the publication of the following documents was decided upon. The transcripts were not originally made with this intention, and it is only in the hope that they will, in some way, be of service to students of the History of Wales that they are published.

Upon a suggestion of Mr. Stepney-Gulston's, the whole of the known documents issued by Owen Glyndwr are included. The kindness of Sir E. Maunde Thompson, K.C.B., and of the Royal Society of Literature relieved me of the task of copying the letters contained in Adam of Usk's Chronicle. It gives me pleasure to acknowledge their courtesy in readily allowing me to use their text.

An ineffectual search was made for the list of the ports of Wales which Sir John Hanmer made for the Count of March, and after my departure from Paris, continued by my friend M. Pol Diverres (Tangwall). M. Henri Petit, the Curator of the 'Archives de la Haute-Vienne' at Limoges, also very kindly searched the MSS. of the Counts of March. It was stated that the document was in existence some twenty years ago, but his search was also in vain.

The reference numbers of the documents at the Archives Nationales, Paris, are, for convenience, given at the head of each document. Full references are also given of sources of the remaining letters.

In a few years the quincentenary of Owen Glyndwr's death will remind us of the close of his struggle, and it may not be inappropriate here, to express the hope that, that anniversary, will see a National tribute to Owen's greatness.

My gratitude is due to the Rev. George Eyre Evans, of Aberystwyth, for his valuable advice; to Mr. Ernest J. Waters, Eurwern, Carmarthen, for kindly copying for me portions of the Alcwyn Evans Mss. in his possession; to Mr. Stepney-Gulston for the benefit of his wide knowledge of heraldry; to Mr. E. E. Hughes, M.A., of the University College, Cardiff, for his advice and kindly criticism while the book was in the press; to the Rev. J. Fisher, B.D., Cefn; to Mr. Walter Spurrell, for the care and interest which he took in the work; and especially to M. Pol Diverres, whose kindness and courtesy I cannot too highly estimate.

It is also a pleasure to acknowledge the courtesy which I received from the Director of the Archives Nationales, Paris, and his staff; from Mr. Henry Farr, the Chief Librarian; Mr. Ifano Jones, of the Welsh Department, and the assistants of the Reference Department of the Free Library, Cardiff; and to Mr. D. Rhys Phillips, Welsh Librarian, Swansea.

Eryl, Llandebie,
Gwyl Garmon, 1909.

FACSIMILES.

ERRATA.

Page xxxii., for footnotes 2, 2, read 2, 3.
Page 32, for Confederationium, read Confederationum.
Page 123, line 7, for apparently, read probably.
Page 125, line 28, for 1415, read 1414.

TREATY BETWEEN LLYWELYN FAWR AND PHILIP AUGUSTUS.

THERE is a certain amount of difficulty in deciding the year during which Llywelyn issued this letter forming an alliance with Philip Augustus. The choice lies between A.D. 1212 and A.D. 1216; but a definite decision can only be made with some hesitation.

In the year 1212, Pope Innocent, as the result of his interdict against King John, called upon Philip Augustus to make war upon John in order to reduce him to the 'subjection of the Holy Church.' At the same time the Pope absolved the Welsh princes from their oaths to John and removed the interdict from Wales. Hence both the Welsh princes and Philip would, in 1212, be acting under Papal authority against John. This may have suggested to Philip the idea of making overtures for common action against John. The letter implies that the decision to form an alliance was due to the influence of the church. Though it is quite possible that the phrase 'in an assembly of clergy and upon the holy relics' may only refer to the usual method of making a binding agreement. Again, the reference to the 'large tract of land and the strongly fortified castles which had lately been occupied by fraud and guile' would seem to refer to the cession of Perfeddwlad in 1211. In 1212, Llywelyn and the princes of Wales 'unanimously rose against King John and bravely wrested Perfeddwlad from him, which he had previously taken from Llywelyn ab Iorwerth.' That is, in 1212, all the princes of Wales were confederated against John, and in a short time after all the losses of 1211 were made good. Hence it is very probable that this alliance between Llywelyn and Philip was concluded late in the year 1212.

There are, however, grounds for hesitating to accept this date. When the chronicler of the *Brut* refers to the five years truce which John made with Philip after his defeat at Bouvines in 1214, he does not refer to any agreement between Wales and France; nor does he refer to a council of the chieftains of Wales and wise men of Gwynedd before the famous council at Aberdovey in 1215. That council solved the dispute between the princes of the Deheubarth—Maelgwn ab Rhys, Rhys Gryg, and their two nephews—concerning their shares of the lands of the Lord Rhys. It is also clear that an agreement was arrived at concerning the part which Wales would take in the civil war in England. For the *Brut* declares that Gwenwynwyn of Powys, when he deserted Llywelyn, "treated with contempt the oath which he had plighted to the chieftains of England and Wales"; and as the Dauphin's forces had landed in England as early as the seventh of January, 1216, there are some grounds for thinking that one of the objects of the Council of Aberdovey was to consider an alliance with Philip Augustus. But it must be pointed out that in deference to the changed relations between John and Pope Innocent in 1215, Philip Augustus studiously avoided giving any countenance to his son's expedition to England in any public or official manner.

Louis the Dauphin, however, landed with more forces "about Trinity Sunday,"[1] 1216. It is unnecessary here to detail his struggle with John, nor after that monarch's death with the royal party, which was concluded by the Treaty of Lambeth, in Sept., 1217. Llywelyn's opportunity to strike came when Reginald de Braos joined the king. This immediately brought Rhys ab Gruffydd and his brother Owain upon Reginald. They took the "whole of Buallt except the castles," and Llywelyn moved down to support them. He intended to destroy the town of Brecon, but he allowed the town to escape through the intervention of "young Rhys," on receiving a fine of 100 marks and five hostages. Lly-

[1] *Brut y Tywysogion*, Rolls Edition, p. 290.

welyn moved from Brecon over the Black Mountains, and encamped in Llangiwg. Reginald de Braos and his brother William, seeing no chance of withstanding Llywelyn, surrendered, and were allowed the castle of Senghenydd. Llywelyn now moved to Dyfed, and while preparing to take Haverford by assault, Iorwerth, bishop of Menevia, secured peace for the men of Rhos and Pembroke, on the payment of 1000 marks and of giving 20 hostages. These were to be surrendered by Michaelmas, failing which, the men of Rhos and Pembroke were to do homage to Llywelyn.

While Llywelyn was thus consolidating his power, Louis was concluding the Treaty of Lambeth with Henry III. Though Louis secured good terms for himself, it is clear that the Cymric Chronicler considered that he had violated an agreement with his prince. For "on that occasion," that is, after the treaty had been signed, "William Marshall fought against Caerleon, and took it; for the Welsh had not consented to the above pacification, supposing the agreement to have been forgotten or disregarded."[1] This can only mean an understanding between Louis and Llywelyn. It cannot mean an agreement with the barons, as it is stated that the pacification is between Henry III. and Louis, son of the King of France. This agreement would then be Llywelyn's Treaty with Philip, which stated that no peace would be made by Llywelyn with the English unless foreknown to Philip,[2] and it is only reasonable to infer that the same condition applied to Philip and hence to Louis.

Hence while there are strong reasons in support of the earlier date, the absence of any reference to a Council of Princes before 1215, and to any agreement between Wales and France till 1217, decides in favour of the later rather than the earlier date.

---

[1] Ygkyfrwg hynny yd ymladawd Gwilim Marscal a Chaer Llion ac y goreskynnawd kany chytsyngassei y Kymry ar dagnefed uchot gan dybygu ebrgofi y cymod [neu ydielwi]. *Brut*, p. 275.

[2] Cf. pp. 4, 58.

BULLS OF URBAN IV. TO THE BISHOP OF MENEVIA.

IT is clear from the context of these bulls that they were issued to bring to being a Crusade which would attempt to terminate the struggle between the Saracens and the Christians in Palestine. Throughout Urban refers only to his solicitude for the Holy Land and the condition of that country, which is 'ravaged by Saracen fury and Tartar rage.' The Holy Land requires assistance against the infidel. It is a shame to Christendom that it calmly stands by, while 'the country which Christ chose as a special patrimony and heritage for himself' is ravaged by Saracen unbelievers. His statements agree, in general, with the condition of the remaining portions of the Latin Kingdom in Palestine, during Urban's short pontificate (1261—1264). In 1259, the Tartars captured Damascus, and shortly afterwards surrounded Acre. However, every apprehension of danger from them, vanished—at least for a time—in 1260. Sultan Kutuz of Egypt came against them, and they were totally defeated by him at Ain Talut. This defeat terminated their progress in that direction, but the peril of the Latin Kingdom was still serious, as the new Sultan of Egypt turned his strength against the Christians of Palestine.

The Mameluke mercenaries of the Egyptian sultans, inspired by their leader Bibars, had been accustomed, since they destroyed the Ayoubite power in Egypt, to set up and murder sultans as they saw best, and Sultan Kutuz was no exception. On his return from Ain Talut, he too was murdered, for Bibars, finding himself strong enough, had intrigued to succeed him. Bibars Elbondukari was a Turkoman slave, who through his military prowess had become captain of the Mamelukes. He was the soul of the opposition against Louis IX. of France during his first crusade, and it was probably the military skill of Bibars which led to the surrender of the French army at Damietta in 1250. In 1262, he commenced his attacks upon the Latin Kingdom of Palestine—or what was left of it. Town after town fell into his hands. It was evident that the triumph of the Saracens was imminent. Hence, it is clear from Urban's statements in the Bulls and the general condition of affairs in the Holy Land, that Urban had in view a crusade to assist the Holy Land against Bibars.

Besides it is well known that Louis IX. had another holy war continuously before his mind—a crusade which would retrieve his disastrous first. It is not clear when Louis first sent an ambassador to the Pope, requesting the assistance of the church on behalf of this war; but there are several reasons which support the theory that these documents may be the result of such an appeal. If Louis made such a request to Pope Urban IV., and undertook the organization of another crusade, it would only be natural that the bulls to the western dioceses should be distributed from Paris. This would account for the large number of bulls of the same date stored among the National Archives of France—many in duplicate—as these to the Bishop of Menevia. The arrangements for a crusade fell through, or it may have been inexpedient to forward them, and these documents were therefore retained at Paris.

The Bulls are interesting as indicative of the support the Holy See expected from Wales. Urban demands an annual tax for a period of five years of the hundredth part of the income of the whole of the clergy of Wales. This tax must be remitted to him in full, without any deduction for cost of collection or transmission. The bishop is also to provide ten horsemen and fifteen men, fully and suitably equipped, and to pay their expenses. The clergy are to exhort their congregations diligently, and carefully explain to them the message of the cross.

The Bishop of St. Davids or his deputies are given full authority to induce people to volunteer for the crusade or in any way assist the war. There is a graduated scale of remissions, and full authority is given to the bishop to grant them, according to the support received. Men who volunteer for the war, and who pay their own expenses, and men who provide substitutes equal to themselves in every respect at their own cost, are granted full pardon for their sins. Indulgences might also be granted to the limit of 'one hundred days plenary indulgence.' The crusaders are immune from ecclesiastic punishment during their period of service, and those who assist are also immune during their period of indulgence. In addition to whatever Urban, or any duly accredited person, may grant by his authority, the chief enticement is that 'your devotion may be followed by the palm of glory which is given as a reward to those who wage war for God.'

These documents have some importance, when we regard them in the light of Gerald's famous struggle for the supremacy of St. Davids. That struggle terminated sixty years before Urban issued these bulls; yet it is perfectly clear from the bulls, that the Holy See regarded the Diocese of Menevia as the premier see of Wales. Indeed, there is some reason for inferring more than seniority in precedence, for Urban demands from the Bishop of Menevia the same quota of men for the crusade which he has asked from other metropolitan sees.

Bishop Beck's attitude in 1284 also gives some proof to this inference. In that year he objected to a visitation of his diocese by Archbishop Peckham, on the ground that the suit instituted by Giraldus at Rome, in 1199, with reference to the supremacy of St. David's, was still pending. The objection was disregarded, and till Owen Glyndwr's letter to Charles VI. of France, in 1406, that is the last we hear of the question of the supremacy of St. Davids.

THE LETTERS OF OWEN GLYNDWR.

THE opening years of the fifteenth century were years of great discontent in Wales. The long smouldering indignation caused by changed social conditions, and by the oppression of the Marcher barons was ready to burst into open revolt. The bards, who for many years had forgotten the joy of battle and adventure, in poems of love and nature, again called the nation to arms, and gave expression to the national longing for a ruler of their own race.[1] The time seemed opportune, Richard II. had just been deposed, and the new king was on all sides beset with difficulties. Within the realm, he had to contend with the partizans of the late king and of the descendants of Edward III., who were senior to him in descent. In Ireland, the power of the Lord Deputy was not supreme even within the Pale; while outside the Pale the Irish were independent, and were constantly fighting against the English colonies on their coasts. Scotland was also openly hostile, and Henry could only expect difficulties from France. For, though on the occasion of the marriage of Richard II. with Isabella of France, in 1396, a treaty had been made agreeing to a truce of twenty years, it was also stipulated, that should Richard die childless, Queen Isabella and her dowry were to be returned to her father. Immediately on hearing of Richard's death, King Charles VI. took care to declare that he would abide by the terms of the treaty, that is, not that he agreed to the truce, but that he would have the right to make war on

---

[1] Llyma fyd rrag sy(th)fryd sais
Mynych iawn a ddamunais;
Kael Arglwydd llam arwydd llain
O honon ni nyhunain.—*Iolo Goch*, p. 194.

Henry whenever he pleased. Henry made every attempt to solve all difficulties with France peaceably. At Henry's request ambassadors were appointed by both countries to treat, but the instructions of the French ambassadors were indicative of the intentions of their King. They were not to speak of Henry as 'king,' and the English ambassadors were to be styled as 'the envoys on the part of England.'[1] Indeed, while these ambassadors were arguing in the church of Lenlyngham, outside Calais, the King of France was strengthening his border fortresses, he had closed the Somme to English merchants, and was collecting a large force at Harfleur,[2] with the object of making a descent on South Wales to seize the castles of Pembroke and Tenby, which had been granted to Isabella by King Richard by the treaty of 1396. The Count of St. Pôl, who had married Matilda Courtenay, Richard's half-sister, was placed in command. It was clear that France was preparing for war, and Henry attempted to postpone the evil day as long as possible, in order to gain strength. Such, in short, were the conditions under which Owen's attempt to make Wales an independent state became a factor in European politics.

It would be difficult to decide whether Owen Glyndwr revolted owing to Lord Gray's duplicity, or that the Welsh revolted and then chose Owen for their leader. This need not be discussed here, but it can be pointed out that Owen's name does not appear in the early stages of the revolt, as, for instance, in Henry's first proclamation against the Welsh rebels on the 19th of September, 1400.[3] On the other hand, the Chronicle history of Henry V. states, that the Welsh rose against the King and then chose Owen to lead them.[4] The earlier negotiations of the struggle can only be indicated. Presumably the earliest reference is the report of the Cham-

---

[1] Wylie, I., 123. [2] *Cronique de Traison*, 168. [3] Ellis' Second Series *Original Letters*, II., 2. [4] *Ibid.*

berlain of Carnarvon, early in 1401, to the King's Council. John Saughall, the Constable of Harlech, has received a warning that there was an arrangement between Meredydd ab Owen and the men of the 'Owtiles' of Scotland to land at 'Abermouth and Eve (Barmouth and [?] Aberdovey) betwixt this and midsomer neghst with her power, and that the same Meredydd should prively warn her friends to make hem ready with hors and harneys again the same tyme.' Great preparations were being made; cattle were sold to buy horses and harness. Meetings were being held in 'dissolate places and wild,' but their 'counsaelle be holden yet secret fro us, wherthrogh yong peple are more wilde in governance.'[1] In the June following some Scottish ships appeared on the coast of Wales, but Henry Percy, the Governor of North Wales at that time, was ready for them. The Scotch ships were met by Henry's ships at sea and pursued, one of them entered Milford Haven and was captured there.[2] The negotiations which the King made with the Lords of the Isles in Cumberland, while returning from a privateering raid on the north-east coast of Ireland, probably gives a reason why no further assistance was obtained from that quarter.[3]

Owen is not mentioned in this report, though it is possible Meredydd was his son.[4] Later in the year, however, that is, on the 29th November, 1401,[5] we have letters from Owen showing that he desired to place himself in communication with the King of Scotland and the Lords of Ireland. The messengers seem to have intended to reach Scotland by way of Ireland, for while in Ireland, they were taken with the letters upon them and beheaded. Their general trend is the same, Owen requires assistance against their mutual foes the Saxons, 'for it faileth me much in men-at-arms.' He appeals to Robert

---

[1] Ellis' *Original Letters*, II., 8. [2] Nicholas' *Ord. Privy Council*, I., 153. [3] Adam of Usk, 61; *Rotuli Scotiae*, II., 255. [4] Cf. notes, p. 129. [5] Adam of Usk, 71–3, cf. p. 103–5, 111–113.

of Scotland on the ground of their reputed common ancestry,[1] and to the lords of Ireland, on the ground that, if he is able 'to manfully wage this war on our borders . . . you and all the other chieftains of Ireland will in the meantime have welcome rest and calm repose.' Owen must about this time, also have sought for assistance from France. For, early in 1402, a certain knight, 'David ap Ieuan Goch, of the County of Cardigan, who for full twenty years had fought against the Saracens with the King of Cyprus and other Christians, being sent by the King of France to the King of Scotland on Owen's behalf, was taken captive by English sailors, and imprisoned in the Tower of London.'[2] That is, even as early as 1402, Owen had foreseen the assistance Charles VI. might be to him, for it would be Charles' advantage to embarrass Henry as much as possible in Scotland, Wales, and in the English possessions in France.

So far, however, negotiations in France and Brittany would only secure for Owen assistance from privateers, for England and France were nominally at peace. But there was an enormous amount of privateering and piracy, especially in the narrow seas. As Henry wished to maintain the truce as long as possible, the blame for the piracy was laid upon the Bretons, for Brittany was still an independent state. Early in 1403 the arrangements for such assistance must have been fairly complete. In the early months of that year, Owen wrote to his 'very dear and entirely well beloved Henry Don,'[3] to be prepared to come to him shortly, with the greatest possible force 'to the place where you hear that we are burning our enemies by destroying them during the march.' Owen explains that he had not warned him of the previous occasion he had come to the marches of Caermarthenshire early in 1401,[4] 'because, from great apprehension and danger, it behoved us to rise without

---

[1] Cf. notes, p. 126. [2] Adam of Usk, 71. [3] Cf. p. 105, 113.
[4] Ellis' *Original Letters*, II., 8.

forewarnings.' At any rate by the 3rd of July, 1403, 'Oweyn Glyndour, Henri Don, Res Duy, Res ap Gr. ap Llewellyn, Res Gethin,' and their men had won the town and castle of Carmarthen,[1] and a few days later burnt the town. We know that on the 5th of July, all Carmarthenshire, Kidwelly, Carnwyllion, and Iscennen were sworn to Owen at Dryslwyn Castle.[2] It seemed only a question of time for the remaining castles of Ystrad Towy—Carreg Cennen, Llandovery, and Dynevor—to fall into his hands. Assistance from France was slow in coming, but on the 'Wednesday next after the Feast of St. Michael the Archangel,' (3rd October) 1403, for on that day the Constable wrote that 'Henry Don, and all the rebels of S. Wales, with the men of France and Bretagne were coming towards the castle and town of Kidwelly with all their array, and there have destroyed all the grain belonging to your poor lieges, on every side around your said Castle and the town; and that the greater part of your poor commons there have taken their departure and gone into England, with their wives and young children, and the rest are within your said Castle in uncertainty about their lives.'[3] The castle was not taken, but the walls were injured; it must have been held in a state of siege for at least three years, as nearly all relief seems to have been sent there by water. The French privateers wintered around the coast. Late in the year, under the command of Jean d'Espayne, they attacked Carnarvon, but were driven off. In conjunction with Owen, a second assault was delivered towards the beginning of January.[4] Full preparations—'engines, sowes, and ladders of great

[1] Ellis' *Original Letters*, II., 8. [2] Hingeston's *Royal and Historical Letters*, p. 138; Ellis, II., 19. [3] Hingeston, 160. [4] Ellis, II., 31–7. There is a peculiar reference in Nicholas' *Orders of Privy Council*, I., 220, to this assault on Carnarvon, which implies that Jean d'Espayne was bought off by the English Government. Minutes of Council for 23rd April, 1404: "Et pur remuer John de . . . . chivaler de France qui ovec certeins niefs et vesselx armez avoit mys assege as ditz chastiel et ville de Carnervan et Harlagh pur la sauve garde et defense de roialme CCC. li.

length '—had been made for the siege. Meanwhile, the remaining castles—Rhuddlan, Llanbadarn, Harlech, Criccieth, Kidwelly, Cardigan, Cardiff—were closely blockaded. They were able to hold out mainly because supplies could be sent by sea.[1] By the April following, Owen, with part of the French force, had entered Shropshire. On the 21st the town of Shrewsbury sent a pitiful appeal to the king for help,[2] and such was the general anxiety and alarm, that the peasants of the Eastern counties of England believed that Owen would shortly march upon Northampton.[3]

It is unnecessary to detail the struggle and Owen's successes. 'Meanwhile,' says John Fordun, 'a hundred Welshmen could easily defeat a thousand English, and a thousand Welshmen ten thousand English.' 'In three years they had expelled all their enemies from Wales, took all the castles built by the English, and destroyed them, three only excepted, Aberystwyth, Conway, and Harlech.'[4] This, it is true, is an exaggeration, but it is an illustration of how a Scotch contemporary was informed of the condition of Wales. A clearer conception is found from the returns of King Henry's own property, the Duchy of Lancaster, the Manors of Monmouth, Ogmore, Ebbwy, Kidwelly, Iskennen, and Brecon, returned no dues for the years 1404, 1405, 1406, and 1407. In 1408 the Manor of Monmouth yielded £90, the Manors of Ogmore and Ebbwy £6 13s. 4d., and the others nothing. In 1409, the Manors of Ogmore and Ebbwy yielded £6, and the others nothing.[5] It is not till 1411 that the dues again reach their average. Adam of Usk estimates the loss of revenue to King Henry at £60,000.[6] In reality the loss was much greater, as the castles had to be garrisoned and relieved from

---

[1] Nicholas' *Orders of Privy Council*, I., 220: "John Stevens of Bristol is commissioned to relieve Aberystwyth (Llanbadarn), Cardigan, Carnarvon, and Harlech." [2] *Ibid.*, II., 77. [3] *Traison de Richard*, II., 275. [4] *Scotichronicon*, II., 450. [5] Duchy of Lancaster Records; Wylie, IV., p. 157, sqq. [6] Adam of Usk, p. 257.

English funds. Taking everything into consideration, it seems safe to infer that by the commencement of 1404, Owen, directly or indirectly through his subject barons, now ruled the whole of Wales.

Meanwhile the hollow negotiations between Henry and Charles VI. of France were pursuing their dilatory course. But the death of the Duke of Burgundy on the 27th of April, 1404, at Hal, near Brussels, removed all opposition to the designs of the Duke of Orleans, and brought matters to a head, especially as Queen Isabel had been returned to her father. A 'quick change' had taken place in the attitude of that prince towards Henry. When Henry was in exile at the court of Charles, the Duke of Orleans had favoured Henry's attempt to obtain the crown of England, and they had made a secret compact with one another, vowing to support each other in every possible way. Despite this, early in November, 1402, Henry received from the Duke a challenge,[1] dated the August previous, to meet him in the lists. This challenge may have been the outcome of the peculiar chivalry of the age, though coincident events make that doubtful. On the 25th of February, 1404, both the Duke and the Count of St. Pôl challenged Henry in terms that could not be mistaken. A quarrel was to be forced. Apart from the general reasons for war, the Count of St. Pôl had married Richard's half-sister, and the eldest son of the Duke of Orleans was betrothed to Isabella, after her return to France. Hence the Duke may have wished to secure the lands granted to Isabella by Richard on the occasion of their marriage. The preparations for war which the French were making were well known in England,[2] and Henry was also constrained to take similar measures, and even to expel all foreigners from his court. Owen must have been aware of the trend of affairs in France, if not the objective of the preparations.

---

[1] Hardy's *Syllabus of Rymers Foedera*, p. 550. [2] Hingeston's *Original and Historical Letters of the Reign of Henry IV.*, 28, 187.

In the spring of 1404 he summoned a parliament to meet at Dolgelly, and perhaps as the result of the decision of this body, he issued on the 10th of May, 1404, to Griffith Yonge[1] and to John Hanmer, a commission with full powers to conclude an offensive alliance with Charles VI. against 'Henry of Lancaster.'[2] Accompanying them as their notary was Benedict Comme, 'a clerk of the diocese of St. Asaph.'[3] They arrived at Paris early in June, for on the 14th Charles VI. issued a commission to the Count of March and the Bishop of Chartres to meet the Welsh ambassadors, and to complete the treaty.[4]

The ambassadors were well received, for the French King remembered that a certain Welsh squire, Owen of Wales, had served France valiantly against the English, and Owen Glyndwr was of the same race as that knight. The ambassadors brought from Owen a request for active support, in the form of 'money, harness, and men.' King Charles seems to have made many enquiries concerning the conditions, life, and customs of Wales. Hanmer left before the treaty was concluded, but it had been decided to assist Owen. He took with him as presents for Owen from Charles a gilded helmet, a cuirass, and a sword, for King Charles understood that 'Owen loved arms above all things.' These were tokens of more substantial assistance. Before leaving Hanmer wrote out for the Count of March a list of the 'most famous ports in Wales, and the most fertile districts through which they might enter more freely.'[5] The treaty was concluded on the 4th of July, 1404, being sealed by the French ambassadors and Griffith Yonge. By this 'Charles, King of the French,' and 'Owen, Prince of the Welsh,' mutually bound themselves in an offensive and defensive alliance against Henry of Lancaster and his adherents. They also made provision,

---

[1] Afterwards Owen's Bishop of Bangor; Cf. Notes for a sketch of his life. [2] Cf. p. 23. [3] Cf. p. 31. [4] Cf. p. 28–9. [5] *Chroniques de St. Denys*, III., Cap. IX., p. 164 sqq ; Hingeston, 270.

that should any difficulties arise between them, they could be adjusted amicably, 'according to their merits and legitimately reformed.' Owen ratified the treaty at his 'castle of Llanbadarn' on the 12th of January following.[1]

There, probably, were Welsh agents, attempting to secure help, in Brittany and France, even before Owen had issued his commission to Yonge and Hanmer. For on the failure of the privateering raid which William de Chastel, Lord of Chateau Neuf, near St. Malo, made on Dartmouth on the 15th of April, 1404, there were Welshmen among the captives.[2] Now that the treaty was concluded, no time was lost in the attempt to give Owen active assistance. Even seven days before the treaty was sealed, Louis, Duke of Bourbon, appealed to Henry III., King of Castile and Leon, to provide him with forty armed ships, as quickly as possible, for King Charles, his ally had ordered the Count of March to proceed forthwith to Brittany with one thousand lances and five hundred crossbowmen, in order to sail thence to Wales. The ships should be in Brest by the 15th of August, at which date it was intended that the expedition should sail, 'to harass, and damage the English, our enemies.' It is not clear that they obtained the desired assistance from Spain, but the expedition remained in Brest till November, as there was no money forthcoming from Paris.[3] When they did sail they thought it too late to sail for Wales, and also the force was insufficient, so they 'explored the coast of England.'[4] The wind was contrary and they failed to make for Dartmouth. They, however, fell in with seven trading vessels and gave chase. The ships made for Plymouth, and being unable to reach that port, the vessels were abandoned, and the crews rowed themselves ashore.

---

[1] Cf. p. 39. [2] Rymer's *Foedera*, viii., 358. [3] *Chroniques de St. Denys*, III., 144 sqq; *Extrait des Chroniques de Monstrelet*, I. p. 69, sqq. [4] *Ibid.*

Plymouth was then attacked and burnt, and after Plymouth 'the small island of Salmouth,' as both places were practically defenceless. For their bravery here the Count of March made 'new knights' of his brothers, Louis, Duke of Bourbon, Jehan, Lord of Clarency, and a few others. After some time they turned for France, but were caught in a furious storm, which lasted for three days. Twelve vessels were lost, and some sixty men. The remainder were able to reach St. Malo in safety. Thus this expedition, owing to the carelessness and waste of the French court, despite the great preparations, was not even as effectual as many of the piratical raids of the period.

Owen's position now seemed secure. Later in the year a second parliament was held at Machynlleth, when David Gam attempted to kill Owen. Though his forces were defeated at Mynydd Camstwn, the total defeat of the English at Craig-y-dorth, near Monmouth, compensated for that reverse. John Trevor, the able and clear-sighted Bishop of St. Asaph, had also thrown in his lot with Owen. However, on the 11th of March, a Welsh force received a serious reverse at Grosmont. A Welsh force attacked Grosmont, and being caught unawares by an English force under Prince Henry, Lord Talbot, William Newport, and Sir John Greindre were defeated, leaving 800 slain on the field.[1] There is some contradiction in Henry's letter, as the burning of four houses cannot be termed the burning even of a part of a small town. Fordun, also, states that the battle was won by treachery.[2] Later in the year there was another fight near Usk. Owen seems to have had a strong supporter in that district—a John ab Howel, an Augustinian canon.[3] This man is given the credit of securing for Owen the support of the men of Glamorgan and Gwent. A Welsh force being attacked near 'Brinbiga upon the River Usk,'

---

[1] Ellis' *Original Letters*, II., 39–41. [2] *Scotichronicon*, II., 452–459. [3] *Ibid.*

and after a bitter struggle were overcome, seventy being slain, among them the 'eloquent canon John ab Howel.'

But these defeats would have been of small importance had the French alliance and the invasion been successful. Early in 1405, Jean de Hangest, Lord of Hugueville who had been captured by the English at Marck, was released. He immediately threw himself heart and soul into the task of fulfilling King Charles' promise to Owen, and pledged his estate at Ayencourt, near Montdidier, to secure funds for the enterprise. With the help of Jean de Rieux, the Marshal of France, a force of 800 men-at-arms, 600 crossbowmen, and 1200 light infantry was collected.[1] After securing the consent and assistance of the Estates of Brittany, they sailed from Brest on the 23rd of July, 1405, for Wales.[2] The Marshal de Rieux was in command, Jean de Hangest, Lord of Hugeville, was in command of the crossbowmen, and a Strabo de la Heuse as one of the captains. They had a rough passage, owing to which they lost a large number of horses. At last, early in August, they reached Milford Haven and were met by a Welsh force of 10,000 men. Haverfordwest was attacked and destroyed, but the castle still held out. Tenby was called upon to surrender in the name of Queen Isabel, the rightful owner, and attacked; but the appearance of the English fleet caused them to retire. Carmarthen was taken and destroyed. The combined force then entered Glamorgan, and visited 'the Round Table, that is to say the noble abbey which is near the road to Caerwent.'[3] Ultimately the combined army met the English forces, tradition states, at Woodbury Hill, between the Severn and the Teme. Neither side seemed prepared to attack. At last famine compelled the Welsh and French to retire upon Caerwent. After making further preparations, the King entered

---

[1] *Chroniques de St. Denys*, III., 144 sqq. [2] *Chronicum Brittanicum* [printed in Morice], *Histoire de Bretagne*, I., 115. [3] *Chroniques de St. Denys*, III., Chapter xviii.

Wales, and though able to relieve Coity,[1] was compelled to retire with the loss of all his baggage. Towards the beginning of November, portion of the French forces returned home, leaving 'le Begue de Belay' with 500 archers and 1200 light infantry to winter in Wales.[2] But in March, they also returned, landing at St. Pôl-de-Leon in Brittany, after having suffered considerable losses owing to the attacks of the English admiral during the voyage across.[3] The failure of this expedition must have been exceedingly disappointing to the national leaders. The struggle was difficult as it was, and in all probability the French force, not only was but of little assistance to Owen, but both by wasting his supplies and by their lack of enterprise, especially in not attacking the English forces when they met, did Owen an injury, and caused a loss of prestige from which he did not recover.

Early in 1406, if not during the last few months of the year 1405, Owen had sent two envoys to France. Their purpose is clear in the light of Owen's last extant letters. The envoys, Morris Kery and Hugh Eddouyer, a Dominican friar, returned to Owen with a kindly letter assuring him of the health of the French Royal Family and of their friendship towards him. Charles then proposed that Owen should become united with him in spiritual as in temporal matters, and as ignorance on the part of the ruler means ignorance also on the part of the subjects, Charles proceeds to give Owen the French account of the Papal schism. If Owen would agreee to acknowledge Benedict XIII., the Avignon Pope, then Charles would use his influence with Benedict to secure that all the loyal prelates and beneficed clergymen in Wales shall be confirmed in their present livings, and that when vacancies arise, those persons only who are loyal to Owen shall be appointed to the vacancies. After receiving this despatch, Owen

[1] *Eulogium*, Hist. III., 408. [2] *Chroniques de St. Denys*, III., Chap. xviii. [2] *Annales Ric. II. et Hen. IV.*, 419.

submitted it to his Council, and at their advice, to the 'nobles of his race' and the 'prelates of the Principality.' The result was that they decided to recognize Benedict as the true Pope. Further, that Charles should use his influence with the Pope in support of certain proposals, which Owen made to reform the church of Wales. In the first place, all ecclesiastic censures 'against us, our subjects, or our land,' issued by Benedict or by Clement, were to be removed, and that Benedict was to confirm all the official acts of the clergy, from the time of Gregory XI., which might otherwise endanger or prejudice him and his subjects. Owen then proceeds to state his policy with reference to the church. The cathedral church of St. Davids has 'by the fury of the barbarous Saxons,' been made subject to Canterbury. He therefore requires that St. Davids be restored to its old position as the metropolitan church of his principality, with the Bishops of Exeter, Bath, Hereford, Worcester, Leicester (i.e. Coventry and Lichfield), St. Asaph, Bangor, and Llandaff as suffragans.[1] No one is to be appointed to any benefice or other dignity in Wales, unless he can speak 'our language.' The appropriations by English colleges or monasteries of Welsh churches are to be revoked and annulled, and they cannot in future have any patronage in Wales. Two universities shall be established, one for North Wales and another for South Wales, in places where his ambassadors may again decide upon. But Henry of Lancaster and all his adherents, for their manifold wrong-doings against the church, are to be declared heretics, and tortured in the usual form. While Owen, his heirs and his subjects of whatever nation, as long as they fight against the 'said intruder,' are to be granted full remission of their sins, which is to endure as long as the war between Owen and Henry continues. But the friendship of France was now little more than a form of words. Charles did take some action, perhaps owing to

[1] Cf. p. 53, 97.

the Earl of Northumberland's importunity.[1] On the 2nd of October, 1406, he issued a proclamation calling upon all men ' good and true ' to rise and drive the usurper Henry from the throne, and set up the Earl of March, who was the true heir. He then states that the late expedition to Wales would have been more effectual had he known that help was really needed.[2] But Owen's acknowledgment of the supremacy of the Avignon Pope did produce some of the results naturally subsequent to such action. For in Volume 92 of the Registers of the *Supplicitiones*, in the Vatican Archives, we find two rolls of appeals to Benedict XIII. from Wales, while his nomination of Griffith Yonge as Bishop of Bangor in 1404, was annulled, in 1414, on account of his adherence to the schism.[3]

While Owen was negotiating with France, he was also in correspondence with the Percies. His friendship with the Hotspur seems to have commenced shortly before Henry Percy was relieved of the Governorship of North Wales,[4] when he met Owen to discuss terms of submission. Some correspondence was conducted, by the King's consent, through the Earl of Northumberland and Sir Edmund Mortimer. Owen seems to have been ready to submit. But the King's Council were too divided to come to a conclusion on the matter.[5] However, it seems fairly clear King Henry feared that there was an understanding between them as early as October, 1402. During the previous summer, though the King had marched into Wales with some 30,000 men, he had retired miserably without effecting any success. The Percies, on the other hand, had been singularly successful on the Scottish border, and among their captives was the

---

[1] Waurin's *Receuil des Chroniques*, II., 102. [2] Add Ms. 30663; also *Chroniques de St. Denys*, III., 428. [3] Cf. Notes for Yong's life, p. 123. [4] Henry Percy was Governor of North Wales from 23rd Oct., 1399 (*Patent Rolls*, 1 Henry IV., 4, 6) to June 1401 (Nicholas' *Orders of Privy Council*, II., 57. [5] Nicholas' *Orders of Privy Council*, II., 59; I., 175.

Earl of Douglas, whom Henry Percy retained as his own captive in Northumberland. The King demanded that Hotspur should surrender Douglas to him. Henry Percy in reply, came to London to answer the King's demand in person. A quarrel ensued, the King demanded Douglas, and Henry Percy requested that his brother-in-law, Edmund Mortimer, who had been captured at Pilleth, should be ransomed. The King refused as the ransom would go to aid his enemies. The outcome was that the King declared that Mortimer was a traitor, having yielded himself voluntarily to the Welsh, and so was Percy also, for he had not captured Owen when he had the chance.[1] Whether this refers to the time Owen and Percy met to discuss terms of surrender or not is not clear, but it was soon evident that Henry's tenure of the throne was becoming more insecure. In a short time Mortimer[2] openly declared himself against King Henry. A secret agreement existed between Henry Hotspur, Edmund Mortimer, and Owen, to put the Earl of March on the throne, and to allow Owen to be the independent Prince of Wales. Even as late as the third of October, 1403, one of the messengers, a John Morys,[3] in the service of Thomas Percy, Earl of Worcester, was still with Owen. Probably also, the 'Jankyn Tyby,'[4] who came from the 'Northe contri' with, it was believed, letters from Henry Percy, was a messenger in the same negotiations. The plot seemed to have every hope of success, but Hotspur revolted and tried to effect a junction with Owen, but the latter was in Carmarthenshire. The king met the Percies at Shrewsbury. George Dunbar, the Scotch Earl of March, finally persuaded Hotspur to attack without waiting for Owen to come up, and the death of Hotspur in that fight brought this dream to an end.

The idea of placing the young Earl of March on the

[1] *Chronicon:* Ed. J. A. Giles, 1848, p. 31. [2] He had also married Owen's daughter. [3] *Patent Rolls*, 5 Henry IV., 135. [4] Ellis' *Original Letters*, II., 9.

throne was not however forgotten. The Duke of York, who had favoured Henry Percy's plot, actively favoured a second, which his sister, the widowed Constance, Lady Le Despenser, carried out. About the middle of February, 1405, she succeeded in escaping with the two young Mortimers out of Windsor Castle, intending to make for Wales. She and her escort were caught up near Cheltenham, captured, and brought back to Windsor. Consequently, Henry took care that the two sons of the late Earl of March were better guarded than before.

Owen, however, had not terminated his negotiations with the Earl of Northumberland. By April 19th, 1405,[1] it was clear that the Earl was ready to rebel against Henry, and shortly afterwards was in Scotland plotting a rebellion. Subsequent events indicate that he must have kept Owen informed of his movements, for during the summer Owen sent 'lord Griffith, Bishop of Bangor,' and another bishop, namely of St. Asaph (John Trevor), to Scotland, where they discussed the means of acting in concert against King Henry, and probably also the conditions under which they would do so. With them were Thomas, Lord Bardolf, and the Abbot of the Praemonstratentian Abbey of Welbeck.[2]

While the Earl of Northumberland was in Scotland, the Earl of Douglas was still in the Tower. In Scotland intrigues were proceeding for the succession, and it was important to Douglas that he should be at hand when King Robert died. He had married Margaret, Robert's eldest daughter, and it was expected that he would succeed his father-in-law. There were frequent proposals to ransom him, but the money was not forthcoming. However, on the 27th of August, of 1405,[3] permission was granted to Sir William Borthwick and Lord Lorne to

---

[1] He disregarded the order to attend the King's Council of this date: John Hardyng's *Chronicle*, 362. [2] *Scotichronicon*, II., 441. [3] *Rotuli Scotiae*, II., 176.

come to England to negotiate. They offered to deliver the Earl of Northumberland to King Henry in return for Douglas.[1] Their design failed, for the Earl and Bardolf received a timely hint, and escaped into Wales.[2] They must have been in Wales throughout the winter, for on the 28th of February, 1406, at the house of David Daron, Dean of Bangor, at Aberdaron, in far off Lleyn, Owen, the Earl, and Edmund Mortimer met, and when they had decided upon and drawn up their treaty, they probably went into the little church of St. Hywyn, above the dark waters of the rock-girt bay, where the Daron ends its short course, and heard the Dean say mass. The holy office over, they, 'steadfastly gazing upon the sacred body of the Lord and touching the Holy Gospels,' took from David their vows to observe, keep, and firmly maintain this strange compact.

The treaty seems to have been largely based upon the treaty with Charles VI. of France. They form an offensive and defensive alliance against anyone whomsoever. If any differences arise between them, they arranged for their peaceful adjustment. And if according to the will of God, as the prophet declares, the three lords are the men among whom the government of Great Britain is to be divided,[3] they wish to take the precaution to prevent future strife by allotting to one another the country, and by defining the boundaries. Owen and his heirs were to have Wales, that is, modern Wales, together with the portions of counties of Gloucester, Worcester, and Stafford, and the counties of Monmouth, Hereford, Salop, and Chester. The Earl's share was to be the counties north of a line drawn from Worcester directly east to the sea; but the counties Durham and Cumberland are not mentioned. Edmund Mortimer was to have English counties south of such a line. Finally, they are united against all enemies, saving Owen's ally, the King of France.

---

[1] *Hypodigma Neustria*, 418. [2] *Ibid.* [3] Cf. pp. 108, 109, 116, 117.

A few weeks after the treaty was signed, the French army, where his hopes to a large extent were laid, returned to France, and Owen had to wage a single-handed struggle to maintain his position. The Earl and Bardolf remained in Wales till the 19th of June, 1406.[1] They tried to obtain sympathy in England, but without success.[2] Owen had already sent envoys to France, and by the middle of July the Earl and Lord Bardolf also, reached Paris, by way of Brittany.[3] The Earl prayed for assistance, but no help was forthcoming.[4] The Earl, lured perhaps by inaccurate information, made one more desperate venture. During the severe winter of 1407–8, from Scotland he crossed the border into England, and fell fighting amid the melting snows on Bramham Moor on Sunday, the 19th of February, 1408. A year later Sir Edmund Mortimer died of fever during the siege of Harlech, and that castle capitulated in February, 1409.

Owen seems to have kept up some kind of independence to the end. It is hardly possible that a man whom the English represented as 'a starving and deserted fugitive, lurking in herns and halks, and chewing gravel and mud,' could keep David Gam prisoner, and continue to send envoys to Charles VI. of France. On the 21st of May, 1408,[5] two Welsh envoys arrived at Paris, appealing for assistance against the English. Probably Bishop John Trevor was one of these, for he died at Paris in 1410.[6] They received 200 archers and 300 men-at-arms under Le Borgne (*i.e.*, The One-eyed) de la Heuse.[7] This Strabo de la Heuse was a Norman knight, and had been one of the French captains in the expedition of 1405.[8] There is, however, no proof that the troops arrived in Wales. Late in 1413, Owen sent his last embassy to Charles, for, from the 3rd of December to the 22nd of February, 1414, 'Griffith, Bishop of Bangor, and Philip

[1] *Rolls of Parliament*, Henry IV., iii., 606. [2] *Anglea Sacra*, II., 369.
[3] Hardyng's *Chronicle*, 364. [4] *Monstrelet Chroniques en Guerre*, I., 130.
[5] *Monstrelet Chroniques*, I., 256–9. [6] *Dictionary of National Biography.*
[7] *Monstrelet*, I., 256–9. [8] Cf. p. xxxi.

Haunier, esquire,' [1] were ambassadors from him at the French court. On the 5th of July, 1415,[2] Henry V. commissioned Sir Gilbert Talbot to treat with him with the view to his submission, and on the 24th of February, 1416,[3] with his son Meredydd ab Owen. Because on the 21st of September, 1416,[4] on the sixteenth anniversary of the commencement of the struggle, Owen's stirring career had closed. He was buried ' in the night season by his followers. But his burial being discovered by his adversaries, he was laid in the grave a second time, and where his body was bestowed may no man know.' [5]

Owen's long struggle was over, and despite the long fight, he failed to realize his ideals, as in course of time a small country would always be wanting in Owen's great need, ' namely men,' to continue a long struggle. One of his aims has been realized, an aim which proves that he was in greater sympathy with the educational movements of this time than most of his contemporaries. When we consider Owen's fight for his own people and its failure, the closing lines of the elegy, which his friend Iolo Goch wrote on his death, are singularly appropriate :

A gwawr drist o'r garw dro,
Brydnawn ar Brydain yno ;
A'r gair i Gymry try hwyl,
Wrth archoll frwydr o'th orchwyl,
A'r gwiw rwysg a'r goresgyn,
A'r glod i'r MARCHOG O'R GLYN.

---

[1] Cf. p. 110, 118. [2] Rymer's *Foedera*, ix., 283. [3] *Ibid.*, 331. [4] Panton Ms., 22 : Annales Owenni Glyndwr ex liber vet : script per Lewys Morgannwg. *Historical Mss. Reports*, Part III. : MCCCCXV. ydd aeth Ow : mewn difant yn gwyl Fathau yn y Cynhaeaf. [5] *Chronicon Adae de Usk*, 129.

CONFEDERACIO LOELINI PRINCIPIS NORWALLIE CUM DOMINO REGE FRANCIE.

Plate II.

J655. 14.
AE^{III} 66.

CONFEDERACIO LOELINI PRINCIPIS NORWALLIE CUM DOMINO REGE FRANCIE.

EXCELLENTISSIMO domino suo Philippo, Dei gracia, illustri Francorum regi, Loelinus princeps Norwallie fidelis suus, salutem et tam devotum quam debitum fidelitatis et reverentie famulatum, quid retribuam excellentie nobilitatis vestre pro singulari honore et dono inpreciabili, quo vos, rex Francorum, imo princeps regum terre, me fidelem vestrum non tam munifice quam magnifice prevenientes, litteras vestras, sigillo aureo impressas, in testimonium federis regni Francorum et Norwallie principatus, michi, militi vestro delegastis, quas ego in armatiis ecclesiasticis, tanquam sacrosanctas relliquias conservari facio, ut sint memoriale perpetuum et testimonium inviolabile quod ego et heredes mei, vobis vestrisque heredibus inseparabiliter adherentes, vestris amicis amici erimus et inimici inimicis. Idipsum a vestra regia dignitate erga me et meos amicos regaliter observari, modis omnibus expecto postulans et expeto, quod ut inviolabiliter observetur, congregato procerum meorum concilio, et communi cunctorum Wallie principum assensu, quos omnes vobiscum in hujus federis amicicia colligavi, sigilli mei testimonio me vobis fidelem in perpetuum promitto, et, sicut fideliter promitto, fidelius promissum adimplebo. Preterea ex quo vestre sullimitatis litteras suscepi, nec treugas nec pacem, nec etiam colloquium aliquod cum Anglicis feci. Sed, per Dei gratiam, ego et omnes Wallie principes unamiter confederati, inimicis nostris, imo vestris, viriliter restitimus et a jugo tirannidis ipsorum magnam partem terre et castra munitissima, que ipsi per fraudes et dolos occupaverant, per auxilium Domini in manu forti recuperavimus, recuperata in Domino Deo potenter possidemus, unde postulantes expetimus universi Wallie principes, quod sine nobis nec treugas nec pacem cum Anglicis faciatis, scituri quod nos, nullo pacto vel precio, nisi precognita voluntatis vestre benevolencia, eis aliquo pacis seu federis vinculo copulabimur.

In dorso.—Confederacio Leolini, principis Norwallie cum domino rege Francie.

BULLAE PRO TERRA SANCTA EPISCOPO MENEVENSI INSCRIBUNTUR.

J445. 8[ter.]

BULLAE PRO TERRA SANCTA EPISCOPO MENEVENSI INSCRIBUNTUR.

I.

URBANUS episcopus servus servorum Dei, venerabili fratri [Ricardo] episcopo Menevensi salutem et apostolicam benedictionem. Inter occupationes multiplices et immensas quibus assidue angimur et distraimur supra vires, de subsidio Terre Sancte vehementius cogitantes ad hoc attenta solicitudine et attentione sollicita instantius vigilamus ut ejusdem terre succursui oportuno provideatur remedio et crucis ac crucifixi negotium auctore Domino feliciter dirigatur. Nam, licet nonnulli predecessores nostri romani pontifices grandis ad hoc diligentie studio ferventer institerint, nos tamen qui statum illius terre presentialiter novimus, quique ipsius discrimina experienta palpavimus manuali eo affectuosius cupimus eidem terre celeri et efficaci subsidio subveniri quo terra eadem in graviori est hoc tempore necessitatis articulo constituta. Cum igitur nos centesimam omnium ecclesiasticorum proventuum totius Wallie usque ad quinquennium eidem terre de fratrum nostrorum consilio duxerimus concedendam, fraternitati tue per apostolica scripta mandamus quatinus hujusmodi centesimam annuatim usque ad predictum quinquennium per te vel per alium seu alios integre colligens, quicquid collectum fuerit nuntiis ejusdem terre vel eorum procuratoribus seu alterius eorumdem absque diminutione qualibet assignare procures per eos in dicte terre subsidium convertendam. Contradictores autem si qui fuerint vel rebelles per censuram ecclesiasticam appelatione remota compescas ; non obstante si prelatis, personis, capitulis, collegiis, conventibus et locis aliquibus exemptis et non exemptis a sede apostolica sit indultum quod ad exhibendum alicui subsidium pecun-

iij° Oct : A.D. 1263.

iarium minime teneantur, quodque ad id compelli non possint. Omnes autem de dicta Wallia clericos et laicos cujuscumque conditionis, ordinis et dignitatis existant qui olim pro dicte terre subsidio crucis signaculum publice deferant, moneas efficaciter et inducas eos ad redimendum vota sua vel ad transfretandum censura simili appelatione postposita cohercendo. Verum quia, sicut accepimus, nonnulli executores plerisque personis et locis ecclesiasticis regularibus et secularibus exemptis et non exemptis ejusdem Wallie a memorata sede concessi super quibusdam concessionibus de redemptionibus votorum crucesignatorum necnon de legatis, datis, obventionibus, relictis subventioni terre predicte ac aliis deputatis ad subventionem eandem in premissa Wallia per nos et predecessores nostros romanos pontifices seu alios de mandato sedis predicte factis, modum in colligendis predictis excedant, aliasque in talibus perniciose versentur, nos nolentes illa sub dissimulatione transire ne in grave quod absit vergant ejusdem terre pro subtractionem vel diminutionem prefati subsidii detrimentum, nolumus ut in predicta Wallia omnibus executoribus, eisdem personis et locis deputatis a predicta sede super hujusmodi concessionibus, ex parte nostra firmiter inhibere procures ne quoquomodo ad colligenda premissa procedant eos si contra tuam inhibitionem procedere forte presumpserint a presumptione hujusmodi per eandem censuram, appellatione postposita compescendo. Et nichilominus qua auctoritate quibusve personis et locis sub qua forma et in qua quantitate fuerint predicta concessa et que et quot et in quibus locis ab eisdem executoribus fuerint collecta pro eis diligentius inquirens ea nobis per tuas litteras studeas fideliter intimare. Nos enim concessiones predictas aliquem vigorem habere ac illarum pretextu quicquam percipi nolumus donec per tuum insinuationem sciamus super premissis plenius veritatem ac de hiis prout expediens fore viderimus disponamus. Tu autem interim redemptiones, legata, relicta, data et obventiones hujusmodi per te vel per alium seu alios quos ad hoc idoneos esse cognoveris integre colligens, quicquid de hiis collectum fuerit nuntiis dicte terre vel eorum procuratoribus seu alterius eorumdem, convertendum in ipsius terre subsidium assignare totaliter non omittas. Omnes etiam crucesignatos et crucesignandos pro dicte terre subsidio quos sub nostra et apostolice sedis protectione suscipimus, non permittas per te vel per alium seu alios contra immunitates et priviligia crucesignatis ab eadem sede concessa ab aliquibus indebite molestari ; molestatores hujusmodi per eandem censuram, sublato cujuslibet appelationis obstaculo compescendo. Ad hec cum predicatio crucis in memorata Wallia pro ejusdem terre succursu, tibi per alias sub certa forma litteras sit commissa, nos volentes ut negotium hujusmodi eo efficatius prosequaris quo majori per nos fueris auctoritate munitus, injungendi libere per te vel alium seu alios omnibus predicatoribus et ex executoribus crucis ecclesiasticis, secularibus et religiosis pro Terre sancte subsidio in dicta Wallia a sede apostolica deputatis aut in posterum deputandis ut in omnibus que promotioni dicti negotii expedire cognoveris tibi assistant, obediant, pareant et intendant, assumendi etiam aliquos ecclesiarum prelatos, aliosque religiosos et seculares ejusdem Wallie de quibus expedire videris ut in hiis que spectant ad ipsius negotii promotionem tibi assistant, intendant et obedient at tam predicatores et executores predictos quam prelatos aliosque religiosos et seculares hujusmodi ad hec, si necesse fuerit, auctoritate nostra appellatione remota cogendi, faciendi etiam quinque clericis qui tecum in ipso negotio laborabunt, beneficiorum, prebendarum et ecclesiarum suarum proventus per te vel per alium seu alios cotidianis distributionibus dumtaxat exceptis integre ministrari ; ac si in ecclesiis quas seu in quibus ea obtinent personaliter residerent et contradictores per censuram ecclesiasticam appellatione postposita compescendi, consuetudinibus vel statutis contrariis ecclesiarum ipsarum juramento confirmatione apostolica vel quacumque alia firmitate vallatis nequaquam obstantibus libera sit tibi de nostra permissione facultas, presentium quoque auctoritate concedimus ut predicatores crucis quos ad id duxeris deputandos ne hujusmodi eorum predicationibus impedimentum vel aliquod obstaculum ingeratur, questuariis universis et aliis quibuslibet predicare volentibus proponendi aliquid populo dum ab ipsis predicatoribus crucis negotium proponetur licentiam penitus interdicere valeant ac compescere per censuram ecclesiasticam sublato cujuslibet appelationis obstaculo, temeritatem eorum qui secus duxerint presumendum ; concedimus insuper tibi ut cum ad aliquam villam vel ecclesiam predicte Wallie ecclesiastico interdicto suppositum te declinare contigerit, possis interdictum hujusmodi suspendere ac divina officia dum ibidem moram traxeris in eadem ecclesia propter crucis predicationem, exclusis excommunicatis et hiis qui causam interdicto dederint, celebrare ac facere celebrari ; et cum ad loca interdicta te declinare contigerit, crucesignatis et crucesignandis dummodo excommunicati non fuerint nec causam dederint interdicto audiendi te presente divina officia in illis ecclesiis in quibus possunt ex privilegiis sedis apostolice nunc temporis celebrari, licentiam valeas impertiri. Preterea absolvendi per te vel alium seu alios eos qui contra prohibitionem predicte sedis vel legatorum ejus sepulchrum Dominicum visitarunt ac illos qui portaverunt ferrum, arma, lignamina et merces prohibitas Sarracensis vel alias contra christianos dederunt eis consilium, auxilium vel favorem ; quoslibet etiam clericos in prelataris dignitatibus vel personatibus institutos necnon presbyteros qui contra constitutionem ecclesie leges vel physicam audiverunt ab excommunicationum sententiis quibus propter hoc tenentur astricti et dispensandi cum illis qui excommunicati vel suspensi alias immiscentes se divinis, irregularitatem aliquam incurrerunt, dumtamen crucesignati existant, vel crucem recipiant et in dicte terre subsidium personaliter transfretent, seu in propriis expensis alios illuc pro se ydoneos dirigant bellatores, aut alias partem de bonis suis prefato subsidio congrue juxta tue et illorum quibus hoc commiseris discretionis arbitrium subministrent, absolvendi quoque per te vel per alium seu alios quos ad hoc ydoneos esse cognoveris, a voto crucis omnes crucesignatos hactenus in subsidium terre predicte et crucesignandos deinceps qui propter suorum infirmitatem aut debilitatem corporum inhabiles vel impotentes fuerint ad pugnandum vel ad transfretandum in ipsius terre succursum, dummodo secundum proprias facultates velint redimere vota sua; commutandi quoque per te vel per alium seu alios in hujusmodi votum crucis vota peregrinationis et abstinentie illorum qui pro dicto subsidio signum crucis assumpserint et dispensandi cum quinquaginta clericis ipsius Wallie defectum natalium patientibus dummodo non sint de adulterio vel incestu aut de regularibus proc[r]eati, nec paterne incontinentie sectatores sed bone conversationis et vite, aliasque eis merita suffragentur ad dispensationis gratiam obtinendam qui signo crucis assumpto transfretaverint personaliter in dicte terre subsidium vel illuc bellatores ydoneos destinaverint aut alias partem de bonis suis predicto subsidio congrue juxta tue discretionis arbitrium ministrabunt, quod quilibet eorum hujusmodi non obstante defectu possit ad omnes ordines promoveri et ecclesiasticum beneficium obtinere etiam si curam habeat animarum; absolvendi insuper durante commisso tibi hujusmodi crucis negotio per te vel per alium aut alios idoneos juxta formam Ecclesie omnes illos quos pro violenta injectione manuum in viros religiosos et clericos seculares vel etiam pro incendio incidisse compereris in canonem sententie promulgate, dummodo injurias et dampna passis satisfaciant competenter et non sit adeo gravis et enormis excessus quod propter hoc sit merito sedes apostolica requirenda, ac de mandato tuo vel illorum quos ad hoc duxeris deputandos signum crucis receperint in subsidium dicte terre, ituri personaliter vel missuri illuc ydoneos bellatores aut alias partem de bonis suis congrue juxta tue et illorum quibus hoc commiseris pro hujusmodi subsidio discretionis arbitrium ministrabunt; et dispensandi cum clericis hujusmodi ligatis sententiis qui se immiscuere divinis ac injungendi eis penitentiam salutarem ; absolvendi etiam ab excommunicationis vinculo juxta formam Ecclesie illos qui pro violenta injectione manuum et incendiis in promulgate sententie canonem inciderunt et pro quorum gravi et enormi excessu sedes foret merito requirenda predicta, dummodo injurias et dampna passis satisfaciant competenter, et tales crucis assumpto signaculo ad mandatum tuum in subsidium dicte terre se duxerint personaliter transferandos, plenam et liberam concedemus auctoritate presentium facultatem. Nichilominus concedentes ut clerici et laici predicte Wallie crucesignati et crucesignandi decimas non ecclesiarum ratione pacifice detinentes fructus earum perceptos hactenus in dicte terre subsidium convertere valeant per se ipsos vel tibi aut illis quibus hoc specialiter commiseris secura conscientia exhibere, liberumque sit tibi dimittendi per te vel per alium seu alios clericis et laicis eisdem quintam partem decimarum hujusmodi perceptarum hactenus ita quod ad aliam restitutionem earum minime teneantur sed exinde remaneant penitus absoluti dummodo decimas easdem ecclesiis ad quas spectare noscuntur duxerint libere in posterum dimmittendas. Ceterum volumus ut premissa omnia et singula exequi libere valeas non obstante si personis vel locis aut ordinibus aliquibus a memorata sit sede indultum quod interdici, suspendi vel excommmunicari non possint per litteras apostolicas plenam et expressam ac de verbo ad verbum non facientes de indulto hujusmodi mentionem et quibuslibet aliis indulgentiis, privilegiis seu litteris ab eadem sede obtentes vel in posterum obtinendis per que predicta impediri vel differi valeant et de quibus seu quorum totis tenoribus mentionem fieri oporteat in nostris litteris specialem et constitutione *de duabus dietis* edita in consilio generali.

Datum apud Urbemveterem v nonas octobris, pontificatus nostri anno tertio.

In dorso.—Pro Terra Sancta Wallia inscribitur episcopo Menevensi.

J445. 26 quarter.

II.

URBANUS episcopus, servus servorum Dei, venerabili fratri [Ricardo] episcopo Menevensi salutem et apostolicam benedictionem. De summis celorum Dominus terram sue Nativitatis et Passionis aspiciens, dum per singulos dies in illa variis provocatur injuriis nec exsurgit populus quem Ipse redemit ad vindicandum crucis obprobrium ex eo precipue non immerito addi ad dolorem suorum vulnerum reputat quod locus ille sanctissimus in quo ipsum celi Regem virgo puerpera genuit, continue vexacionis lassatur, angustiis et successivis dissidiis laceratur, nunc in illum Sarracenica furente sevita, nunc in eundem furoris immanitate Tartarici sexui vel etati parcere nescia seviente. Ad hoc enim precipue filiorum lucis intentio tendere circa id debent eorum assidue revolvi precordia et sollicitudo versari ut illius terre quam in hereditatem sibi Dei Filius preelegit, abhominationes expiare conentur et potenti manu resistere polluentibus ipsam filiis tenebrarum. Hec profecto dissimulari non debent vel obtusis auribus preteriri ne Redemptor noster cuncta previdens, falli nescius, ingratitudinis vitio redemptos laborare comperiens ab eis faciem iratus avertat, eosque velut indignos paterna gratia derelinquat; non sint igitur filii devotionis immemores quod ipse Christus in terra illa in forma servi carnem nostre mortalitatis indutus, crucis non metuit subire tormentum ut mortem nostram moriendo destrueret et vitam resurgendo fidelibus repararet. Quesumus diligenter attendant qualiter illa miserabilis regio depressa jacet diris angustiata flagellis, quodque in eam pestis Tartarica supervenit, cujus tanto potius nimirum

iv° Oct: A.D. 1263.

futuri vicinique formidantur incursus, quanto gravius ille sevus et dampnabilis Tartarorum populus terram quam sue subicit servituti intolerabilibus exactionibus opprimens sic illius incolas torquet immaniter et affligit quod degentes sub eorum tirampnide libentius metas mortis eligerent, quam sic muendo tanta subire genera tormentorum. Exurgant itaque fidei zelatores ad defensionem dicte regionis ejusdem Redemptoris martirio consecrate nec ad id tepescant eorum animi set servientibus desideriis accendantur. Hoc enim ipse Dei filius inter cetera sollicitudinis humane servitia gratissimum reputat et ob id illa rependit premia que principaliter affectare debemus et petere, dum in valle positi presentis miserie indulta nobis excurrimus tempora servitatis. Cum igitur de te, quem habere credimus timorem Domini et amorem, quique multiplicibus donis virtutem preditus, laudabiliter scis et vales proficere ubi labores impendis, magnam in domino fiduciam habeamus, sperantes ut in prosecutione presentis negotii constanter militans illud efficacibus studiis et plenis debeas affectibus promovere, fraternitatem tuam rogamus et hortamur attente, in remissionem tibi peccaminum injungentes, quatinus hujusmodi predicte terre statum Christi fidelibus in Wallia per te vel per alium seu alios ecclesiarum prelatos et clericos, religiosos et seculares, cujuscumque dignitatis vel ordinis fuerint, quos ad hoc idoneos esse cognoveris, diligenter exponens eisque proponens sollicite verbum crucis, ipsos juxta datam tibi a Domino gratiam intentis inducas monitis et sedulis predicationibus exhorteris, ut cogitantes prudenter quantum nunc indigeat ipsorum prefata terra succursu ad subventionem ejus promptis intendant animis et viribus totis exurgant, crucisque suscepto signaculo illuc spiritualibus armis et materialibus premuniti, de divina quoque sperantes potentia, cum festinatione procedant, et ut circa id eo libentius et animosius intendant quo exinde dona spiritualia temporalibus procul dubio preferenda perceperint potiora. Nos de omnipotentis Dei misericordia et beatorum Petri et Pauli apostolorum ejus auctoritate confisi, et illa quam nobis Deus licet indignis ligandi atque solvendi contulit potestate, omnibus vere penitentibus et confessis qui hujusmodi laborem in propriis personis subierint et expensis, plenam suorum peccaminum veniam indulgemus ; eis autem qui non in propriis personis illuc accesserint set in suis dumtaxat expensis juxta facultates et qualitates suas viros idoneos destinaverint et illis similiter qui licet in alienis expensis in propriis tamen personis accesserint plenam suorum concedimus veniam peccatorum. Hujus quoque remissionis volumus et concedimus esse participes juxta quantitatem subsidii et devocionis affectum omnes qui ad subventionem ipsius terre de bonis suis aliquam portionem vel alias consilium et auxilium impedirint opportunum ; volumus eciam crucesignatos illo privilegio illaque immunitate gaudere que in generali crucesignatorum indulgentia continetur. Ut autem commissum tibi hujusmodi ministerium facilius et utilius exequi valeas, tibi et predictis quos in hoc co-operatores eligeris convocandi ob id quocienscumque et ubicumque videris expedire, cleros et populos locorum in quibus te vel ipsos proponere contiggerit verbum crucis ut processionaliter cum devotione conveniant et predicationibus vestris intersint, cleros eosdem ad id si necesse fuerit per censuram ecclesiasticam appellatione postposita compellendi ac pro eisdem predicationibus ferias prout expedire videris indicendi, concedendi quoque omnibus vere penitentibus et confessis qui ad easdem convocationes et predicationes vestras accesserint, centum dierum indulgentiam plenam concedimus auctoritate presentium potestatem, non obstantibus si aliquibus cujuscumque ordinis vel dignitatis existant, quod interdici, suspendi vel excommunicari nequeant a sede apostolica sit indultum et quibuslibet indulgentiis, privilegiis seu litteris ab eadem sede obtentis vel obtinendis per que predicta impediri vel defraudari possint et de quibus specialem oporteat in nostris litteris fieri mentionem. Taliter igitur tu et alii quibus hujusmodi predicationis officium duxeris committendum, mandatum apostolicum super hoc exequi procuretis, quod palmam glorie que bellum Dei gerentibus in retributionem ab ipso impenditur, vestra devotio consequi mereatur.

Datum apud Urbemveterem iiij. nonas octobris, pontificatus anno tertio.

In dorso.—Pro Terra Sancta.

J451. 10.

III.

URBANUS episcopus, servus servorum Dei, Venerabili fratri [Ricardo] episcopo Menevensi salutem et apostolicam benedictionem. Volentes omnes crucesignatos et crucesignandos in Wallia pro subsidio Terre sancte singularis privilegii prerogativa gaudere crucesignatis et crucesignandis hujusmodi, ut per litteras apostolice sedis vel legatorum ejus impetratas hactenus quarum non sit auctoritate processum et impetrandas imposterum, nisi dicte sedis littere impetrande plenam et expressam fecerint de presentibus mentionem extra dioceses in quibus ipsi et eorum bona consistunt in causam trahi vel ad judicium evocari non possint, dummodo parati sint coram eorum ordinariis de se querelantibus exhibere justicie complementum auctoritate presentium indulgemus. Nulli ergo omnino hominum liceat hanc paginam nostre concessionis infringere, vel ei ansu temerario contraire. Si quis autem hoc attemptare presumpserit, indignationem omnipotentis Dei et beatorum Petri et Pauli apostolorum ejus se noverit incursurum. **Idus Oct: A.D. 1263.**

Datum apud Urbemveterem, idus octobris, pontificatis nostri anno tertio.

In dorso.—Pro Terra Sancta.

J451. 10[ter.]

IV.

Idus Oct: A.D. 1263.

URBANUS episcopus servus servorum Dei, venerabilibus fratribus archiepiscopis et episcopis, ac dilectis filiis ceteris ecclesiarum prelatis per Walliam constitutis, salutem et apostolicam benedictionem. Terram sanctem quam unigenitus Dei filius, Dominus Jehsus Christus in proprium sibi patrimonium et hereditatem elegit, conspicientes feritate diversorum infidelium immaniter lacerari vias et modos desideranter exquirimus, quibus eidem terre possint oportuna presidia nostro ministerio provenire. Quare de venerabili fratre nostro [Ricardo] episcopo Menevensi quem Dei timorem habere credimus et amorem, quique multiplicibus donis virtutem preditus utiliter scit et valet ubi labores impendit, plenam in Domino fiduciam obtinentes predicationem crucis pro dicte terre subsidio, in Wallie sibi per nostras litteras sub certa forma duximus committendam, cupientes ut negotium ipsum in manibus ejus eo plenius divina clementia faciente proficiat, quo magis insidet cordi nostro et quo majorem necessitatem ad presens eidem terre novimus imminere. Ideoque universitatem vestram rogamus et hortamur attente, vobis nichilominus in remissionem peccaminum injungentes, quatimus prefato episcopo et aliis quos in hoc ipse co-operatores elegerit, circa ipsius negotii prosecutionem ferventer assistere studeatis, habentes ipsum episcopum, immo potius nos in ipso, tamquam nobis intimum in ejusdem prosecutione negotii, favorabiliter in Domino commendatum, ita quod devotionem vestram commendare cum gratiarum actionibus merito valeamus ac nichilominus exinde divine retributionis vobis proveniat incrementum.

Datum apud Urbemveterem, idus octobris, pontificatus nostri anno tertio.

In dorso.—Pro Terra Sancta.

J445. 26bis.

V.

URBANUS episcopus servus servorum Dei, venerabilibus fratribus universis patriarchis, archiepiscopis et episcopis ac dilectis filiis electis, abbatibus, prioribus, capitulis, conventibus et collegiis Sancti Benedicti vel cujuslibet alterius ordinis, necnon decanis, archidiaconis, prepositis, archipresbyteris et aliis ecclesiarum prelatis et rectoribus ac preceptoribus sue administratoribus domorum Hospitalis et Templi, ac Sancte Marie Theotonicorum, exemptis et non exemptis ad quos littere iste pervenerint, salutem et apostolicam benedictionem.

xij Kal: Feb., A.D. 1264.

Cum negocium Terre Sancte venerabili fratri nostro [Ricardo] episcopo Menevensi, viro utique probate fidei et examinate virtutis in Wallia, de fratrum nostrorum consilio, duxerimus specialiter committendum, universitatem vestram monemus, rogamus, et hortamur attente per apostolica vobis scripta districte precipiendo mandantes quatimus ipsum immo potius nos in eo, ob reverentiam apostolice sedis et nostram in eundo, morando, et redeundo, suscipientes honore condigno, sibi extra suam civitatem et diocesim personaliter in predicto negotio laboranti, pro se, decem equitaturis et quindecim personis, in necessariis necnon in securo conductu providere curetis liberaliter et decenter. Ita quod idem quem nos et dicti fratres sue probitatis exigentibus meritis carum habemus multipliciter et acceptum, possit vestre promtitudini testimonium laudabile prohibere ac nos exinde reddere in vestris utilitatibus promptiores alioquin sententias quas ipse per se vel per alios rite tulerit in rebelles ratas habebimus, easque faciemus auctore domino usque ad satisfactionem condignam appellatione remota inviolabiter observari. Non obstantibus aliquibus apostolicis indulgentiis seu privelegiis, sub quavis verborum forma concessis, quibuscumque ecclesiasticis, ordinibus, collegiis universitatibus vel personis quod excommunicari, suspendi vel interdici nequeant seu ad prestandas procurationes legatis et nunciis sedis apostolice coartari sive quibuslibet aliis cujuscumque tenoris existant, que nulli suffragari volumus in hac parte et quibus vis constitutionibus a predecessoribus nostris editis seu consuetudinibus quibuslibet de procurationibus, nuntiis dicte sede sub certis modis et conditionibus exhibendis.

Datum apud Urbemveterem xij. Kalendas februarii, pontificatus nostri anno tertio.

In dorso.—Pro Terra Sancta.

LITTERAE OWYNI
PRINCIPIS WALLIAE.

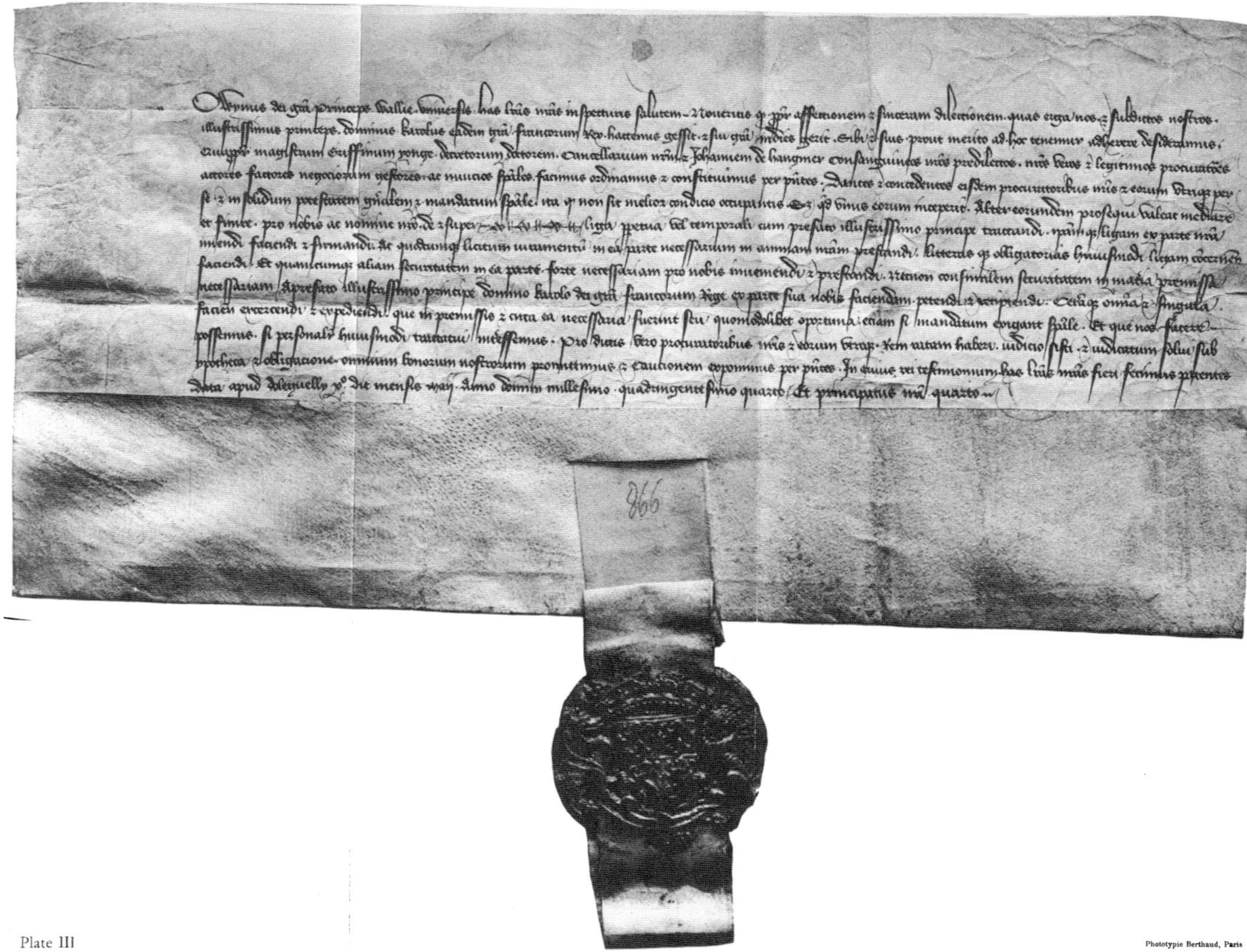

Plate III

Phototypie Berthaud, Paris

J392. 27.

PROCURATIO MAGISTRO GRIFFINI YONGE, DECRETORUM DOCTORIS, ET JOHANNIS HANGMER, AMBAXIATORUM DOMINI OWINI PRINCIPIS WALLIARUM.

x° Maii, A.D. 1404.

OWYNUS, Dei gratia princeps Wallie, universis has litteras nostras inspecturis salutem. Noveritis quod propter affectionem et sinceram dilectionem quas erga nos et subdictos nostros illustrissimus princeps dominus Karolus eadem gratia Francorum rex hactenus gessit et sui gratia in dies gerit, sibi et suis, prout merito ad hoc tenemur, adherere desideramus. Quapropter magistrum Griffinum Yonge, decretorum doctorem, cancellarium nostrum et Johannem de Hangmer consanguineos nostros predilectos, nostros veros et legitimos procuratores, actores, factores, negociorum gestores ac nuncios speciales facimus, ordinamus et constituimus per presentes ; dantes et concedentes eisdem procuratoribus nostris et eorum utrique per se et in solidum potestatem generalem et mandatum speciale ita quod non sit melior condicio occupantis, sed quid unus eorum inceperit alter eorundem prosequi valeat mediare et finire pro nobis ac nomine nostro de et super liga perpetua vel temporali cum prefato illustrissimo principe tractandi ipsamque ligam ex parte nostra iniendi, faciendi et firmandi ac quodcumque licitum juramentum in ea parte necessarium in animam nostram prestandi, litterasque obligatorias hujusmodi ligam concernentes faciendi et quamcumque aliam securitatem in ea parte forte necessariam pro nobis inveniendi et prestandi, necnon consimilem securitatem in materia premissa necessariam a prefato illustrissimo principe domino Karolo Dei gratia Francorum rege ex parte sua nobis faciendam petendi et recipiendi, ceteraque omnia et singula faciendi exercendi et expediendi que in premissis et circa ea necessaria fuerint seu quomodolibet oportuna eciamsi mandatum exigant speciale et que nos facere possemus si personaliter hujusmodi tractatui interressemus. Pro dictis vero procuratoribus nostris et eorum utroque rem ratam haberi, judicio sisti et judicatum solvi sub ypotheca et obligacione omnium bonorum nostrorum promittimus et caucionem exponimus per presentes.

In cujus rei testimonium has litteras nostras fieri fecimus patentes.

Data apud Doleguelly, x^o die mensis maii, anno domini millesimo quadringentesimo quarto et principatus nostri quarto.

In dorso.—Procuratio magistri Griffini Yonge, decretorum doctoris, et Johannis Hangmer ambaxiatorum domini Owini principis Walliarum.

J623. 96[bis.]

CONFEDERATIONES INTER OWYNUM PRINCIPEM WALLIARUM ET KAROLEM REGEM FRANCORUM.

NOS Jacobus de Borbonio, comes Marchie, procurator et nuncius specialis serenissimi principis domini mei metuendissimi domini Karoli Dei gracia Francorum regis et nos Griffinus Yonge, decretorum doctor, cancellarius et Johannes de Hangmer scutifer consanguinei, ambaxiatores, procuratores et nuncii speciales illustris et metuendissimi domini nostri Owini principis Walliarum, prout de potestatibus et procuratoriis utrique nostrum datis per dominos nostros supradictos plene constat per litteras patentes ipsorum dominorum quarum tenores inferius sunt inserti, ad infrascripta a dictis dominis deputati et commissi, notum facimus universis quod nos virtute mandatorum dictorum dominorum nostrorum regis et principis et potestatum per eos nobis attributarum et datarum de et super ligis, confederacionibus et amiciciis inter ipsos dominos regem et principem iniendis et formandis, invicem convenimus in certis capitulis seu articulis continentibus formam que sequitur et tenorem: xiiij[a] Julii: A.D. 1404.

Primo quod ipsi domino rex et princeps erunt amodo ad invicem conjuncti, confederati, uniti et ligati vinculo veri federis et vere amicicie certeque et bone unionis, potissime contra Henricum de Lencastria utriusque ipsorum adversarium et hostem suosque adherentes et fautores. Item quod alter ipsorum dominorum honorem et commodum alterius volet, prosequetur ac eciam procurabit, dampnaque et gravamina que ad unius noticiam devenerint per dictum Henricum ejusque complices, adherentes et fautores aut alios quoscumque alteri inferenda impedient bona fide ; alter quoque ipsorum apud alteram aget et faciet ea omnia et singula que per bonum, verum et fidum amicum bono, vero et fido amico agi et fieri debent et pertinent, fraude et dolo cessantibus quibuscumque. Item si et quociens alter eorum sciverit vel cognoverit prefatum Henricum de Lencastria seu adherentes aut fautores suos aliquid gravaminis sive dampni procurare vel machinari contra alium, ipse sibi quamcitius commode fieri poterit ea significabit et ipsum de et super hoc advisabit ut adversus malicias suas prout ei visum fuerit sibi valeat providere. Soliciti quoque erunt quilibet ipsorum dominorum impedire gravamina et dampna predicta bona fide. Item quod quilibet dominorum predictorum nullatenus pacietur quod aliqui subditorum suorum det, faciat, aut procuret dicto Henrico de Lencastria, fautoribusve aut adherentibus suis auxilium vel consilium aliquod seu favorem, nec quod ipsi juvent cum ipsius stipendiis neque eciam sine stipendiis contra aliquem eorumdem dominorum; quod si contra facere presumerent, taliter punientur quod ceteris cedet in exemplum. Item quod aliquis dominorum regis et principis predictorum non faciet seu capiet treugas nec faciet pacem cum dicto Henrico Lencastrie quin alter, si voluerit, comprehendatur in ipsis treugis sive pace, nisi in eisdem treugis vel pace renuerit sive noluerit comprehendi et de qua noluntate seu recusacione constabit illi qui dictas treugas sive pacem tractare voluerit infra mensem postquam alteri treugas seu pacem predictas signifcaverit per suas patentes litteras suo sigillo sigillatas. Item quod omnes subditi regni Francie cum eorum navigiis, mercimoniis sive mercanciis, rebus et bonis quibuscumque recipienter et recolligentur ac pacientur moram facere sine fraude in omnibus terris et portubus subditis dicto principi Walliarum, et eciam omnes subditi prefati domini principis similiter cum eorum navigiis et mercimoniis sive mercanciis, rebus et bonis quibuscumque recipientur et recolligentur pacienturque moram facere in omnibus terris et portubus regni Francie sine fraude ; dumtamen subditi hujusmodi hinc inde habeant litteras testimoniales sub sigillis dominorum predictorum seu justiciariorum aut officiariorum suorum de et super subjectione et fidelitate eorumdem confectas. Item quod si discordia, violencia, pugna, riota, spoliacio vel alia quevis injuria in mari sive in terra inter subditos dictorum dominorum, quod absit, committatur seu oriri contigerit, causeque super hoc emergent amicabiliter secundum merita earumdem et locorum existenciam ubi premissa committentur per dominos utriusque partis vel justiciarios et officiarios suos ad quos spectabit tractentur et per eos commissa hujusmodi legitime reformentur discordieque predicte pacificentur. Item quod quocienscumque alter prefatorum dominorum pro parte alterius fuerit requisitus confederaciones predictas sic per eorum procuratores factas et initas tenebitur per suas litteras cum promissionibus debitis ratificare, confirmare, ac eciam validare. Item quod quelibet pars procuratorum predictorum promittet et jurabit in animam domini sui tactis sacrosanctis envangeliis, quod confederaciones et lige contente in articulis supradictis per ipsos dominos et eorum subditos firmiter bona fide tenebuntur. Ab istis autem confederacionibus et ligis excipiuntur pro parte dictorum dominorum nostrorum regis et principis omnes illi qui racione generis seu subjectionis, dumtamen subditi prefati Henrici Lencastrie non existant aut pretextu ligarum precedencium erant sibi antea federati. Quequidem capitula nos Jacobus de Borbonio, comes Marchie, necnon Griffinus Yonge et Johannes de Hangmer, procuratores et nuncii supradicti, dominorum nostrorum regis Francorum et principis Walliarum predictorum nominibus rata et grata habentes ipsa omniaque et singula in eis et quolibet ipsorum contenta et declarata alter alteri quisque videlicet pro suo dominorum nostrorum predictorum et nomine ipsius et pro ipso, promittimus bona fide juramusque in animas eorumdem dominorum nostrorum, ad sancta Dei envagelia per nos et utrumque nostrum tacta bene et fideliter tenere, attendere et complere ac eciam firmiter et inviolabiter observare.

In quorum omnium et singulorum fidem et testimonium presentes litteras seu presens publicum instrumentum fieri et duplicari et per notarios publicos infrascriptos publicari mandavimus et sigillorum nostrorum una cum signis et subscripcionibus dictorum notariorum publicorum fecimus appensione muniri. Tenor vero litterarum procuratoriarum dicti domini nostri Francorum regis sequitur et est talis :

" Karolus, Dei gracia Francorum rex, universis presentes litteras inspecturis salutem ; notum facimus quod nos de fidelitate diligentique industria dilectorum et fidelium consanguinei et consiliariorum nostrorum Jacobi de Borbonio comitis Marchie et Johannis episcopi Carnotensis plenissime confidentes, ipsos facimus, constituimus, nominamus et eligimus procuratores nostros generales et certos nuncios speciales et eorum quemlibet in solidum ita quod non sit melior condicio occupantis sed quod unus eorum inceperit alter prosequi valeat et finire ad tractandum nomine nostro et pro nobis cum dilectis nostris magistro Grifino Yonge et Johanne de Hangmer consanguineis magnifici et potentis Owini principis Walliarum et ejus ambaxiatoribus et nunciis habentibus ad infrascripta a dicto principe potestatem per litteras ipsius principis sigillo suo sigillatas, ligas, confederaciones et amicicias perpetuas vel ad tempus inter nos ex una parte et dictum principem Walliarum ex altera prout eisdem procuratoribus utriusque partis videbitur faciendum, de et super ipsis ligis, confederacionibus et amiciciis et de modis ipsorum conveniendum, ipsasque cum illis modis, convencionibus et promissionibus de quibus ipsi procuratores utriusque partis invicem convenirint firmandum et concludendum ac quodcumque licitum et debitum juramentum in animam nostram necnon quamcumque securitatem ad hoc necessariam querendum, inveniendum, prestandum atque dandum, similesque a parte dicti principis querendum, recipiendum et acceptandum. Dantes et concedentes dictis procuratoribus nostris et eorum cuilibet in solidum plenam, generalem et liberam potestatem et mandatum speciale premissa et generaliter omnia et singula faciendi, gerendi, exercendi et expediendi que circa ea et eorum dependencias necessaria fuerint et quomodolibet oportuna et que nos faceremus et facere possemus si presentes ad hec personaliter interessemus, eciamsi mandatum exigerent magis speciale; promittentes bona fide ratum, gratum et firmum habere quicquid per dictos procuratores nostros et eorum quemlibet in solidum in premissis et circa premissa actum factumque fuerit ac eciam firmatum et conclusum sub ypotheca et obligacione omnium bonorum nostrorum presencium et futurorum.

In cujus rei testimonium nostrum, presentibus litteris fecimus apponi sigillum. Datum Parisius die xiiij[a] junii, anno Domini millessimo cccc[mo] quarto et regni nostri vicesimo quarto."

Item sequitur tenor litterarum procuratoriarum dicti domini principis Walliarum in hec verba:

" Owynus, Dei gracia princeps Wallie, universis has litteras nostras inspecturis salutem. Noveritis quod propter affectionem et sinceram dilectionem quas erga nos et subdictos nostros illustrissimus princeps dominus Karolus eadem gratia Francorum rex hactenus gessit et sui gracia in dies gerit, sibi et suis, prout merito ad hoc tenemur, adherere desideramus. Quapropter magistrum Griffinum Yonge, decretorum doctorem cancellarium nostrum et Johannem de Hangmer consanguineos nostros predilectos, nostros veros et legitimos procuratores, actores, factores, negociorum gestores ac nuncios speciales facimus, ordinamus et constituimus per presentes; dantes et concedentes eisdem procuratoribus nostris et eorum utrique per se et in solidum potestatem generalem et mandatum speciale ita quod non sit melior condicio occupantis, sed quod unus eorum inceperit alter eorumdem prosequi valeat mediare et finire pro nobis ac nomine nostro de et super liga perpetua vel temporali cum prefato illustrissimo principe tractandi ipsamque ligam ex parte nostra iniendi, faciendi et firmandi ac quodcumque licitum juramentum in ea parte necessarium in animam nostram prestandi, litterasque obligatorias hujusmodi ligam concernentes faciendi et quamcumque aliam securitatem in ea parte forte necessariam pro nobis inveniendi et prestandi, necnon consimilem securitatem in materia premissa necessariam a prefato illustrissimo principe domino Karolo Dei gracia Francorum rege ex parte sua nobis faciendam petendi et recipiendi, ceteraque omnia et singuli faciendi exercendi et expediendi que in premissis et circa ea necessaria fuerint seu quomodolibet oportuna eciamsi mandatum exigant speciale et que nos facere possemus si personaliter hujusmodi tractatui interressemus. Pro dictis vero procuratoribus nostris et eorum utroque rem ratam haberi, judicio sisti et judicatum solvi sub ypotheca et obligacione omnium bonorum nostrorum promittimus et caucionem exponimus per presentes.

In cujus rei testimonium has litteras nostras fieri fecimus patentes.

Data apud Doleguelly, x° die mensis maii, anno domini millesimo cccc° quarto et principatus nostri quarto."

Actum et datum Parisius in domo habitacionis magnifici viri domini Ernuadi de Corbeya, militis, cancellarii Francie, anno Domini millesimo quadringentesimo quarto, indictione duodecima, die decima quarta mensis julii; presentibus dicto domino Cancellario Francie necnon reverendis in Christo patribus et dominis dominis Phillippo Noviomensi, Petro Meldensi et Johanne Atrebatensi episcopis ac eciam magnifico et potenti Ludovico de Borbonio Comite Vindocinensi, nobilibusque viris dominis Roberto de Braquemont et Roberto d'Amilly, militibus dicti serenissimi principis regis Francorum cambellanis, testibus ad premissa vocatis.

[*Locus monogrammatis*]

EGO Johannes de sanctis Belvacensis diocesis, apostolica et imperiali auctoritatibus publicus notarius, prefatique domini nostri Francorum regis notarius et secretarius, qui premissis omnibus et singulis dum ut premittitur agerentur et fierent per dominos procuratores superius nominatos una et cum suprascriptis testibus presens fui eaque fieri vidi et audivi, ad requestam et de consensu ipsorum dominorum procuratorum huic presenti publico instrumento super hiis confecto et sub eadem forma verborum duplicato, quod scribi et grossari per alium feci pluribus aliis ocupatus negociis, collacione per me facta cum notario publico infra scripto de originalibus litteris supra insertis cum eodem presenti publico instrumento ipsum publicando me subscripsi et signum meum apposui consuetum.

[*Locus signi*]

Et ego Benedictus Comme, clericus Assavensis diocesis, publicus apostolica auctoritate notarius premissis omnibus et singulis dum sic ut premictitur per dictos dominos procuratores agerentur et fierent una cum magnificis dominis testibus ac venerabili viro notario supradicto, presens interfui eaque sic fieri vidi et audivi et ideo hoc presens publicum instrumentum per alium me aliunde occupato fideliter scriptum ad requisicionem et de consensu eorumdem dominorum procuratorum duplicatum publicavi signoque et nomine meis solitis et consuetis signavi, rogatus et requisitus in fidem et testimonium omnium premissorum.

In dorso.—Confederaciones facte et inite inter dominum Owinum, principem Walliarum et dominum nostrum regem per procuratores, anno Domini M^{o} cccc^{o} iiij^{o}, die xiiij^{a} mensis julii.

J623. 96.

CONFIRMATIO CONFEDERATIONIUM INTER OWYNUM ET KAROLEM.

xij° Januari: A.D. 1405.

OWYNUS Dei gratia princeps Wallie, universis has litteras nostras inspecturis salutem. Noverit universitas vestra nos litteras patentes infrascriptas ligam et confederacionem inter illustrissimum principem dominum Karolum Dei gratia Francorum regem et nos per procuratores suos et nostros in hac parte initas et contractas continentes recepisse in hac verba:

"Nos Jacobus de Borbonio, comes Marchie, procurator et nuncius specialis serenissimi principis domini mei metuendissimi domini Karoli, Dei gratia Francorum regis, et nos Griffinus Yonge decretorum doctor, cancellarius et Johannes de Hanmer, scutifer, consanguinei, ambaxiatores, procuratores, et nuncii speciales illustris et metuendissimi domini nostri Owyni principis Walliarum prout de potestatibus et procuratoriis utrique nostrum datis per dominos nostros supradictos plene constat per litteras patentes ipsorum dominorum quarum tenores inferius sunt inserte ad infrascripta a dictis dominis specialiter depputati et commissi, notum facimus universis quod nos virtute mandatorum dictorum dominorum nostrorum regis et principis et potestatem per eos nobis atributarum et datarum de et super ligis, confederacionibus et amiciciis inter ipsos dominos regem et principem iniendis et firmadis invicem convenimus in certis capitulis seu articulis continentibus formam que sequitur et tenorem:

Primo quod ipsi domini rex et princeps erunt amodo ad invicem conjuncti, confederati, uniti et ligati vinculo veri federis et vere amicicie certeque et bone unionis potissime contra Henricum de Lencastria utriusque ipsorum adversarium et hostem suosque adherentes et fautores. Item quod alter ipsorum dominorum honorem et commodum alterius volet, prosequetur ac eciam procurabit, dampnaque et gravamina que ad unius noticiam devenerint per dictum Henricum ejusque complices, adherentes et fautores aut alios quoscumque alteri inferenda impedient bona fide, alter quoque ipsorum apud alteram aget et faciet ea omnia et singula que per bonum verum et fidum̄ amicum bono, vero et fido amico agi et fieri debent et pertinent fraude et dolo cessantibus quibuscumque. Item si et quociens alter eorum sciverit vel cognoverit prefatum Henricum de Lencastria seu adherentes aut fautores suos aliquid gravaminis sive dampni procurare vel machinari contra alium, ipse sibi quamcicius commode fieri poterit ea significabit et ipsum de et super hoc advisabit ut adversus malicias suas prout ei visum fuerit sibi valeat providere; soliciti quoque erunt quilibet ipsorum dominorum impedire gravamina et dampna predicta bona fide. Item quod quilibet dominorum predictorum nullatenus pacietur quod aliquis subditorum suorum det, faciat aut procuret dicto Henrico de Lencastria fautoribusve aut adherentibus suis auxilium vel consilium aliquod seu favorem nec quod ipsum juvent cum ipsius stipendiis neque eciam sine stipendiis contra aliquem eorundem dominorum. Quod si contra facere presumerent taliter punientur quod ceteris cedet in exemplum. Item quod aliquis dominorum regis et principis predictorum non faciet seu capiet treugas nec faciet pacem cum dicto Henrico Lencastrie quin alter si voluerit comprehendatur in ipsis treugis sive pace nisi in eisdem treugis vel pace renuerit sive noluerint comprehendi, et de qua noluntate seu recusacione constabit illi qui dictas treugas sive pacem tractare voluerit infra mensem postquam alteri treugas seu pacem predictas significaverit per suas patentes litteras suo sigillo sigillatas. Item quod omnes subditi regni Francie cum eorum navigiis, mercimoniis sive mercanciis, rebus et bonis quibuscumque recipientur et recolligentur ac pacientur moram facere in omnibus terris et portubus regni Francie sine fraude dum tamen subditi hujusmodi hinc inde habeant litteras testimoniales sub sigillis dominorum predictorum seu justiciorum aut officiariorum suorum de et super subjectione et fidelitate eorumdem confectas. Item quod si discordia, violencia, pugna, riota, spoliacio, vel alia quevis injuria in mari sive in terra inter subditos dictorum dominorum, quod absit, committatur seu oriri contigerit, causeque super hoc emergerit amiciabiliter secundum merita eorumdem et locorum existenciam ubi premissa committentur per dominos utriusque partis vel justiciarios et officiarios suos ad quos pertinebit tractentur et per eos commissa hujusmodi legitime reformentur, discordieque predicte pacificentur. Item quod quocienscumque alter prefatorum dominorum pro parte alterius fuerit requisitus confederaciones predictas sic per eorum procuratores factas et initas tenebitur per suas litteras cum promissionibus debitis ratificare, confirmare ac eciam validare. Item quod quelibet pars procuratorum predictorum promictet et jurabit in animam domini sui, tactis sacrosanctis envangeliis quod confederaciones et lige contente in articulis supradictis per ipsos dominos et eorum subditos firmiter bona fide tenebuntur. Ab istis autem confederacionibus et ligis excipiuntur pro parte dictorum dominorum nostrorum regis et principis omnes illi qui racione generis seu subjectionis, dum tamen subditi prefati Henrici Lencastrie non existant aut pretextu ligarum precedencium erant sibi antea federati. Quequidem capitula nos Jacobus de Borbonio, comes Marchie, necnon Griffinus Yonge et Johannes de Hanmer, procuratores et nuncii supradicti, dominorum nostrorum regis Francorum et principis Walliarum predictorum nominibus, rata et grata habentes ipsa omniaque et singula in eis et quolibet ipsorum contenta et declarata alter alteri quisque videlicet pro suo dominorum nostrorum predictorum et nomine ipsius et pro ipso promittimus bona fide juramusque in animas eorundem dominorum ad sancta Dei envangelia per nos et utrumque nostrum tacta, bene et fideliter tenere, attendere et complere ac eciam firmiter et inviolabiter observare.

In quorum omnium et singulum fidem et testimonium presentes litteras seu presens publicum instrumentum fieri et dupplicari et per notarios publicos infrascriptos publicari mandavimus et sigillorum nostrorum una cum signis et subscripcionibus dictorum notariorum publicorum fecimus appensione muniri."

Tenor vero litterarum procuratoriarum dicti domini nostri Francorum regis sequitur et est talis:

"Karolus Dei gratia Francorum rex, universis presentes litteras inspecturis salutem. Notum facimus quod nos de fidelitate diligenti et industria dilectorum et fidelium consanguinei et consiliariorum nostrorum Jacobi de Borbonio comitis Marchie et Johannis episcopi Carnotensis plenissime confidentes ipsos facimus, constituimus, nominamus et eligimus procuratores nostros generales et certos nuncios speciales et eorum quemlibet in solidum ita quod non sit melior condicio occupantis, sed quod unus eorum inceperit alter prosequi valeat et finire, ad tractandum nomine nostro et pro nobis cum dilectis nostris magistro Griffino Yonge et Johanne de Hanmer, consanguineis magnifici et potentis Owyni principis Walliarum et ejus ambaxiatoribus et nunciis, habentibus ad infrascripta a dicto principe potestatem per litteras ipsius principis sigillo suo sigillatas, ligas, confederaciones, et amicicias perpetuas vel ad tempus inter nos ex una parte et dictum principem Walliarum ex altera, prout eisdem procuratoribus utriusque partis videbitur faciendum de et super ipsis ligis confederacionibus et amiciciis et de modis ipsorum conveniendum ipsasque cum illis modis convencionibus et permissionibus de quibus ipsi procuratores utriusque partis invicem convenerint firmandum, concludendum ac quodcumque licitum et debitum juramentum in animam nostram necnon quamcumque securitatem ad hoc necessarium querendum, inveniendum, prestandum atque dandum ; similesque a parte dicti principis querendum, recipiendum et acceptandum ; dantes et concedentes dictis procuratoribus nostris et eorum cuilibet in solidum plenam, generalem et liberam potestatem et mandatum speciale premissa et generaliter omnia et singula faciendi, gerendi, exercendi et expediendi que circa ea et eorum dependencias necessaria fuerint et quomodolibet oportuna et que nos faceremus et facere possemus si presentes ad hec personaliter interessemus eciamsi mandatum exigerent magis speciale, promittentes bona fide ratum, gratum et firmum habere quidquid per predictos procuratores nostros et eorum quemlibet in solidum in premissis et circa premissa actum factumque fuerit ac eciam firmatum et conclusum sub ypotheca et obligacione omnium bonorum nostrorum presencium et futurorum.

In cujus rei testimonium nostrum presentibus litteris fecimus apponi sigillum. Datum Parisius die xiiij[a] junii, anno Domini millesimo quadringentesimo quarto et regni nostri xxiiij[o]."

Item sequitur tenor litterarum procuratoriarum dicti domini principis Walliarum in hec verba :

" Owynus Dei gratia princeps Wallie, universis has litteras nostras inspecturis salutem. Noveritis quod propter affectionem et sinceram dilectionem quas erga nos et subditos nostros illustrissimus princeps dominus Karolus eadem gratia Francorum rex hactenus gessit et sui gratia in dies gerit sibi et suis prout merito ad hoc tenemur adherere desideramus. Quapropter magistrum Griffinum Yonge, decretorum doctorem, cancellarium nostrum et Johannem de Hanmer, consanguineos nostros predilectos, nostros veros et legitimos procuratores, actores, factores, negociorum gestores ac nuncios speciales facimus, ordinamus et constituimus per presentes, dantes et concedentes eisdem procuratoribus nostris et eorum utrique per se et in solidum potestatem generalem et mandatum speciale ita quod non sit melior condicio occupantis sed quod unus eorum inceperit alter eorum prosequi valeat, mediare et finire pro nobis ac nomine nostro de et super liga perpetua vel temporali cum prefato illustrissimo principe tractandi ipsamque ligam ex parte nostra iniendi, faciendi et firmandi ac quodcumque licitum juramentum in ea parte necessarium in animam nostram prestandi, litterasque obligatorias hujusmodi ligam concernentes faciendi et quamcumque aliam securitatem in ea parte forte necessariam pro nobis inveniendi et prestandi, necnon consimilem securitatem in materia premissa necessariam a prefato illustrissimo principe domino Karolo Dei gratia Francorum rege ex parte sua nobis faciendam petendi et recipiendi ceteraque omnia et singula faciendi, exercendi et expediendi que in premissis et circa ea necessaria fuerint seu quomodolibet oportuna eciamsi mandatum exigant speciale et que nos facere possemus si personaliter hujusmodi tractatui interessemus ; pro dictis vero procuratoribus nostris et eorum utroque rem ratam habere, judicio sisti et judicatum solvi sub ypotheca et obligacione omnium bonorum nostrorum promittimus et cauciones exponimus per presentes.

In cujus rei testimonium has litteras nostras fieri fecimus patentes. Data apud Dolegelle x° die mensis maii, anno Domino millesimo quadringentisemo quarto, et principatus nostri quarto."

Actum et datum Parisius in domo habitacionis magnifici viri domini Ernaudi de Corbeya militis, cancellarii Francie, anno Domini millesimo quadringentesimo quarto, indictione duodecima, die xiiij[a] mensis julii, presentibus dicto domino cancellario Francie, necnon reverendis in Christo patribus et dominis dominis Philippo Noviomensi, Petro Meldensi, et Johanne Atrebatensi episcopis ac eciam magnifico et potenti Ludovico de Borbonio, comite Vindocinensi, nobilibusque viris dominis Roberto de Braquemont et Roberto d'Amilli, militibus dicti serenessimi principis regis Francorum cambellanis testibus ad promissa vocatis.

Ego Johannes de Sanctis, Belvacensis diocesis, apostolica et imperiali auctoritatibus publicus notarius prefatisque domini nostri Francorum regis notarius et secretarius qui premissis omnibus et singulis dum, ut premittitur, agerentur et fierent per dominos procuratores superius nominatos una cum suprascriptis testibus presens fui eaque fieri vidi et audivi ad requestam et de consensu ipsorum dominorum procuratorum ut huic presenti publico instrumento super hiis confecto et super eadem forma verborum dupplicato quod scribi et grossari per alium feci, pluribus aliis negociis occupatus, collacione per me facta cum notario publico infrascripto de originalibus litteris procuratoriarum supra insertis cum eodem presenti publico instrumento ipsum publicando me subscripsi et signum meum apposui consuetum.

Et ego Benedictus Comme, clericus Assavensis diocesis publicus auctoritate apostolica notarius, premissis omnibus et singulis dum sic ut premictitur per dictos dominos procuratores agerentur et fierent una cum magnificis dominis testibus ac venerabili viro notario supradicto presens interfui, eaque sic fieri vidi et audivi, et ideo hoc presens publicum instrumentum per alium me aliunde occupato, fideliter scriptum ad requisicionem et de consensu eorumdem dominorum procuratorum, dupplicatum publicavi, signoque et nomine meis solitis et consuetis signavi rogatus et requisitus in fidem et testimonium omnium premissorum."

Nos vero factum procuratorum nostrorum in hac parte ratum et gratum habentes ligam et confederacionem premissas quantum in nobis est ratificamus et confirmamus per presentes.

In cujus rei testimonium has litteras nostras fieri fecimus patentes. Data in castro nostro de Llanpadarn xij° die januarii, anno Domini millesimo quadringentisimo quinto et principatus nostri sexto.

In dorso.—Confederationes facte et inite inter dominum nostrum regem et Owinum principem Walliarum anno Domini M°· cccc°· v°·.

J516 B. 40.

LITTERA AD KAROLEM REGEM FRANCORUM.

Ultimo die Martii: A.D. 1406.

SERENISSIME princeps, humili recommendacione premissa scire dignemini quod nacio mea per plures annos elapsos per rabiem barbarorum Saxonum suppedita fuit ; unde ex quo ipsi regimen habebant licet de facto super nos oportuit cum eis ambulare. Sed nunc, serenissime princeps, ex innata vobis bonitate, me et subditos meos ad recognoscendum verum Christi vicarium luculenter et gratiose multipliciter informastis. De qua quidem informacione vestre excellencie regracior toto corde ; et quia prout ex hujusmodi informacione intellexi, dominus Benedictus, summus pontifex, omnibus viis possibilibus offert se ad unionem in ecclesia Dei faciendam, confidens eciam in jure ejusdem et vobiscum, quantum michi est possibile concordare intendens, ipsum pro vero Christi vicario pro me et subditis meis per litteras meas patentes hac vice majestati vestre per latorem presencium presentandas recognosco. Et quia, excellentissime princeps, rabie barbarica, ut prefertur, hic regnante, ecclesia Menevensis metropolitica violenter ecclesie Cantuarensi obedire coacta fuit et in subjectione hujusmodi adhuc de facto remanet et alia quamplura in convenientia per hujusmodi barbaros ecclesie Wallie illata extiterunt que pro majori parte in litteris meis patentibus de quibus prefertur plenius sunt inserta, super quorum expedicione penes dominum summum pontificem habenda magestatem vestram actencius deprecor et exoro, ut sicut nos a tenebris in lucem erigere dignati estis, similiter violenciam et oppressionem ecclesie et subditorum meorum extirpare et aufferre, prout bene potestis, velitis. Et vestram excellentissimam magestatem in prosperitate votiva diu conservet Filius Virginis gloriose. Scriptum apud Pennal, ultimo die marcii.

Vester ad vota
Owynus princeps Wallie.

In dorso.—Serenissimo et illustrissimo principi domino Karolo, Dei gracia, Francorum regi.

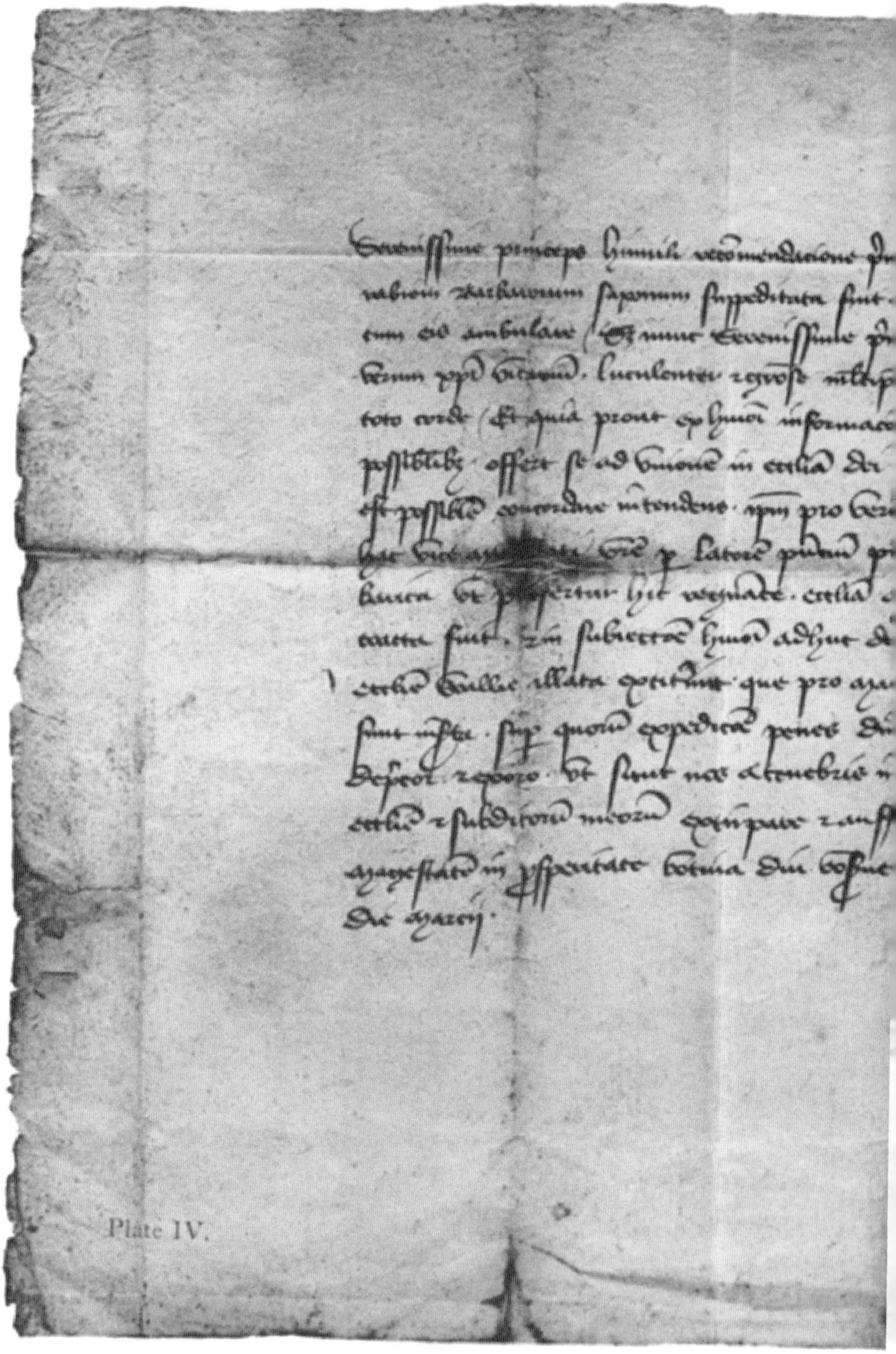

Serenissime princeps humili recomendacione pre
variorum [illegible] sapientum suppeditata sunt
tum eis ambulare Et nunc Serenissime pr
[illegible] luculenter [illegible]
toto corde Et quia prout ex huiusmodi informac
possibilibus offert se ad unione in ecclia dei
est possibile concordare intendens ipsi pro bene
hac vice [illegible] per latore presentem pr
[illegible] ut [illegible] hic regnare ecclia
tractata sunt. Cum subiectos huiusmodi adhuc de
eccle Wallie illata extiterunt que pro ma
sunt iniste. super quorum expedicione penes dn
desidero [illegible] ut sicut nox et tenebris in
ecclie et subditorum meorum [illegible]
majestatem in prosperitate [illegible] diu conservet
die Marcij.

Plate IV.

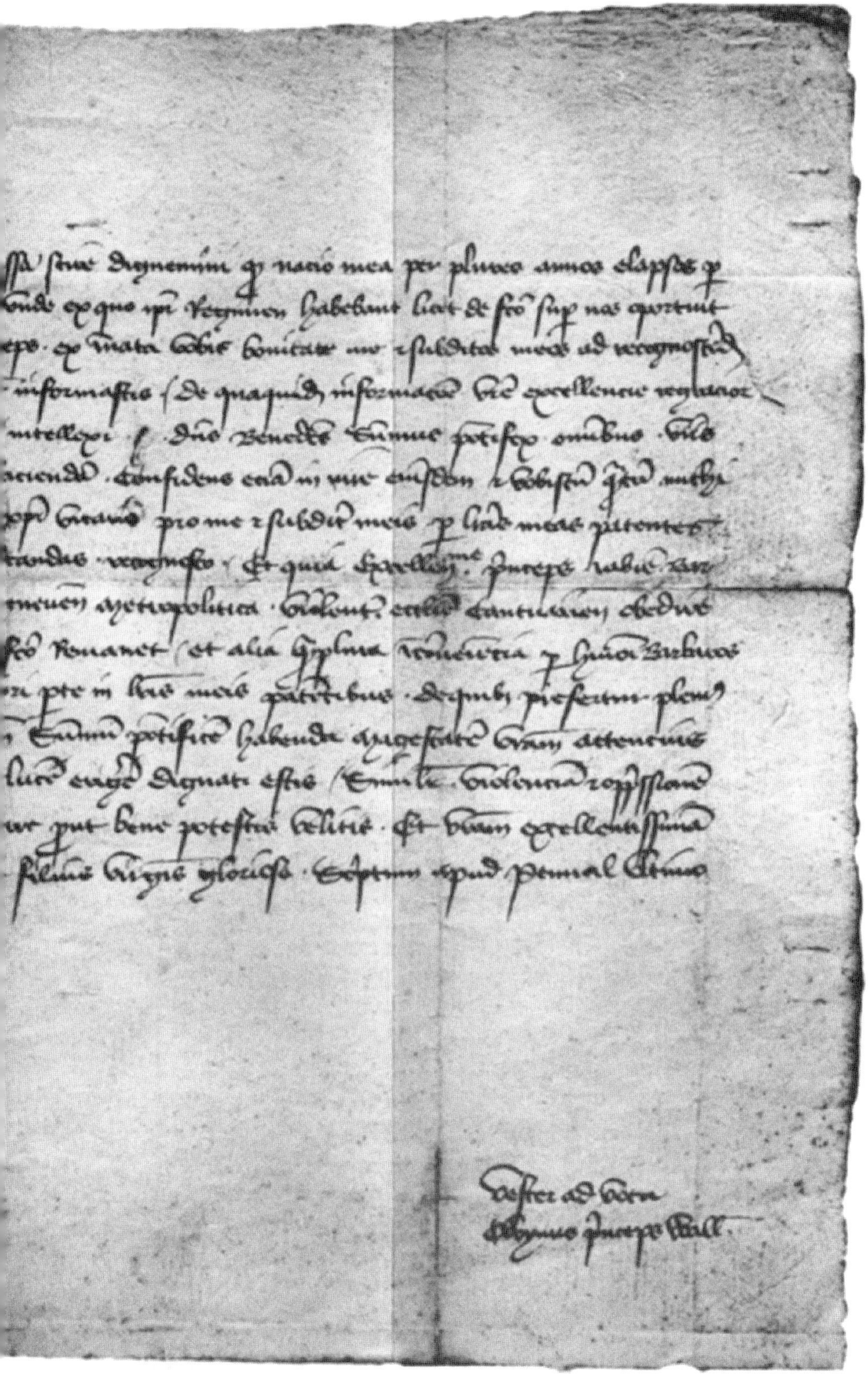
...ssa sunt dignemini quod nacio mea per plures annos elapsos q...
...onde ex quo ipi regimen habebant licet de sco sup nas qportunt
...epe. ex mata vobis bonitate me r subditos meos ad recognoscend...
... informastis / de quaquidem informacione vre excellencie regracior
... intelligi / dno Benedco summo potifice omnibus vrs
...aciendo. considerans etiam in vrā eundem r vobiscum qua mihi
...ospd vratis pro me r subditis meis p lras meas patentes
...tandus recognosco. Et quia excellencie vestre habui...
...menen metropolitica. violent. ecclie cantuarien obedire
...sco Romanet / et alia quplima remedia p hu... ...
...n pte in lris meis patentibus. decipimt presentium pleni...
... summo potifice habenda magestate vram attenciu...
...lud erga dignati estis / Cum vt. violencia r oppressione...
...ur put bene potestis velitis. Et vram excellentissima...
... filium regns gloriosa. Scriptum apud Penal ... Anno ...

vester ad vota
Owynus princeps Wall'

J516. 29.

LITTERA PER QUAM OWYNUS REDUXIT SE ET TERRAS AD OBEDIENCIAM DOMINI NOSTRI PAPE xiii$^{mi.}$

Ultimo die Martii: A.D. 1406.

ILLUSTRISSIMO principi domino Karolo Dei gracia Francorum regi, Owynus eadem gracia princeps Wallie, reverencias tanto principi debitas cum honore. Noverit excellencia vestra nos articulos infrascriptos ex parte vestra per fratrem Hugonem Eddouyer, ordinis predicatorum et Mauricium Kery, familiares et nuncios nostros nobis viij^{o} die marcii anno a Nativitate Domini millesimo quadringentesimo sexto presentatos recipisse formam continentes infrascriptam et tenorem : Et primo premissa cordiali salutacione ex parte domini nostri regis et presentatis ejus litteris exponent dicto domino principi qualiter dominus noster rex multum desiderat scire bonum statum suum et felices successus in negociis suis, rogatque eum ut quociens se facultas offeret de hoc velit sibi scribere quoniam recipiet magnam complacentiam ; et demum informabit eum de bono statu dicti domini regis, regine et liberorum suorum ac aliorum dominorum principum regalis prosapie et quomodo dominus rex et alii domini regalis prosapie habent et habere proponunt sinceram dilectionem et cordialem amicitiam ad dictum principem, zelantes ejus honorem, statum prosperum et bonum, et de hoc dictus dominus princeps potest securissime confidere. Item exponent eidem domino principi qualiter dominus noster rex, qui sincere et caritative diligit eum, multum desiderat quod sicut sunt colligati et confederati in temporalibus quod ita essent in spiritualibus et in factis ecclesie ut unanimes in domo Domini valerent ambulare. Ideoque rogat dominus rex eundem dominum principem affectuose ut velit attendere ad justiciam domini pape Benedicti tercii decimi, universalis ecclesie summi pontificis, ac ipsam agnoscere et ab omnibus subditis suis agnosci facere, et tenet dominus rex quod erit ad salutem anime sue et subditorum suorum, et securitatem ac firmitatem status sui et eorum confederationes in utilitate fidei et caritate Christi fundate erunt firmiores et vallidiores. Item licet omnes fideles christiani teneantur se informare de veritate scismatis, tamen inter omnes magis tenentur principes, et quia eorum opinio potest plures trahere in errorem et maxime subditos qui se habent conformare cum opinione sui superiores et quia eorum eciam interest ex debito procurare totis conatibus ut tale scisma totaliter extirpitur paxque et unio in Dei ecclesia habeatur et quod ille qui verus est Christi vicarrius a cunctis Christi fidelibus agnoscatur et recipiatur et ille qui est intrusus et conatur ansu nephario sanctam sedem apostolicam usurpari expellatur et ab omnibus fidelibus abiciatur ut antichristus et ad hoc possethenus laborare astringuntur secundum decreta sanctorum patrum, ad quod non sine magnis sumptibus et expensis laboravit dictus dominus rex et laborat indefesse. Item exponent dicto domino principi quod ipse non dubitat quin si ipse fuisset informatus ab inicio sufficienter qualiter Bartholomeus de Prinhano tunc archiepiscopus Barensis, violenter et per notoriam impressionem fuit intrusus in sede apostolica, non adhesisset ille parti, sed seductus et deceptus per ignoranciam facti, tenuit illam partem ; quoniam propter distanciam patrie sue a Roma, scit dominus rex quod potuit faciliter decipi et male informari ; et ideo dominus rex ad informandum animum suum et conscienciam suam ipsum duxit informare de sequentibus per que satis poterit sibi apparere de justicia domini pape Benedicti et se movere ad recognoscendum justiciam suam et eciam apparere de inconvenientibus que alias possent sibi contingere in statu suo, quod absit. Et primo est verum quod felicis recordacionis dominus Gregorius xj tunc temporis unicus et indubitatus romanus pontifex obiit Rome de anno Domini millesimo trecentesimo septuagesimo octavo, vicesima septima mensis marcii, quo tempore remanserunt in urbe predicta sexdecim cardinales, quatuor Ytalici, videlicet cardinalis Florentinus, cardinalis Sancti Petri, Cardinalis Mediolanus et cardinalis de Ursinis, et duodecim citramontani, scilicet cardinalis Lemovicensis, cardinalis de Agrofolio, cardinalis Gebennsis qui fuit postea electus in papam, cardinalis Glandatensis, cardinalis Pictavensis qui adhuc vivit, cardinalis Majoris monasterii, cardinalis Vivariensis, cardinalis de Britania, cardinalis Sancti Eustacii, cardinalis de Luna, nunc summus pontifex, cardinalis Sancti Angeli et cardinalis de Vernhio; ultra tamen cardinalem Ambianensem qui tunc temporis erat legatus in Florencia super certo tractatu tunc pendente inter dictum dominum Gregorium et Florentinos, et ad istos solum et in solidum et nullum alium pertinebat electio romani pontificis secundum canones et decreta sanctorum patrum. Item est notorium et manifestum quod dictus Bartholomeus fuit electus per violenciam et notoriam impressionem sequitur, nam mortuo dicto domino Gregorio, dum dicti cardinales celebrarent juxta morem exequias et novenam ipsius domini Gregorii officiales urbis sepius requisiverunt dictos cardinales et in coram et in particulare ut vellent eligere Romanum vel Ytalicum cum comminacione quod alias dubitabant de maximis et irreparabilibus scandalis. Et ut ipsi cardinales timore perterriti facilius conscenderent eorum requeste, commoverunt populum ad tumultum et rumorem et incitaverunt ad arma; et ut non esset qui posset comprimere talem rumorem seu sedicionem, expulerunt omnes nobiles potentes de urbe. Et cum transacta hujusmodi novena dicti cardinales intraverunt conclave pro electione Romani pontificis celebranda, populus in maxima multitudine et armatus pro majori parte intraverunt cum eis palacium Sancti Petri ubi erat conclave, clamando et vociferando: "Romanum volumus, vel ad minus Ytalicum," cum orrida vocifferacione et occupaverunt totum palacium; et licet fuerint pluries requisiti quod exirent dictum palacium, nunquam voluerunt exire, nec potuerunt expelli, ymo nec permiserunt dictum conclave murari juxta morem, nec ipsum palacium claudi, nec de die nec eciam de nocte, sed semper steterunt ibi, vociferando ut supra. Et ut majorem incuterent timorem dictis cardinalibus, et populus magis incitaretur ad furorem, fecerunt pulsari campanes ecclesie Sancti Petri juxta quam erat conclave et campanas Capitolii ad martellum ; et dum cardinales erant in ista pressura, fuerunt avisati pluries per custodes conclavis et alios ab extra quod nisi statim et sine aliqua mora eligerent Romanum vel Ytalicum, erant in periculo quod omnes inciderentur per frustra. Et tunc, sic perterriti, pro eritando mortis periculo et alias non facturi prout dixerunt omnes quasi tribus exceptis ex arrupto et sine alia discussione nominaverunt dictum Bartholomeum Ytalicum et eum elegerunt in papam ; et demum finaliter dictus populus qui continue erat in palacio sic clamando et percussiendo dictum conclave specialiter subtus solarium cum maximo furore irruerunt in ipsum conclave, eum frangendo per tres partes et clamando " per la clavalata de Romano le volemo," et intraverunt dictum conclave quanti potuerunt recipi taliter quod dicti cardinales vix potuerunt se salvare et liberare de morte et credunt indubite quod fuissent omnes interfecti nisi quia unus ex dictis cardinalibus suggessit populo quod cardinalis Sancti Petri erat electus sed nolebat consentire. Et dum populus se occuparent ad ipsum compellandum alii cardinales exiverunt ut melius potuerunt et fugerunt cum habitibus dissimulatum aliqui extra civitatem aliqui ad castrum Sancti Angeli et aliqui ad domos proprias. Et dicti Romani ulterius de vacancia rapuerunt vaxellum, vestes et alia bona dictorum cardinalium que repererunt in dicto conclavi et aliquorum domos fuerunt depredati et de istis clare memorie dominus Karolus tunc rex Francie, pater dicti domini nostri regis ultra testimonium dictorum cardinalium fuit per multas personsas notabiles et fidedignas plenissime informatus et faciliter potest' quilibet informari quia manifesta et notaria fuerunt. Item in crastinum Bartholomeus et officiales urbis predicti mandaverunt dictos cardinales quorum aliqui erant in Castro Sancti Angeli et aliqui in urbe dispersi in diversis latibulis absconsi ad se venire ut eundem Bartholomeum intronisarent, qui premissis pluribus excusacionibus in quibus non potuerunt exaudiri, cum tunc non adesset eis possibilitas exeundi Romam jamdicto rumore qui adhuc durabat pavefacti, ad ipsum Bartholomeum venire sunt coacti et postquam ad eum venerunt ad ipsum intronisandum, coronandum, reverencias papales exhibentes et ut Romano pontifici sibi asistentes, electionemque suam regibus et principibus denunciandum et intimandum simili metu compulsi, quoniam si premissa denegassent, fuissent in tanto periculo sicut ante, et tenent indubie quod fuissent omnes interfecti, saltim citramontani. Item omnes dicti cardinales ut primum potuerunt, exiverunt civitatem Romanam et nemine dempto omnes simpliciter dicesserunt a dicto Bartholomeo et quamprimum fuerunt in libertate sua in loco securo per solempnes viros fecerunt sibi exponi veritatem hujusmodi electionis et qualiter non erat papa sed intrusus et moneri quod vellet deponere illum statum quem sic indebite usurpaverat et consulere saluti anime sue cunctorum Christi fidelium ac obviare tot malis et scandalis que alias possent contingere, quod dictus Bartholomeus nimia ambicione detentus renuit et contempsit. Et deinde dicti cardinales habito tamen prius super hoc maturissimo consilio, publicaverunt dictum Bartholomeum non esse papam sed intrusum et violentum occupatorem sedis apostolice, ipsumque sentencias excommunicationis et anathematisacionum contra tales occupatores et mussores (?) sedis apostolice per sanctos patres latas et promulgatas incurrisse et demum post premissa; ne ecclesia diuctius esset sine capite, omnes concorditer elegerunt dominum Clementem vii tunc cardinalem Gebennensem. Item omnes dicti cardinales, tam ytalici quam citramontani uniformiter deposuerunt et testificati sunt cum juramento et sub periculo anime sue quod metu mortis cohacti et ut solum possent sibi salvare vitam nominaverunt dictum Bartholomeum et ipsum elegerunt in papam alias non facturi et quod intronisacionem, coronacionem reverencias, exhibicionem et alia que dicto Bartholomeo fecerant et litteras que pro tunc regibus et principibus super electionem dicti Bartholomei scripserant existentes in civitate Romana fecerant simili metu cohacti et non intencione nec proposito ex hiis aliquid juris sibi tribuendi aut ipsum in statu usurpato confirmandi ; et ad informandum clare memorie dominum Karolum tunc regem Francie, patrem dicti domini nostri regis de predictis venerunt tres ex dictis cardinalibus, scilicet Lemoricensis, Pictavensis et de Agrifolio qui viva voce predicta sibi exposuerunt et ea fuisse et esse vera et pro ipsis tocius collegii nomine a quo eciam mittebantur cum juramento et sub periculo anime sue, deposuerunt et factum super hoc per totum collegium recollectum et juratum tradiderunt. Item est verum quod ultra premissa.omnes ex dictis cardinalibus qui depost mortui sunt, tam ytalici quam citramontani quilibet singulariter in fine dierum suorum, in sua tamen sana memoria existentes testificati sunt sub periculo anime sue dictum Bartholomeum fuisse et esse intrusum et non fuisse nec esse papam ; de quibus presertim in tali passu cum essent viri omnes multum solemnes, probi et maxime litterature, non est presumendum quod fuerunt immemores sue salutis et cum secundum decreta sanctorum patrum ipsi cardinales sint testes et produces electionis Romani pontificis et qui soli sciunt veritatem quia soli intersunt in electione pape et nullus alius cum eis ipsis est in hoc simpliciter fiandum (?) et credendum. Item dictus dominus Karolus qui inter ceteros principes orbis tempore suo fuit magne prudencie, multum catholicus, devotus et Deum timens, et auditis dictis cardinalibus qui hac de causa venerant ad eum, fecit ad se evocari dominos principes sue prosapie, multos notabiles prelatos et barones regni sui, multos solemnes clericos tam de universitate Parisiensi quam aliis quibus exponi fecit ea que sibi per dictos cardinales fuerant exposita et eciam que pro parte dicti Bartholomei fuerant sibi intimata ; qui, materia hinc inde bene discussa et pluribus deliberacionibus habitis, prout ejus arduitas requirebat consuluerunt dicto domino Karolo quod electio dicti Bartholomei erat violenta, impressiva et simpliciter nulla, electioque dicti domini Clementis erat canonica. Quorum consilio et deliberacione audita, dictus dominus Karolus decrevit obedire dicto domino Clementi et a subditis suis obedire facere ipsiusque partem fovit, dictumque Bartholomeum tanquam invasorem sedis apostolice abjessit ; et post dicti domini Karoli obitum dictus dominus noster rex, inherendo vestigiis progenitorum sui, obedivit dicto domino Clementi tanquam vero Romano pontifici, quamdiu vixit et post ejus mortem domino Benedicto ejus vere successori. Et simili modo dominus Johannes tunc rex Castelle qui ut securius procederet misit Romam proprios ambaxiatores ad habendum ibidem informacionem de veritate facti eciam cum Romanis ac admisit et audivit ad plenum ambaxiatores dicti Bartholomei super omnibus que voluerunt proponere tam in facto quam in jure, et auditis relacione dictorum ambaxiatorum suorum de hiis que Rome repererant, domino cardinali de Luna qui erat tunc legatus ad eum pro parte dictorum Clementis et collegii et ambaxiatoribus dicti Bartholomei, discussaque et diceptata diucius materia inter utramque partem et demum habita plenissima deliberacione cum prelatis, principibus baronibus et viris litteratis regni sui, presentibus ambaxiatoribus utriusque partis, se determinavit pro dicto domino Clemente cum toto regno suo. Idem fecit dominus Johannes tunc rex Aragonum. Idem rex Portugalie mortuus. Idem rex Navarre. Idem eciam fecit regina Johanna, regina Jherusalem et Cicilie, licet dictus Bartholomeus esset de sua civitate Neapolitana oriundus, cui et propter nacionem et favores quos ab ipso sperabat habere libenter obedivisset si salva consciencia potuisset. Idem rex Socie et rex Cipri, duces Barrensis et Lothaingie et comes Sabaudie. Idem comes Fundorum ytalicus. Idem nunc civitas Januensis et multi alii principes et communitates, et finaliter omnes qui voluerunt audire et admictere legatos utriusque partis et de earum justicia ac veritate facti equaliter informari et merita utriusque electionis equa lance librari. Item et multi anticardinales creati per dictum Bartholomeum et suos successores se reduxerunt ad partem istam, videlicet cardinalis Yspanie ultimo deffunctus, quem dictus Bartholomeus creaverat et fecerat legatum suum in Castella ; cardinalis de Malapetra, cardinalis de Silisco et prelati alii quamplures, et tamen nunquam aliquis de ista parte se reduxit ad aliam. Item dictis dominus Clemens quamdiu vixit una cum dicto collegio cardinalium omnem operam possibilem dederunt quod omnes principes informarentur de veritate facti et justicia utriusque partis, mictendo legatos et ambaxiatores ad reges et alios principes christianos et post obitum dicti domini Clementis, idem fecit dominus Benedictus ejus successor. Dictus autem Bartholomeus et ejus successores quantum potuerunt impediverunt quod sibi obedientes non audirent partem istam astringendo eciam aliquos ad hoc juramento specialiter certos principes Almanie. Item de anno proxime preterito dictus dominus Benedictus confisus de justicia sua et desiderans summo opere ponere pacem in ecclesia dolens intrinsecus tanquam verus pastor de periculo ovium suarum, misit Romam ad Bonifacium tunc intrusum solemnes ambaxiatores et fecit sibi offeri in presencia suorum anticardinalium viam mutue convencionis ipsorum duorum et collegiorum suorum, viam discussionis justicie, informacionem veritatis et omnem aliam viam racionabilem et possibilem per quam unio posset haberi eciam usque ad renunciacionem inclusive casu pro dictus Bonifacius sic vellet facere; que omnia ipse Bonifacius simpliciter refutavit et quod fuit deterius ambaxiatores dicti domini Benedicti, non obstante salvo conductu quod habebant, fuerint capti Rome et reclusi in strictis carceribus in castre Sancti Angeli, a quibus non potuerunt expediri nisi mediante financia v^{m} ducatorum. Hiis tamen non obstantibus, ipso Bonifacio mortuo et isto moderno jam intruso, fecit diligenciam et multum laboravit de simili modo, requirendo et summando istum intrusum modernum, sed ipse noluit ejus ambaxiatores admittere, nec eis salvum conductum concedere, prout hec clare patent in litteris dicti Benedicti quam dicto principi ostendant. Et ultra hoc dictus dominus Benedictus dolens visceraliter per diffugia ipsius intrusi istud detestabile cisma sic procelari ecclesiam lacerari et animas fidelium periclitari, non parcens senili etati sue pro ipsa unione commodius et efficacius procuranda intravit Ytaliam et est nunc in civitate Januensi ubi obtulit et offert omnes vias possibiles, dispositus eciam exponere vitam corporalem pro ipsa unione obtinenda. Item principes Alamanie premissis pensatis et consideratis, licet usque ad hec tempora renuissent admittere et audire nuncios et ambaxiatores dicti domini Benedicti et informacionem justicie sue recipere, obtulerunt nunc se paratos ejus nuncios admictere et audire et informacionem justicie sue recipere et ultra reges Boemie et Ungarie ab obediencia dicti intrusi jam se substraxerunt. Item habuit nova dictus dominus noster rex de partibus Ytalie, quod intrusus cum ejus anticardinalibus fugiit de Roma per modum contentum in littera cujus copiam dicto domino principi ostendent. Item consideret dictus dominus princeps quanta dampna potest sibi procurare dictus intrusus quamdiu erit sub obediencia sua, presertim ex quo intendit favere Henrico Anglie ponendo in terra sua prelatos et beneficiatos anglicos, denegando sibi dispencaciones opportunas in matrimoniis et aliis et adinvenire plures vias et modos per quos dominum suum posset periclitari, quod absit, et circa hoc habet considerare quid fecerit, regi Ungarie quem eciam inauditum privavit regno Ungarie et dedit Laudislao, qui se asserit regem Cicilie; quid eciam regi Boemie, quem procuravit privare per electores imperii regno Romanorum et Ruppertum de

Bavaria per eos electum confirmavit. Ea propter dominus noster rex rogat et exortatur vicerose dictum dominum principem ut velit premissa considerare et bene ponderare, specialiter violenciam et notorietatem impressionis que fuit in electione dicti Bartholomei et in aliis actibus subsequtus quamdiu cardinales fuerunt sub posse Romanorum, testimonium uniforme et juramenta omnium cardinalium quod vix in aliquo alio scismate legitur quod omnes cardinales essent ab una parte et signanter Ytalicorum qui libencius adhesissent intruso eo quia Ytalicus si salva consciencia potuissent et specialiter in mortis articulo deliberaciones et determinaciones dicti domini Karoli patris dicti domini nostri regis et aliorum principum supradictorum tam mature et tam solemniter factas oblaciones dicti domini Benedicti tam jurisdicas et tam racionabiles ac reffutaciones intrusi per quas ostendit diffidenciam de jure suo non modicam et ipsis bene ponderatis quod velit attendere ad justiciam dicti domini Benedicti et ipsum agnoscere in verum Christi vicarium et universalem pastorem Dominici gregis, et eidem ut tali veraciter et filialiter obedire et a suis subditis obediri facere. Et videtur dicto domino nostro regi quod hoc erit ad salutem anime sue, subditorum suorum, conservacionem status sui ; et de hoc idem dominus rex qui sincere zelatur salutem suam, prosperitatem et conservacionem honoris et status sui ipsum visceraliter et sub vinculo ac federe amicicie et dilectionis singularis, quam ad eum habet, rogat et requirit significando sibi quod si premissa deducat ad execucionem, faciet eidem domino regi maximam complacenciam et se repputabit ad sua beneplacita peramplius obligatum ; et si forte dictus dominus princeps, prelati et alii viri ecclesiastici terrarum sibi subditarum formidarent quod ex hujusmodi reductione possent certa prelaturas et alia beneficia ab intruso et suis predecessoribus obtenta et alias gracias cujuscumque condicionis subditis suis concessis pro tempore futuro turbari vel quod dominus Benedictus vellet aliquid innovare, dominus noster rex offert se procuraturum erga dictum dominum Benedictum quod omnes prelati et beneficiati confirmabuntur, omnesque gracias, dispensaciones et alie etc. ratificabuntur et concedentur in forma eis grata et secura ; quodque dictus dominus Benedictus providebit de prelaturis et aliis beneficiis ibidem vacantibus et vacaturis personis sufficientibus dicto domino principi fidis et gratis et non sibi emulis aut suspectis. Et subsequentur ex deliberacione consilii nostri convocari fecimus proceres de prosapia nostra et prelatos principatus nostri ac alios in hac parte evocandos et tandem post diligentem examinacionem et disputacionem articulorum premissorum et materie eorumdem per prelatos et clerum sufficienter factas, concordatum et conclusum existit quod nos, confidentes in jure domini Benedicti, sacrosancte Romane ac universalis ecclesie summi pontifices, presertim eo quod pro pace et unione ecclesie prosequtus est et in dies, ut intelleximus, prosequitur, considerantesque duram servitiem, adversarii ejusdem Benedicti tunicam Christi inconsutilem dillacerantis ac ob sinceram dilectionem quam erga vestram excellenciam gerimus specialem, predictum dominum Benedictum ut verum Christi vicarium in terris a nobis et subditis nostris recognoscendum fore duximus et recognoscimus per presentes. Et quia, illustrissime princeps, infrascripti articuli statum nostram et ecclesie Wallie refformacionem et utilitatem notorie concernunt, vestram regiam magestatem humilime rogamus quatinus expedicionem eorumdem graciose penes prefatum dominum Benedictum summum pontificem promovere dignemini. Et primo si sensure ecclesiastice contra nos et subditos nostros seu terram nostram per prefatum dominum Benedictum aut Clementem predecessorem suum late existant, quod ipse Benedictus easdem relaxet. Item quod quecumque et qualiacumque juramenta per nos seu quoscumque alios principatus nostri illis qui se nominaverunt Vrbanum et Bonifacium nuper deffunctos seu eisdem adherentibus qualitercumque prestita relaxat. Item quod confirmet et ratificet ordines collatos, titulos prelatorum, dispensacionesque et officia tabellionum ac alia quecumque in quibus periculum animarum aut prejudicium nobis et subditis nostris in ea parte evinire seu generari possent a tempore Gregorii xi. Item quod ecclesia Menevensis que a tempore sancti David archiepiscopi et confessoris fuit metropolitana et post obitum ejusdem successerunt eidem archiepiscopi ibidem xxiiij, prout in cronicis et antiquis libris ecclesie Menevensis nomina eorumdem continentur et hic pro majori evidencia eadem exprimi fecimus, videlicet, Eliud, Keneu, Morwal, Menevie, Haerunen, Elwayd, Gvrnuen, Llevdiwyt, Gvrwyst, Gvgavn, Cledavc, Ainan, Elave, Maelyswyd, Sadernuen, Catullus, Alathvy, Nouis, Sadernuen, Diochwael, Asser, Arthuel, David secundus, et Sampson, pristina statui restituatur ; quequidem ecclesia metropolitana infrascriptas habuit et habere debet ecclesias suffraganeas, videlicet, Exoniensem, Battoniensem, Herefordensem, Wygorniensem, Legicestrensem, cujus sedes jam translata est ad ecclesias Coventrensem et Lichfeldensem, Assavensem, Bangorensem, et Landavensem ; nam ingruente rabie barbarorum Saxonum qui terram Wallie eisdem usurparunt, ecclesiam Menevensem predictam suppeditarunt et eam ancillam ecclesie Cantuariensis de facto ordinarunt. Item quod idem dominus Benedictus provideat de metropolitano Menevensi ecclesie et aliis ecclesiis cathedralibus principatus nostri, prelaturis, dignitatibus et beneficiis ecclesiasticis, curatis scientibus linguam nostram dumtaxat. Item quod dominus Benedictus in corporaciones, uniones, annexiones et appropriaciones ecclesiarum parrochialium principatus nostri, monasteriis et collegiis anglicorum quorumcumque auctoritate hactenus factas revocet et annullet et quod veri patroni earumdem ecclesiarum locorum ordinariis ydoneas personas presentare valeant ad easdem seu alias conferre. Item quod dominus Benedictus concedat nobis et heredibus nostris principibus Wallie quod capella nostra de cetero sit libera et gaudeat privilegiis, exempcionibus et immunitatibus quibus gaudebat temporibus progenitorum nostrorum principum Wallie. Item quod habeamus duas universitates sive studia generalia, videlicet unum in Northwallie et aliud in Swthwallie, in civitatibus, villis seu locis per ambaxiatores et nuncios nostros in hac parte specifiendis et declarandis. Item quod dominus Benedictus contra Henricum Lencastrie intrusorem regni Anglie et usurpatorem corone ejusdem regni et sibi adherentes, eo quod ecclesias tam cathedrales quam conventuales et parochiales voluntarie combusit et comburi procuravit, archiepiscopos, episcopos, prelatos, presbyteros, religiosos tam possessionatos quam mendicantes inhumaniter suspendi, decapitari et quartirizari fecit et fieri mandavit et quod scismaticus existit, cruciatam concedere dignetur in forma consueta. Item quod idem dominus Benedictus concedat nobis et heridibus nostris, subditis et adherentibus nobis cujuscumque nacionis fuerint dumtamen fidem teneant ortodoxam, qui guerram contra prefatum intrusorem sustinemus plenam remissionem omnium peccatorum et quod remissio hujusmodi duret guerra inter nos, heredes, et subditos nostros et prefatum Henricum, heredes et subditos suos durante.

In cujus rei testimonium, has litteras nostras fieri fecimus patentes. Data apud Pennal ultimo die macii anno a Nativitate Domini millesimo quadringentesimo sexto et principatus nostri sexto.

In dorso.—Littera per quam Owynus, princeps Wallie reduxit se et terras et domina sua ad obedienciam domini nostri pape xiij^mi.

TRANSLATIONS.

LLYWELYN TO PHILIP AUGUSTUS KING OF FRANCE.

TO our most excellent lord Philip, by the grace of God, the illustrious King of the French, Llywelyn, Prince of North Wales, his friend, sends greeting and such devotion as the debt of fealty and respectful service, which I will repay the excellency of your nobility, on account of the singular and priceless gifts, which you, King of the French, even prince of that country of kings, outstripping me, your friend, not more munificently than magnificently, have sent me by your knight, your letters, impressed by your golden seal in witness of the alliance of the kingdom of the French and the principality of North Wales, which I, before an assembly of clergy, even upon the sacrosanct relics swear to observe as they will be a perpetual memorial and an inviolable testimony, that I and my heirs, cleaving inseparably to you and your heirs, shall be to your friends' friends, to your enemies' enemies. This itself therefore stipulating, I expect and ask from your kingly dignity to be royally observed in every manner towards me and towards my friends, and in order that it may inviolably be observed, having called together a council of my chieftains, and with the common consent of all the princes of Wales, all of whom I have joined with you in the friendship of this treaty, I promise you, under witness of my seal, fidelity in perpetuity, and as I thus faithfully promise I will carry out my promise more faithfully. Moreover, since I received letters of your excellency, I have made neither truce, nor peace, nor any negotiation whatever with the English. But, by the grace of God, I and all the princes of Wales, unitedly confederated, will manfully resist our enemies, even yours, and by the help of God and with a strong hand, we will recover from the yoke of the tyrants themselves the great part of the land and the strongly fortified castles, which they by fraud and guile have occupied. And being recovered, we will powerfully hold [them] in the Lord God, whence stipulating, we, the princes of all Wales, desire that without us, neither truce nor peace will ye make with the English, [for] let it be decreed, that by no pact or reward, unless by the foreknown kindness of your wish, will we be joined to them in any peace or treaty.

Endorsement.—The Covenant of Llywelyn, Prince of North Wales, with the Lord King of France.

BULLS ISSUED TO RICHARD, BISHOP OF ST. DAVIDS, ON BEHALF OF THE HOLY LAND.

I.

URBAN, Bishop, servant of the servants of God, sends to the venerable brother [Richard] Bishop of Menevia greeting and apostolic blessing.

Among the manifold and exceeding great labours, by which we are grievously distressed and distracted beyond measure, we are more pressingly concerned with providing assistance for the Holy Land, meditating with strained solicitude and anxious attention to this purpose, namely, that steps be taken to provide assistance for the said land by some suitable means, and that work of cross and crucifix may, with the help of God, be happily directed. For, although some of our predecessors, the great Roman pontiffs, urged forward this project with fervent zeal, yet, we ourselves, knowing the present condition of that land as we do, and since we know by the severe experience in this matter in hand, we desire, all the more, that swift and effective assistance be sent to relieve the serious jeopardy in which the same land is placed. Since by the advice of our brethren, we have determined that the hundredth part of the increase of all the clergy of the whole of Wales should be granted to that land, for a period of five years. We, therefore, by apostolic authority, command your brotherhood that the aforesaid hundredth part shall be collected by you, by another or others, in full, even to the fifth year, and that whatsoever the amount collected, it shall be given over to the ambassadors of the same land, their procurators, or one of them, without any diminution whatsoever, and that by them, it shall be converted into a subsidy for the same land. Moreover, you should restrain all gainsayers or rebels, if there are any, by apostolic censure, from which there can be no appeal; notwithstanding, let it be allowed to prelates, clergy, chapters, colleges, convents, or any order whatsoever, whether exempt or not exempt from the jurisdiction of the apostolic see, that though they cannot be compelled to do so, they shall, neverthelees, be expected to grant pecuniary assistance to some one.

However, you should effectually warn all the clergy and laity of the aforesaid Wales, of whatsoever condition, order, and dignity, who on a former occasion publicly took the sign of the cross to assist the said land, to arise and induce them by a similar censure to redeem their vows, even to crossing the sea,* a right of appeal against such censure being withheld. But because, according to the information that we have received, some executors have exceeded the amount allowed for the collection to many ecclesiastic persons and places, regular and secular, of the aforesaid Wales, who may be exempt or not exempt from the jurisdiction of the said see over certain concessions concerning the redemption of the vows of crusaders and concerning legacies, gifts, titles or profits granted to assist or allotted for the assistance of the aforesaid country in the said Wales, by us and our predecessors in the Roman pontificate, or by others according to the mandate of the aforesaid see already given, and that they have shamefully used other grants in such manner. We, unwilling to transgress under that dissimulation, lest, God forbid, they tend to the serious loss, diminution, and detriment of the aforesaid subsidy, wish that, in the aforesaid Wales, you should undertake to check strongly on our part all the executors deputed by the same rectors or religious places over any concessions from the said see, lest they in any manner proceed

* *I.e.*, actively taking part in the Crusade.

to collect the aforesaid dues. If perchance they will have presumed, from any presumption under the same censure that they can proceed contrary to your inhibition, an appeal against the restraint will be disregarded.

Nevertheless, you should the more diligently seek and faithfully endeavour to find out from us by letter, by what authority, to what persons and places, under what form, and to what extent the above-mentioned were granted; and how many and in what places were they to be collected by the same executors. For, we do not desire that the above-mentioned concessions, and anything whatsoever obtained under a pretext of those concessions, should have any force until by your favour, we shall ascertain the truth concerning these premises more fully, and shall have arranged concerning them as we may deem expedient. However, in the menatime, you will collect in full, the ransoms, legacies, gifts, and tithes of any kind, personally, through another or others, whom you will have known to be suitable for that purpose; and you shall not fail to assign the amount collected from these in full to the ambassadors of the same land, their procurators, or one of them, to be used as a subsidy for that land.

Again, it is not allowed that personally or through another or others, you can unduly molest the crusaders or intending crusaders, who wish to assist the said land, and whom we have taken under our protection and that of the Apostolic see, to any degree contrary to the immunities and privileges granted by the same see to crusaders, and that, by the same censure, the right of any appeal whatsoever for restraining is taken away from those who molest. To this purpose, since the preaching of the cross is entrusted to you in the said Wales by letters under fixed forms, we, wishing that you more zealously pursue an undertaking of this nature, entrust you with greater powers, that you, another or others, deputed by the Holy See, or who, in future, may be deputed, shall enjoin, without hindrance, to all preachers and executors of the cross, to all clergy regular and secular, on behalf of assistance for the Holy land in the said Wales, that they are to assist, obey, and help you in all matters which you shall deem to be expedient to the advancement of the said undertaking. That you should even accept any prelates of churches and other regular and secular clergy, whom you will deem to be suitable, that they who see to these matters shall assist, help, and obey you in the advancement of this undertaking, and even the prelates and other clergy regular and secular, of any order, if it shall be necessary, as well as the preachers and executors aforesaid. You shall also choose and ordain five clerks, who shall work with you in the undertaking, that through you, another, or others, the income of their benefices, prebendaries, or churches shall be entirely administered, the daily distributions being to a certain extent excepted, and all right of appeal is withdrawn by our authority. And even if they personally reside in the churches where, or in which, they receive these grants, you have the full power by our permission. There being by no means any right to withstand, gainsayers being restrained by apostolic censure, according to the customs and governing statutes of their churches, confirmed by our decree, or supported by any other authority whatsoever, the right of appeal being disregarded. Also, by the authority of these presents, we grant to the preachers of the cross whom you have chosen for this purpose, that they are to be considered, lest any hindrance or other obstacle withstand their preaching. That they are to preach before all administrators of public monies and others whosoever, who may wish to have something stated to the people while the message of the cross is set forth by the same preachers. They have power to wholly ban the license and to crush the presuming boldness of those who were badly chosen, by ecclesiastic censure, the right of any appeal whatsoever against which being taken away.

Besides, we grant to you fully and freely by the

authority of these presents that should it happen, when you have turned to any town or church placed under an interdict of the church in the aforesaid Wales, you can suspend that interdict, and you may celebrate and cause to be celebrated the holy offices while there in the usual manner, in the same church, on account of the preaching of the cross, the excommunicated and those who gave cause for the interdict being excluded. And whenever it should happen that you come to a place under an interdict, you have the power to grant a licence that they may be able to celebrate the holy offices in those churches on account of the privileges of the apostolic see at this present time, you being present, to crusaders and intending crusaders. The excommunicated, or those who caused the interdict cannot, however, be there listening.

Besides, we grant to you the power of granting absolution, personally, by another or others, to those who contrary to the prohibition of the said see or of its legates have visited the Lord's sepulchre, and to those who have carried weapons, arms, timber, and prohibited goods to the Saracens, or to others who have given advice, aid, or favour to them against Christians ; even to any clerks in prelate dignities, or benefices, or instituted priests, who contrary to the constitution of the church have heard readings or doctrine from the opinions of excommunicated persons. These shall be held to be treated with those, who, excommunicated or suspended, have rushed into an irregularity, mixing other doctrines with holy teaching, while they were crusaders, or while they took the cross, and personally crossed the seas as an aid for the said land, or at their own cost furnished, for that place, on their own behalf, other suitable warriors, or who have assisted others from their own goods for the aforesaid subsidy, suitably according to your discretion and that of others who you may appoint for this purpose. Also, you have the power of absolving, personally, or through another or others, whom you shall have known to be suitable for this purpose, all crusaders, who up to this time were for an aid for the said land and afterwards intending crusaders, from their vows, who on account of infirmity or bodily weakness shall be unable or powerless to fight or to cross the seas to succour the said land, provided that according to their own proper abilities they wished to redeem their vows.

You have also the power of commuting, personally, or through another or others, any vow of the cross into vows of pilgrimages or abstinence, for those who had assumed the sign of the cross on account of the said aid ; and of dispensing with the services of fifty clerks of poor lineage of the said Wales, provided that they are not born of adultery, incest, or illegitimacy, nor follow paternal incontinence, but are of good repute and life ; and to those who supported others by merit to obtain the grace of this dispensation, who, having assumed the sign of the cross, have personally crossed the seas as an aid for the said land, or who have sent suitable soldiers there, or who have supported others partly from goods on behalf of the said subsidy, suitably according to your discretion. For notwithstanding any such defect, he can be admitted to all orders, obtain an ecclesiastic benefice, or he even may have the care of souls.

Also, you have the power of absolving, the sentence having been promulgated according to the canon, and the charge of the work of the cross is entrusted to you, personally, through another or other suitable persons, according to the form of the church, all those whom you shall have known to have sinned by laying violent hands upon religious men or secular clerks, or on account of passion, provided that they make full satisfaction for those wrongs and injuries, being past, and have so far left such serious and grave offences, because the apostolic see shall on this account require according to the merits of the case. And by your command, or those deputed whom you have chosen for that purpose, they shall take the sign of the cross as an aid for the said land, and shall go there personally, or shall cause suitable soldiers to be sent there, or they shall partly from their own goods support others suitably according to your discretion, or of other whom you have commissioned for that purpose. You have the power of giving dispensation to clerks, being bound by any judgement, who have committed themselves in sacred matters, and of enjoining to them salutary penitence; and even of absolving from the bond of excommunication according to the form of the church those who, through the violent laying on of hands, or through their passions, have received the judgement promulgated in the canon, and on account of which serious outbreaks the aforesaid see shall require punishment. Provided that they give full and complete satisfaction for those injuries and wrongs now past, and having thus taken the sign of the cross by your command, shall give themselves as an aid for that land, personally crossing over the seas for that purpose. Nevertheless, granting that the clergy and laity of the aforesaid Wales, crusaders and intending crusaders have power to convert the tithes to be used as an aid for the said land, but not to the extent of retaining the increase of those churches on account of peace, and even to show to you or to those specially entrusted by you in this matter their reason with a safe conscience. You have, also the right, personally or through another or others, to grant to the aforesaid clergy and laity a fifth part of the tithes so obtained, because they are the least bound to receive that restitution, but accordingly as long as they remain absolved. Provided that they acknowledge that those tithes which they are known to expect, must in future be freely remitted to the same churches.

But it is our desire that you have the power to carry out each and every one of the above premises freely, notwithstanding it is granted by the aforesaid see to any persons, places, or orders, that they cannot be placed under an interdict, suspended, or excommunicated by means of letters apostolic, unless a full and express mention, word by word, is made concerning any indulgence, or other indulgences, privileges, or letters whatsoever obtained, or shall in future be obtained from the same see, through which aforesaid they have the power to frustrate or change, and concerning which, or the whole tenor of which, special mention must be made in our letters, and issued in the general council according to the constitution *de duabus dietis.*

Given at Orvieto the third day of October (1263) in the third year of our pontificate.

II.

URBAN, Bishop, servant of the servants of God, to the venerable brother [Richard] Bishop of Menevia, greeting and apostolic blessing. The Lord, beholding from the highest heavens the land both of His Birth and Passion, is daily angered by various injuries, while the people whom He Himself redeemed do not arise to avenge the cross. On that account, especially, He considers that by want of merit, shame is added to the dolour of his wounds, because that most holy country, where a virgin gave birth to the King of Heaven himself, is being continually worn out by vexations, and is torn by very cruel and successive oppressions. Now, by the savage fury of the Saracens, now, by the fierce rage of the Tartar race, a people, so cruel, as to be ignorant even of sparing age. Therefore, it is but right that special attention of the sons of Light be drawn to this purpose ; that their hearts and solicitude be assiduously directed concerning this country, so that they may devote themselves to expiate the abominations of that land, which the Son of God especially chose as a heritage for Himself, and by a strong hand resist the sons of darkness. This having been accomplished, they should not dissimulate or with heavy ears be frightened, lest our Redeemer, foreseeing all things, finding the redeemed labouring under the vice of ingratitude, and ignorant of their folly, shall in anger turn his face away from them, and shall depart from such men unworthy of his Father's grace. Therefore, let not the sons of devotion be unmindful, because Christ took upon Himself the flesh of our mortality in that land, as a servant, and did not fear to suffer the torments of the cross, that by dying, he might destroy our death, and by rising to life, he might prepare life for the faithful. We beseech diligently, that they attempt, as that unhappy land lies crushed and most dejected by hard scourgings, because the Tartar plague presses upon it, whose incursions, so much they are stronger and nearer, will indisputably be dreaded so much more seriously. That savage and damnable Tartar nation have subdued that land of His, oppressing it with the unbearable exactions of slavery, so torturing and afflicting its inhabitants that they freely choose the gates of death rather than live under that tyranny, which by living they endure under such a race of torturers. Therefore let the zealous of the faith rise for the defence of that country, consecrated by the death of our Redeemer, and let them not allow their minds to become lukewarm, but let them be kindled with a burning desire to serve. For the Son of God Himself considers, among other duties, human service the most pleasing, and on that account gives that reward as a recompense, which we should principally pursue and seek, while we undergo our period of service granted to us in this low vale of present misery. Therefore, since we have great faith in the Lord, concerning you, whom we believe to have the fear of God and also endowed with the manifold gifts of virtue, we have great faith in the Lord, that in a praiseworthy manner, you know and have strength to make progress where you labour with earnestness, hoping that in the prosecution of the present business you will, constantly fighting, promote it with effective studies and full affection. We pray and earnestly exhort your brotherhood, granting in remission of sins to the faithful in Christ in this manner, as far as granted by you or another or other prelates or clergy of the church, regular or secular, of whatsoever rank they may be. You will exhort with strict warnings and careful homilies those whom you know to be suitable for this purpose, diligently explaining to them and earnestly laying before them the message of the cross, and will lead them near to the grace given to you from God. That earnestly considerating how much the aforesaid land now needs their succour, they will come forward to its assistance with ready courage, and will rise with all their strength, having taken the sign of the cross there, they will be armed with spiritual arms and material. Hoping also for divine power, they will proceed with caution and will more fully and courageously strive for that purpose, so that they will receive from thence spiritual gifts, than which there is hardly any doubt they can obtain better. We, by the mercy of Almighty God and of his blessed apostles Peter and Paul, entrust you with authority, and as God has pleased, He has granted to us the power of binding and of freeing sins, we grant full pardon for their sins to all those who are truly penitent and confess their sins, and who in any way undertake the work in their own persons and expenses. To those who have not sought that land in their own persons, but in that they have sent at their own expense suitable men in ability and quality, and similarly to those, who, although supported at another's expense, but in their own persons, we grant full pardon for their sins. We also wish and concede that all those who have granted some portion of their goods or given other timely advice and help to the assistance of that land to be participators of this remission according to the amount of their aid and the effect of their devotion. We, indeed, wish that all the crusaders shall enjoy that privilege and immunity which is usually granted to crusaders. Moreover, that you will be able to follow more freely and usefully any office given to you, we grant to you and to the aforesaid, whom you may elect as your assistants for this purpose, the right of calling together for this purpose, as often as you may deem expedient, the clergy and people of the places where you or your assistants may preach the message of the cross. So that they may come together processionally, and with devotion, and be present at your preachings. That if it may be necessary for this purpose, the same clergy should be rebuked by apostolic censure, the right of appeal being disregarded.

We grant the power, on account of the same preachings, by the authority of these presents, that you may cause, as often as you may deem expedient, the declaring and conceding one hundred days plenary indulgence to all who are truly penitent and confess, and who shall have supported the same convocations and preachings, notwithstanding, if they proceed from anyone of whatsoever rank or dignity. Because, let it be granted from the apostolic see, that they cannot be interdicted, suspended, or excommunicated, and that they cannot be impeded or defrauded by means of any indulgences, privileges, or letters, held or which may be held by the aforesaid, from the same see, and concerning which special mention should be made in our letters. Therefore, you and those to whom you have determined to entrust the duty of any manner of preaching, shall take care to follow the apostolic command upon this in such a way, that your devotion may be followed by the palm of glory, which is given by Him to those waging the war of God.

Given at Orvieto the fourth day of October (1263) in the fourth year of our pontificate.

Endorsement—For the Holy Land.

III.

URBAN, Bishop, servant of the servants of God, to the venerable brother [Richard] Bishop of Menevia, greeting and apostolic benediction. Wishing that all who have taken the Cross, or who are about to take the Cross in Wales, as an aid for the Holy Land, should enjoy the prerogative of the singular privilege to crusaders or intending crusaders of every rank, so that there may not be, hereafter, any increase of authority by letters permissory of the apostolic see, or letters intending to be permissory, and even of those of his legates, unless in the said letters permissory of the see, they make full and express mention concerning these presents outside the dioceses, in which they determine, that their goods are to be ascribed for the cause. Or, while they are prepared to show full justice before their ordinaries concerning complaints made against them, they cannot be called upon for trial. To them, we grant full indulgence by the authority of these presents. No one, therefore, will be allowed to break this section of our concessions, or at any time oppose it with temerity. If, however, anyone will have presumed to attempt this, let him know that the anger of Almighty God and of his blessed apostles Peter and Paul, will fall upon him.

Given at Orvieto on the fifteenth day of October (1263), in the third year of our pontificate.

Endorsement.—For the Holy Land.

On fold.—F. A.

IV.

URBAN, Bishop, servant of the servants of God, to the venerable brethren, the archbishops, bishops, and other chosen sons, the constituted prelates of the churches throughout Wales, greeting and apostolic blessing. Seeing that the Holy Land, which the only begotten Son of God, the Lord Jesus Christ, chose as a special patrimony and inheritance for himself, is fiercely ravaged by the savagery of divers infidels, we most anxiously seek ways and means by which, through our assistance, suitable garrisons may be obtained for that same country. Wherefore, concerning our venerable brother [Richard] Bishop of Menevia, whom we believe to have the fear and love of God, we grant to whomsoever he may know to be usefully endowed with manifold gifts of virtue, and who will be strong where he expects hardships, placing full faith in the Lord, we have granted to him by our letters under fixed forms a commission for preaching the cross in Wales in favour of an aid for the said land. We hope that the undertaking will prosper to a greater extent in his hands, divine clemency working more fully through him, by which the more he impresses our hearts, and by which we know the very great necessity threatening that same land at present. And for the same reason, we earnestly pray and exhort you all, granting you in remission of sins, to the extent granted to you by the aforesaid bishop and by others, whom he may elect to assist him in the prosecution of this undertaking, commended by us favourably in the Lord. Therefore, because we have power, by merit, to commend your devotion with deeds of friendship, and as far as divine blessing will allow the increase to come to you.

Given at Orvieto on the fifteenth of October, 1263, in the third year of our pontificate.

Endorsement.—For the Holy Land.
On fold.—F. A.

V.

URBAN, Bishop, servant of the servants of God, to all the venerable brethren, the patriarchs, archbishops, and bishops, and the well-beloved and chosen sons, abbots, priors, chapters, convents, and colleges of St. Benedict, or of any other order whatsoever, also to the deans, archdeacons, provosts, archpriests, and other prelates of churches, and to the rectors and preceptors or administrators of the Houses of the Hospital, of the Temple, and of St. Mary of the Teutons, who may or may not be released of their vows, greeting, and apostolic blessing.

Since we have been especially led, by the advice of our brethren to entrust the negotiations for the Holy Land to our venerable brother [Richard] Bishop of Menevia, a man both of tried faith and great virtue in Wales, we warn, pray, and earnestly beseech ye, by apostolic authority, commanding you with a strict injunction as that matter has even preference with us, that you undertake, on account of reverence of the apostolic see and of us, the very worthy honour to travel, to await, and to return, labouring yourself personally outside your estate and diocese in the business aforesaid. That you may see, on your own behalf, to provide ten horsemen and fifteen men, freely and suitably in all needful equipment, even with a safe conduct. Therefore, because he, whom we and our brethren, with their deserving need of probity, have in various ways an accepted friend, is able to defend the praiseworthy witness of your promptitude, and to render us from thence an account on your usefulness, which he, through himself or through others, has borne against the rebel designs. We will grant to them, by the authority of our Lord, even the very deserving satisfaction of being honoured by the unusual title of inviolable. Apostolic indulgences of any kind, or privileges or concessions under any form of words, notwithstanding, they cannot be impeded by any ecclesiastics, orders, colleges, universities, or persons whatsoever that I have excommunicated, suspended, or interdicted, or proceed to the present business by legates or nuncios of whatever kind, that we wish no one to be elected in this respect, and to whom you wish, by constitutions or customs whatever granted by our predecessors concerning procurations, given to nuncios of the said see under certain forms and conditions.

Dated at Orvieto the 21st day of January (1264), in the third year of our pontificate.

Endorsement.—For the Holy Land.

THE RATIFICATION OF THE TREATY BETWEEN OWEN, OF WALES, AND CHARLES VI., KING OF FRANCE.[1]

OWEN, by the grace of God, Prince of Wales, to all who are about to view these our letters greeting. Be it known to all that we have received the letters patent following containing the league and covenant between the most illustrious lord Charles, by the grace of God, King of France, and us, commenced and completed by his ambassadors and ours on this part, in these words :

"We, James de Bourbon, Count of March, procurator and special ambassador of most serene lord prince and our most dreaded master, the lord Charles, by the grace of God, King of France, and we, Griffith Yonge, Doctor of the Canon Law, Chancellor, and John Hanmer, esquire, kinsmen, ambassadors, procurators, and special nuncios to the illustrious and most dreaded lord Owen, Prince of the Welsh, as is fully given by powers and commissions given us of both parties by our lords aforesaid, by letters patent of the same lords, copies of which are inserted below, being specially deputed and commissioned by the said lords, we make known to all that we, by virtue of the commands and powers of our said lords the king and the prince, attributed and given to us by them, concerning and over leagues, covenants, and friendships between the said lords the king and the prince, we have mutually agreed upon the commencing and completing in certain chapters or successive articles, which follows in form and tenor :

[1] The Ratification contains the text of the "Treaty" and "Commission."

In the first place, that the said lords the king and the prince shall be mutually joined, confederated, united, and leagued by the bond of a true covenant and real friendship, and of a sure, good, and most powerful union against Henry of Lancaster, and adversary and enemy of both parties, and his adherents and supporters. Again that one of the said lords shall desire, follow, and even will procure the honour and advantage of the other, and should any damage or injury intended against the one by the said Henry, his accomplices, adherents, supporters, or other whomsoever, come to the notice of one, he shall prevent that in good faith. The one, also, of these shall urge and make with the other each and every thing, which, by a good, true, and faithful friend, ought and pertains to be urged and done to a good, true, and faithful friend, yielding to no one by fraud or guile. Again, if and as often as the one of them shall know or shall understand that any injury or damage is procured or plotted against the other by the aforesaid Henry of Lancaster, or by his adherents or supporters, he shall, as many times as it shall become necessary signify that fact, and shall advise him concerning and over that, so that the other shall be able to prepare against his malice as far as he shall have foreseen ; also, both of the same lords, without distinction, shall be anxious to hinder the aforesaid injury or damage in good faith. Again, if anyone of the said lords be pacified in any manner, if anyone of his subjects gives, makes, or procures aid, advice of any kind, or favour to the said Henry of Lancaster, his followers or adherents, or promise that for rewards, or even without rewards, against any one of their lords. That if they shall presume to withstand, they shall be punished in such manner that shall give an example to the others. Again, that one of the lords, the king and the prince aforesaid, shall not make or take truce nor make peace with the aforesaid Henry of Lancaster, but that the other might be included if he had wished in the same truce or peace, unless he is united or did not wish to be included in the same truce or peace, and he shall determine, concerning such refusal or rejection, who wished to treat for the said truce or peace, within a month after the one shall have signified the said truce or peace, by his letters patent, sealed by his seal. Again, that all the subjects of the kingdom of France, with their ships, merchant or mercenary, chattels, and goods whatsoever shall be taken, collected, and surrendered without fraud, to cause delay in all the lands and ports of the kingdom of France, provided that subjects of every degree have, from this time forth, letters of testimony under the seal of the aforesaid lords, or their justiciars, or their officers, and under their subjection and fidelity. Again, that if strife, violence, battle, riot, pillage, or other injury whatever, and may that not happen, be committed or caused to arise, upon sea or land, between the subjects of the said lords, and should a pretext appear over this, let it be treated amicably according to their merits and extent of places where the offences were committed by the lords of both parties, or their justiciars or officers to whom that pertains, and that offences of every kind committed by them shall be legitimately reformed, and the aforesaid strife pacified. Again, that whosoever of the aforesaid lords on his part shall have required of the other, he will be held by his letters to ratify, confirm, and even to make valid with binding promises the aforesaid covenants thus begun and completed by their ambassadors. Again, that whatever one of the aforesaid ambassadors will promise and vow instead of his lord, having touched the sacrosant gospels, those covenants and binding league in the aforesaid articles shall be held firmly in good faith by those lords and their subjects. However, all those who by reason of their race or subjection, while subjects of the aforesaid Henry of Lancaster, shall not appear, or by pretext of former treaties previously federated, shall be excepted from these covenants and leagues. We, James de Bourbon, count of March, and Griffith Yonge, and John de Hanmer, ambassadors and special nuncios aforesaid, of the lords, the King of the France, and the Prince of Wales aforesaid by name, having each, all and singular in them accepted and received, and in each of them is satisfied, and the one has declared to the other ; and we each promise, in good faith, on his own behalf and of our aforesaid lords, and in his name and for himself, and we swear for our masters, the holy gospels of God having been touched by us and each of us, each article well and faithfully to hold, keep, comply, and even firmly and inviolably observe.

In faith and testimony of each and all of which, we have commanded that these present letters or present public instrument to be made and duplicated, and to be published by the public notaries undermentioned, and we have caused them to be confirmed by appending our seals together with the marks and signatures of the said public notaries."

The true tenor of the letters of commission of our lord, the king of the Franks, follows, and is of this nature :

"Charles, by the grace of God king of the French, to all these present letters may come, greeting. We make known that we, on account of the faithful diligence and industry of our beloved and faithful kinsman, and our councillors, James de Bourbon, Count of March, and John, Bishop of Chartres, having our fullest confidence, we make, constitute, name, and elect them our general ambassadors and assured special nuncios, and each of them, in the whole matter, thus that there may not be a better condition of negotiations, but that which one of them may commence, the other shall have power to follow and complete, for the purpose of negotiating in our name and for us with our beloved friends, master Griffith Yonge and John Hanmer, kinsmen of the magnificent and powerful Owen, Prince of the Cymry, and his ambassadors and nuncios, having for the undermentioned purpose, power, from the said prince, by letter sealed by the seal of the prince himself, to make leagues, covenants, and perpetual or temporary friendships between us on the one part, and the said Prince of the Cymry on the other part, as it may seem to the same ambassadors of both parties, concerning and over the same leagues, covenants, and treaties, and concerning the manner of arranging of them, meetings and concerts concerning which the same ambassadors of both parties will meet mutually for the purpose of confirming, concluding, and of binding whatsoever lawful or due in our stead, seeking, finding, securing, and giving whatsoever security necessary for this purpose; and in like manner seeking, receiving, and accepting from the part of the said prince; giving and conceding to our said ambassadors, and to each of them complete, full, general, and free power and command by special permission, both for making, negotiating, exercising, and preparing generally each and every thing which shall be necessary, both for those purposes and their dependencies, and in whatever manner suitable, and that we shall cause and are able to cause, if we shall be interested personally, for this present purpose even if they require a very special command, promising in good faith to have ratified, accepted, and confirmed whatever shall be made and completed in full by our aforesaid ambassadors, and whoever of them in or around these premises, and even confirm and conclude under conditions and obligation of all our goods present and future.

In testimony whereof we have caused our seal to be attached to these present letters. Dated at Paris the 14th day of June, 1404, and the twenty-fourth year of our reign."

Again, the tenor of the letters of proxy of the said lord prince of Wales follow in these words:

"Owen, by the grace of God, Prince of Wales, to all who will examine these our letters, greeting. Know ye that on account of the affection and sincere regard which the illustrious prince, the lord Charles by the same grace, King of the French, has up to the present time borne towards us and our subjects, and of his grace bears daily, we desire to cleave to him and to his subjects, as by merit we are held to this purpose. Wherefore, we make, ordain, and constitute by these presents Master Griffith Yonge, Doctor of the Canon Law, Chancellor, and John de Hanmer, our well-beloved kinsmen, our true and legal ambassadors, proctors, factors, negotiators, and special nuncios, giving and conceding to our same ambassadors, and to both of them by himself, and in full general power and special command, in such manner that there shall not be a better condition of negotiation, but that which the one of them shall commence the other of them has power to follow, consider, and complete for us, and in our name concerning and over a perpetual or temporal league with the aforesaid most illustrious prince, and of conducting, commencing, making, and confirming the same league on our part, and of undertaking whatsoever suitable oath necessary in that part in our stead, and of the making of letters obligatory of this kind concerning the league, and of giving or granting for us whatsoever other security may incidentally appear necessary on their part, or of seeking and receiving the giving of similar security necessary in the material premises from the aforesaid most illustrious prince, the lord Charles by the grace of God king of the French on his part to us, and of making, granting, and expediting other, all and singular, which were necessary in the premises, and concerning them or whatsoever manner suitable, even if a special injunction appear necessary, and which we are able to make if we had been personally concerned in any way in the negotiation. For the said our true ambassadors and each of them, we promise and place our consent by these presents that ye shall decide, and your decision shall be fulfilled, and the agreement established shall be kept under the pledge and obligation of all our goods.

In testimony whereof we make these our letters patent. Given at Dolgelly the tenth day of May, 1404, and in the fourth year of our rule."

Completed and given at Paris in the house of his magnificence lord Ernaud de Corbeya, Knight, Chancellor of France, on the fourteenth day of July, 1404, in the twelfth cycle, being present the said lord Chancellor of France and the reverend fathers and lords in Christ, lord Philip Noyon, Peter Meux, and John, Bishop of Arras, and even the eminent and powerful Louis de Bourbon, Count of Vendôme, and the noble lord Robert de Braquemont and Lord Robert d'Amilly, Knights of the chamber to the said most serene prince, the King of France, as witnesses to the premises named.

I, John de Sanctis, of the diocese of Beauvais, notary public by apostolic and imperial authority, notary and secretary to the aforesaid and our lord King of France, was present while each and every of the premises as it was brought forward, discussed, and agreed upon by the above-named lords ambassadors, together with the above-mentioned witnesses. I saw and heard them made at the request and with the consent of the same lords ambassadors, as in this present public instrument above, drawn up and under the same form of words duplicated; which I have written and caused to be engrossed by another, being myself occupied with many other negotiations, an examination being made by me, together with the notary public under-mentioned of the original letters of commission above inserted, the same being published with this present public instrument, I therefore have subscribed myself and placed my accustomed sign.

And I, Benedict Comme, clerk of the diocese of St. Asaph, notary public by apostolic authority, was present while each and every of the premises as thus set forth, were discussed and completed by the said lords ambassadors, together with the eminent lords witnessing and the venerable notary aforesaid, and I saw and heard them thus made; and I have caused this present public instrument to be faithfully written by another, as I was occupied in another manner, and with the consent of the same lords ambassadors duplicated. I have signed with my sign and name, as is customary, being asked and required in faith and testimony of all the premises.

We truly ratify and confirm as far as in us lies the premises containing the league and covenant made, established, and accepted on our part by your ambassadors.

In testimony whereof we cause these to be made our letters patent. Given in our castle of Llanbadarn on the twelfth day of January, A.D. 1405, and the sixth of our rule.

Endorsement.—Covenants made and sealed between our lord king and Owen prince of Wales, A.D. 1405.

OWEN'S LETTER TO CHARLES VI.

MOST serene prince, you have deemed it worthy on the humble recommendation sent, to learn how my nation, for many years now elapsed, has been oppressed by the fury of the barbarous Saxons; whence because they had the government over us, and indeed, on account of that fact itself, it seemed reasonable with them to trample upon us. But now, most serene prince, you have in many ways, from your innate goodness, informed me and my subjects very clearly and graciously concerning the recognition of the true Vicar of Christ. I, in truth, rejoice with a full heart on account of that information of your excellency, and because, inasmuch from this information, I understood that the lord Benedict, the supreme pontifex, intends to work for the promotion of an union in the Church of God with all his possible strength. Confident indeed in his right, and intending to agree with you as far as is possible for me, I recognize him as the true Vicar of Christ, on my own behalf, and on behalf of my subjects by these letters patent, foreseeing them by the bearer of their communications in your majesty's presence. And because, most excellent prince, the metropolitan church of St. David's was, as it appears, violently compelled by the barbarous fury of those reigning in this country, to obey the church of Canterbury, and *de facto* still remains in this subjection. Many other disabilities are known to have been suffered by the church of Wales through these barbarians, which for the greater part are set forth fully in the letters patent accompanying. I pray and sincerely beseech your majesty to have these letters sent to my lord, the supreme pontifex, that as you deemed worthy to raise us out of darkness into light, similarly you will wish to extirpate and remove violence and oppression from the church and from my subjects, as you are well able to. And may the Son of the Glorious Virgin long preserve your majesty in the promised prosperity.

Dated at Pennal the last day of March (1406).

Yours avowedly,

OWEN, *Prince of Wales.*

Endorsement.—To the most serene and most illustrious prince, lord Charles, by the grace of God, King of France.

OWEN, PRINCE OF WALES, TO CHARLES VI., KING OF FRANCE, PROMISING OBEDIENCE TO POPE BENEDICT XIII.

TO the most illustrious prince, the lord Charles, by the grace of God, King of the French, Owen by the same grace, sends the reverence due to such a prince with honour. Be it known to your excellency that we have received from you the articles following, brought to us by Hugh Eddowyer, of the Order of Predicants, and Morris Kery, our friends and envoys, on the eighth day of March, A.D. 1406, the form and tenor of which follow:

In the first place they express the cordial greeting on the part of our lord the king, and of his present letter to our said lord the prince. In this manner, our lord the king greatly desires to know of his good state and the happy issue of their negotiations. He requests Owen, that he will write as often as an opportunity offers, as he will receive great pleasure, and he will inform him, at length, concerning the good state of the said lord, the king, of the queen, their children, and of the other lords, the princes of the royal family, how my lord the king, and the other princes of the royal family have and intend to have sincere love, cordial friendship, zeal for his honour, the prosperity and well-being of the state of the said prince, and in this the said lord, the prince, can place the most secure faith.

They also explain to the same lord, the prince, how our lord, the king, who esteems him with sincerity and love, greatly desires that, as they are bound and united in temporal matters, so also will they be united in spiritual things, that they may be able to walk to the house of the Lord together. My lord, the king, also requests the same lord, the prince, that he wishes him to consider, with a favourable disposition, the rights of my lord, the pope, Benedict XIII., the supreme pontiff of the universal church, that he may himself learn and cause all his subjects to be informed. Because my lord the king, holds that it shall be to the health of his soul and of the souls of his subjects, to the security and strength of his state, and that their covenants shall be laid in a stronger and more powerful foundation in the advantage of faith and in the love of Christ. Again, even as all faithful Christians are held to keep themselves well informed concerning the truth of schisms. Princes, however, are so held even more than others, because their opinion can keep many in error, especially their subjects, who must conform with the opinion of their superiors. It is, also, even to their advantage, on account of their duty, to keep themselves informed in all things, that such a schism may be entirely removed and that the Church may have unity in God. Because he, who is the true Vicar of Christ, should be known and acknowledged by all the faithful in Christ, while he, who is an intruder, and known to have by nefarious means usurped the holy apostolic see, shall be expelled and cast aside, by all the faithful, as anti-Christ. To this purpose they should bind themselves to strive, to their utmost, according to the decrees of the holy fathers. To which purpose the said lord, the king, has striven, not without great burdens and expense, and will strive unweariedly.

The envoys explained to the said lord, the prince, because he should not doubt that he had been sufficiently informed from the commencement, how Bartholomew de Prinhano, then Archbishop of Bari,[1] violently and through a infamous riot, was forced into the apostolic

---

[1] Bari is in the province of Pouille, France.

see. He should not have clung to that office, but seduced and deceived through ignorance of the case, he has held the office. My lord the king, knows, that, on account of the distance of his fatherland from Rome, he could easily be deceived and be poorly informed. My lord the king, has, on that account, been induced for the information of his mind and conscience to keep himself informed concerning the events, by which he could satisfy himself concerning the rights of my lord, the Pope Benedict, bestir himself to obtain recognition of those rights, and even to make manifest the disagreements which they can extend to others in his kingdom, which God forbid.

In the first place it is true, that my lord, Gregory XI., of happy memory, at that time the only and undoubted Roman pontiff, died at Rome on the twenty-seventh of March, A.D. 1378. At that time there were dwelling in the aforesaid city sixteen cardinals; four of Italy, namely, the Cardinal of Florence, the Cardinal of St. Peter's, the Cardinal of Milan, and the Cardinal of Mossyne; and twelve non-Italian (citramontane) cardinals, namely, the Cardinal of Limoges, the Cardinal of Aigrefeuille, the Cardinal of Geneva, who afterwards was elected pope, the Cardinal of Glandives, the Cardinal of Poitiers, who yet lives, the Cardinal of Marmontier, the Cardinal of Vivier; the Cardinal of Britain, the Cardinal of St. Eusteche, the Cardinal of Saint Angel, and the Cardinal of Vernhio; besides, however, the Cardinal of Amiens, who at that time was legate in Florence, negotiating certain matters pending between she said lord, Gregory, and the Florentines. To these alone, and to them entirely, and to no one else, pertained the election of the Roman pontiff, according to the canons and the decrees of the holy fathers.

Again, it is notorious and manifest that the said Bartholomew was elected owing to the violent and infamous riot which followed. For, after the death of the said Lord Gregory, while the said cardinals, according to custom celebrated the obsequies and funeral of the same Lord Gregory, the officers of the city, several times, informed the said cardinals, because they hesitated over others, with threats both in public and in private, to the greatest and irretrievable scandal, that they desired the election of a Roman, or an Italian. As the cardinals would more easily bend through fear, they stirred the populace to a tumult, and even sent around a call to arms. So that there should be no one who would be able to suppress such a rumour or sedition, they expelled all the powerful nobles from the city. When the obsequies were over, the said cardinals entered the conclave to proceed with the election of the Roman pontiff, the people in a great multitude and armed for the most part rushed with them into the palace of St. Peter, where the conclave was, clamouring and shouting, 'We want a Roman, or at least an Italian,' with an awful din and filled the whole palace. Indeed they were many times requested to leave the said palace. They refused to leave, nor could they be expelled. Neither did they allow the said conclave to be walled in, according to custom, nor the palace itself closed, but by day and even by night they remained there, shouting as explained above. As they caused great alarm to the said cardinals, to still more incite the populace to fury, they rang the bells of the Church of St. Peter, and those of the Capitol in the near proximity of the conclave. While the cardinals were in this strait, they were several times warned by the guards of the conclave and others from outside, that unless they would immediately and without any further delay elect a Roman or an Italian, they would be in danger, because all would be stirred to anger by this failure [to elect a Roman]. Then thus, terrified on account of the overhanging fear of death, and as they declared that no others could be made, three only excepted, without further discussion they named Bartholomew, an Italian, and him they elected pope. Finally the said populace, who were continually in the palace, thus shouting and ringing, especially as the said conclave was under the clock tower, they rushed into the conclave itself with great fury, breaking into three divisions and shouting: "By the Cavalcade, we will have a Roman." They entered the said conclave, as many as could, in such a manner that the said cardinals were scarcely able to save and free themselves from death. The cardinals believed, without doubt, that all would be slain had not one of the said cardinals hinted to the populace that the Cardinal of St. Peter had been elected, but that he was unwilling to consent. While the populace occupied themselves in compelling him, the other cardinals left as they were best able to and fled, disguised, some left the city, some to the Castle of San Angelo, some to their own homes. Further, the said Romans stole the voting urn, the clothes and other goods of the said cardinals, which they found in the said conclave, and the houses of the others were looted. Concerning these things of infamous memory, the Lord Charles, then King of France, father of our said lord the king, was fully informed, besides from the testimony of the said cardinals, by many notable and trustworthy persons, and anyone could be easily informed, because these things were manifest and well known.

Upon the following day Bartholomew and the aforesaid officers of the city commanded the said cardinals, some of whom were in the Castle of St. Angelo, some, scattered in the city hidden in divers hiding-places, to come to them that they might enthrone the same Bartholomew; they gave many excuses, which were not listened to, since they were frightened by the rumours which continued, and no opportunity was left for them at that time to leave Rome. They were then compelled to come to the same Bartholomew, and after their arrival to assist at his enthronement and coronation, paying the usual homage, as though to the Roman pontiff himself. They were compelled as by fear from denouncing his election and informing their kings and princes. For, if they positively denied the foregoing, they would be in as much danger as previously, and they undoubtedly thought that all would be slain, especially the foreign cardinals.

All the said cardinals, as soon as they were able, left the city of Rome, and, no one withdrawing, they frankly disowned the said Bartholomew. In a secure place, now on the first opportunity, they stated the truth concerning this election, and that he was not really pope, but an intruder, and warned that even if he wished to lay aside that office which he had undoubtedly usurped, he should reflect concerning the salvation of his soul and of all the faithful of Christ, and to withstand all the evils and scandals which might happen to others. This, the said Bartholomew withheld by his excessive ambition, refused and despised. Then the said cardinals, having however first taken ripe advice concerning this position, declared that the said Bartholomew was not the pope, but was an intruder, and occupied the apostolic see by violence. They published and declared, according to the holy fathers, the sentence of excommunication and anathema that he had incurred, and against all such occupants and intruders of the apostolic see. Then after the foregoing, lest the church should any longer be without a head, they unanimously elected the lord Clement VIII., then Cardinal of Geneva.

Again, all the said cardinals, Italian and citramontane, uniformly declared and testified upon oath and under the peril of their souls, that they were driven by fear of death, and as the only hope of saving their lives they nominated the said Bartholomew and elected him pope, and others could not be made. That they had enthroned, crowned, made obeisance to, showed in public, and other things to the said Bartholomew. That then, they wrote letters to their kings and princes concerning the election of the said Bartholomew, shewing that they were compelled, as by fear, and had not granted by intention nor by proposition any of these rights to him, nor had confirmed him in the office he had usurped. Then three of the said cardinals, namely, the Cardinal of Limoges, the Cardinal of Poitiers, and the Cardinal of Aigrefeuille came to inform the lord Charles of renowned memory, then King of France, and father of our said lord the king, concerning the aforesaid. They explained to him openly, face to face, on their own behalf and on behalf of the whole college on whose behalf they had been sent, upon oath, and on the peril of their souls, how matters had been, and the things that were true. They declared and gave the truth concerning this remembered, and vouched for by the whole college.

It is, again, true that besides the foregoing, all of the said cardinals who are since dead, whether Italian or citramontane, each one separately, during their last hours, and manifestly with a clear memory, testified, on the peril of their souls, that the said Bartholomew was and is an intruder, that he neither was nor is pope. It could not be presumed that men, many religious, upright, and of the greatest learning, in such a difficulty, would be forgetful of their salvation; because the cardinals only, according to the decrees of the holy fathers, are the witnesses and voters at the election of a Roman pontiff. They alone know the truth, because they alone are present, and no one else except these men themselves can in this matter be entirely entrusted or believed.

When the said lord Charles V., who above all the princes of the world at this time, was a man of great prudence, strongly catholic and fearing God, had heard the said cardinals, who had come to him concerning this matter, he called together the princes of his race, many notable prelates and barons of his kingdom, and many religious clerks, such as of the University of Paris, who could best explain the matters which had been set forth by the said cardinals. Even those who were in favour of Bartholomew had been informed. The matter having been thoroughly discussed, and after many deliberations, as this difficult subject demanded, they informed the said lord Charles that the election of the said Bartholomew was compulsory, ineffective, and really void, and that the election of the said lord Clement was canonical. Their advice and decision having been heard, the said lord Charles declared that he would be obedient to the said lord Clement, cause his subjects to be obedient, and that he himself would promise on their part; that he cast aside the said Bartholomew as an intruder in the apostolic see. After the death of the said lord Charles, our said lord the king, cleaving to the footsteps of his father, obeyed the said lord Clement as the true Roman pontiff, while he lived, and after his death the lord Benedict, as his true successor. In a similar manner the lord John, then King of Castile, who in order to proceed more safely, had sent his own ambassadors to Rome to obtain the same information concerning the truth of the case even with the Romans. He admitted and heard fully the ambassadors of the said Bartholomew in all things which they wished to place before him, in question of fact, as well as in question of law. Having heard the account of his said ambassadors concerning the matters which they had obtained at Rome, for the Cardinal de Luna was at that time a legate to Castile on behalf of the said Clement, and the college, and from the ambassadors of the said Bartholomew, the matter was more fully discussed and debated between both parties, and finally, after a most complete deliberation with the prelates, princes, barons, and learned men of his kingdom, he decided in favour of the lord Clement with his entire kingdom. So also did the lord John, then King of Arragon; the King of Portugal, now dead; even also Queen Joan, Queen of Jerusalem and Sicily; indeed the said Bartholomew was a native of the state of Naples, whom, both on account of his nation and the favours he hoped to have for himself, he would have obeyed freely, if he had a safe conscience. The King of Scotland, the

King of Cyprus, the Dukes of Barri and Lorraine, the Count of Savoy, the Italian Count of Fuime, the state of Genoa, and many other princes and states also acknowledged the lord Clement. Finally, all who wished to hear and consider the legates of both parties, and to be equally informed of the rights and truth of the case, and to weigh the merits of both elections justly. Also many anti-cardinals created by the said Bartholomew and his successors surrendered to Clement, namely, the Cardinal of Spain, lately deceased, whom the said Bartholomew had created and appointed his legate in Castile; the Cardinal of Malepierre; the Cardinal of Silesia, and many other prelates, but no one ever surrendered to Bartholomew.

While the said lord Clement lived and the same college of cardinals they accomplished all possible duties, because all princes were informed of the truth and rights of both parties, by sending legates and ambassadors to kings and all Christian princes. The lord Benedict, his successor, did the same after the death of the said lord Clement. The said Bartholomew and his successors, as far as they were able, hindered them, so that those who were obedient to him could not hear the other version. He even withdrew many to his administration, especially certain princes of Germany.

Again, since the year last past, the said lord Benedict, trusting to his rights and desiring especially to bring peace into the church, grieving inwardly as the true shepherd concerning the danger of his sheep, sent to Rome, to Boniface, at that time the anti-pope, a solemn embassy, and offered in the presence of his anti-cardinals in the form of a mutual convention of the two themselves, their colleges, to considering justice, for the information of the truth and every other reasonable and possible way by which unity could be obtained, even as far as a renunciation should the case being inconclusive, if the said Boniface would agree thus. Boniface simply rejected all this, and because he was poorer, notwithstanding the safe conduct which he had given, the ambassadors of the said Benedict were seized and placed in strict confinement in the Castle of San Angelo, which they were not allowed to leave except after a ransom of five thousand ducats. These things, however, notwithstanding, Boniface being dead and there being now another anti-pope, he wrought diligently and laboured greatly, by requiring and requesting this present intruder in a similar manner. But he refused to admit the ambassadors, to grant them a safe conduct, just as these things were apparent in the letters of the said Benedict, which they showed to the said prince. Besides this, the said lord Benedict, grieving at heart on account of the evasion of that intruder that this detestable schism should be thus advanced, the church be torn, and the souls of the faithful endangered, not sparing his old age, he entered Italy himself to attempt to procure that unity more favourably and efficaciously. He is now in the state of Genoa, where he has offered and still offers all possible ways, disposed even to lay down his life in order to obtain that unity.

The princes of Germany, thinking and considering the aforesaid, as they had up to the present refused to admit and hear the legates and ambassadors of the said lord Benedict, and to receive information concerning his rights, now stated that they were ready to admit, hear, and receive information concerning his rights. Besides the Kings of Bohemia and Hungary now withdrew themselves from the obedience of the said anti-pope. Our said lord the king had news from the parts of Italy that the anti-pope with his anti-cardinals had fled from Rome, which they showed in letters to the satisfaction of our said lord the prince. Our said lord the prince considered how much compensation he could obtain for himself, the said anti-pope shall be still under his obedience, especially on acccount of the favour which he showed to Henry of England by appointing prelates and English priests in his land, by refusing timely dispensations for marriage and other occasions, and to discover many ways by which his lord could be injured, which God forbid. Besides these things he has to consider what the anti-pope has done to the King of Hungary, whom, even unheard, he deprived of the kingdom of Hungary and gave to Ladislaus, who should have been kept King of Sicily. What also he did to the King of Bohemia, whom he caused to be deprived of the kingdom of the Romans by the electors of the empire, and confirmed their election of Rupert of Bavaria. In addition our lord the king prays and exhorts the said lord the prince, by proxy, that he wishes him to consider and well ponder over the aforesaid, especially the violent and infamous riot which caused the election of the said Bartholomew, and his other actions subsequently, as long as the cardinals were under the power of the Romans; and the testimony, consistent and vouched for, of all the cardinals, which is scarcely read of in any other schism; because all the cardinals were all of the same party, markedly of the Italians, who more willingly would have adhered to the anti-pope, because he was an Italian, if they could have with a free conscience; and especially the deliberation and decision of our said lord Charles, father of our said lord the king, during his last hours, and the other princes aforesaid, so maturely and so solemnly made restitution to the said lord Benedict, so legally and so reasonably made a refutation of the anti-pope, by which he showed not a little hesitancy concerning his own right. These facts you should well ponder over, because he wishes you to consider the rights of the said lord Benedict, and to recognize him as the true vicar of Christ and the universal shepherd of the flock of the Lord, that he can truly and filially obey the same and cause his subjects also to obey.

It seems to our said lord the king that this shall be to the safety of his soul, of his subjects, and the safe-keeping of his realm. Concerning this, the same lord the king, who sincerely zealous, prays heartily for his safety, the prosperity and conservation of his honour, his state and himself, under the bond and treaty of friendship, and of a singular love which he has for him. He requests that he indicate this himself, because if he puts the aforesaid into action, he will give the same lord, the king, great satisfaction, and he will consider himself very well pleased and to his greater obligation. If, by chance the said lord prince, the prelates, the other ecclesiastics of his land, and his subjects dread, because from this kind of restoration, that certain prelates and other beneficed clergy, appointed by the anti-pope and his predecessors, and other favours of whatsoever nature granted on behalf of future occasions to his subjects may be unsettled, or that the lord Benedict may wish to change anything. On that account, our lord the king offers that he will, procure from the said lord Benedict that all the prelates and beneficed clergy shall be confirmed, and all favours, dispensations, &c., shall be ratified and conceded to them in secure and proper form. Also the said lord Benedict shall provide, that when prelacies and other benefices are vacant, or shall be vacant, those persons only who are sufficiently in the faith and good will of the said lord the prince shall be appointed, and not rivals or suspects.

Following the advice of our council, we have called together the nobles of our race, the prelates of our Principality and others called for this purpose, and, at length, after diligent examination and discussion of the foregoing articles and their contents being thoroughly made by the prelates and the clergy, it is agreed and determined that we, trusting in the rights of the lord Benedict, the holy Roman and supreme pontiff of the universal church, especially because he sought the peace and unity of the church, and as we understood daily seeks it, considering the hard service of the adversary of the same Benedict, tearing the seamless coat of Christ, and on account of the sincere love which we specially bear towards your excellency, we have determined that the said lord Benedict shall be recognized as the true

Vicar of Christ in our lands, by us and our subjects, and we recognize him by these presents.

Whereas, most illustrious prince, the underwritten articles especially concern our state and the reformation and usefulness of the Church of Wales, we humbly pray your royal majesty that you will graciously consider it worthy to advance their object, even in the court of the said lord Benedict:

First, that all ecclesiastic censures against us, our subjects, or our land, by the aforesaid lord Benedict or Clement his predecessor, at present existing, the same shall by the said Benedict be removed.

Again, that whatsoever vows and of whatsoever nature given by us or whomsoever of our principality, to those who called themselves Urban or Boniface, lately deceased, or to their adherents, shall be absolved.

Again, that he shall confirm and ratify the orders, collations, titles of prelates, dispensations, notorial documents, and all things whatsoever, from the time of Gregory XI., from which, any danger to the souls, or prejudice to us, or our subjects, may occur, or may be engendered.

Again, that the Church of St. David's shall be restored to its original dignity, which from the time of St. David, archbishop and confessor, was a metropolitan church, and after his death, twenty-four archbishops succeeded him in the same place, as their names are contained in the chronicles and ancient books of the church of Menevia, and we cause these to be stated as the chief evidence, namely, Eliud, Ceneu, Morfael, Mynyw, Haerwnen, Elwaed, Gwrnwen, Llewdwyd, Gwrwyst, Gwgawn, Clydâwg, Aman, Elias, Maelyswyd, Sadwrnwen, Cadell, Alaethwy, Novis, Sadwrnwen, Drochwel, Asser, Arthwael, David II., and Samson; and that as a metropolitan church it had and ought to have the undermentioned suffragan churches, namely, Exeter, Bath, Hereford, Worcester, Leicester, which see is now translated to the churches of Coventry and Lichfield, St. Asaph,

Bangor, and Llandaff. For being crushed by the fury of the barbarous Saxons, who usurped to themselves the land of Wales, they trampled upon the aforesaid church of St. David's, and made her a handmaid to the church of Canterbury.

Again, that the same lord Benedict shall provide for the metropolitan church of St. David's, and the other cathedral churches of our principality, prelates, dignitaries, and beneficed clergy and curates, who know our language.

Again, that the lord Benedict shall revoke and annul all incorporations, unions, annexions, appropriations of parochial churches of our principality made so far, by any authority whatsoever with English monasteries and colleges. That the true patrons of these churches shall have the power to present to the ordinaries of those places suitable persons to the same or appoint others.

Again, that the said lord Benedict shall concede to us and to our heirs, the princes of Wales, that our chapels, &c., shall be free, and shall rejoice in the privileges, exemptions, and immunities in which they rejoiced in the times of our forefathers the princes of Wales.

Again, that we shall have two universities or places of general study, namely, one in North Wales and the other in South Wales, in cities, towns, or places to be hereafter decided and determined by our ambassadors and nuncios for that purpose.

Again, that the lord Benedict shall brand as heretics and cause to be tortured in the usual manner, Henry of Lancaster, the intruder of the kingdom of England, and the usurper of the crown of the same kingdom, and his adherents, in that of their own free will they have burnt or have caused to be burnt so many cathedrals, convents, and parish churches; that they have savagely hung, beheaded, and quartered archbishops, bishops, prelates, priests, religious men, as madmen or beggars, or caused the same to be done.

Again, that the same lord Benedict shall grant to us,

our heirs, subjects, and adherents, of whatsoever nation they may be, who wage war against the aforesaid intruder and usurper, as long as they hold the orthodox faith, full remission of all our sins, and that the remission shall continue as long as the war between us, our heirs, and our subjects, and the aforesaid Henry, his heirs, and subjects shall endure.

In testimony whereof we make these our letters patent. Given at Pennal on the thirty-first day of March, A.D. 1406, and in the sixth year of our rule.

Endorsement.—The letter by which Owen, Prince of Wales, reduces himself, his lands, and his dominions to the obedience of our lord the Pope Benedict XIII.

APPENDIX.

LITTERA OWYNI PRINCIPIS WALLIAE AD REGEM SCOCIE.[1]

TRESHAUT et trespuisant et tresredoute seigneur et cosin, je me recomande a vostre treshautisme roial mageste si humblement come suy dygne en toutz maneres des honors et reverencez. Et, tresredoute seigneur et tressovereygn cosin, pleser seyt a vous et a vostre dit treshautisme majeste dasavoyr que Brutus, vostre tresnoble auncestre et le meyn, estoyt le primer roy corone qui primerment enhabita deinz cest realme dengleterre, qui jadis fuist nomme Brataygne graunt. Le quel Brutus engendera troi fitz, cest assavoir, Albanactus Locrius, et Loctrinus, et Kamber. De quel dit Albanactus vous estez descenduz par droit lyne. De quel dit Kamber les issuez ount reygnes roialment, tanque a Kadualadir, qui estoit le darrein roy corronne de ma dit nacioun, dount je, vostre simple cosin, suy descenduz par droit lyne. Apres que decesse mes auncestres et tout ma dit nacion avons este et ore sumes en oppression et bondage desouz mes et vostres morteles enimys Saczouns, comme vous, tresredoute seigneur et tres-sovereygn cosin, ent avez bone conisance. De quex oppressions et bondages le prophecie dit que je serray delivere par eid socour de vostre dit roial mageste. Mais, tresredoute seigneur et sovereygne cosin, je me grauntement complaigne a vostres ditz roall mageste et tressovereigne cosinage, que moi defaut graundment genz dez armez; pur quoy tresredoute seigneur et tressovereygne cosin, je vous supplie humblement en mez genoils engenuler, si pleiser soit a dit vostre roial mageste, de moy maunder certeyn

29e Nov: A.D. 1401.

[1] Chronicon Adae de Usk, Mss. f. 171—3. Sir E. Maunde Thompson's Edition, pp. 72—74. The chronicler introduces this and the following letter thus:—"Nuncii Oeni cum literis infrascripti tenoris, regi Scocie et dominis Hibernie directis, in Hibernia capti decapitantur."

nombre de gentz darmez de moy eidir et resistre, en laide de Dieux, mes et vostre ennmys susditz ; eiant consideracion, tres redoute seigneur et tressovereigne cosin, a la eschatisme de meschyf et meschifs que je et mes ditz auncestres de Gales susditz avons suffres et meyntes autres passez par mez a vostres mortuels enimys susditz. Entendant, tresredoute seigneur et tressovereigne cosin, que ensi soit que je serray jour de ma vie oblige de fayr service et plesance a vostre dit roial mageste et amender a vous. Et pour ceo que je ne puis vous envoir mes bussoignes en escript vous envoir les portours de cestez de toutz mez bussoygnes pleinement enformez, as quex vous pleaise doner foy et credens de ceo quils vous durront par bouche. De par moy. Tresredoute seigneur et terssovereygn cosin, le trespuisant Seigneur vous [garde].

LITTERA OWYNI PRINCIPIS WALLIAE AD DOMINOS HIBERNIE.

29° Nov: A.D. 1401.

SALUTEM et amoris plenitudinem, domine, reverendissime et consanguinee confidentissime. Sciatis quod maxima dissencio, sive guerra, orta est inter nos et nostros vestrosque mortales inimicos, Saxones. Quam guerram viriliter sustentamus hucusque, fere per duos annos elapsos, ac eciam de cetero intendimus et speramus sustentare et ad bonum et effectualem finem perducere, mediantibus gracia Dei, Salvatoris nostri, vestrisque auxilio atque favore. Sed, quia vulgariter dicitur per propheciam quod, antequam nos altiorem manum in hac parte haberemus, quod vos [et] vestri carissimi consanguinei in Hibernea ad hoc manus porrigetis adjutrices ; quocirca, reverende domine et consanguinee confidentissime, vos corditer et affectuose requirimus quatinus de equestribus et peditibus vestris armatis, ad succurrendum nobis et nacioni nostre, a diu per inimicos nostros predictos oppressis, necnon ad resistendum voluntati fraudabili et deceptabili eorundem inimicorum nostrorum, talem numerum qualem commode et honeste poteritis, salvo in omnibus vestro honorabili statu, nobis, tam cito quam bene videbitis expedire, necessitatem nostram considerando, transmittatis. Istud amore nostro, et sicut in vobis maxime confidamus, licet incogniti vestre reverende persone fuerimus, facere non tardatis, intelligentes, domine et consanguinee reverendissime, quod quamdiu nos valebimus istam guerram fortiter sustentare in partibus nostris, quod vobis satis constat sine dubio quod vos et omnes alii magnates de partibus vestris Hibernie pacem desiderabilem et tranquilitatem placabilem medio tempore impetrabitis. Et quia, domine consanguinee, latores presencium vos plenius viva voce informabunt, eis, si placet, credenciam adhibeatis in omnibus que vobis ex parte nostra dicent, et, qua volueritis, domine et consanguinee reverende, que per nos vestrum humilem consanguineum fieri poterunt, vos mandetis cum fiducia. Domine et consanguinee reverende, vestram reverenciam et dominacionem in prosperis Altissimus conservet longevam. Scriptum apud Northwalliam, penultimo die Novembris.

OWYNUS PRINCEPS WALLIAE AD HENRICUM DON.

[Owen and Blakeney History of Shrewsbury, Vol. I. p. 181—2 (note). The original is said to have been kept among the MSS of Cefn-y-Garlleg in Llansantffraed, Denbighshire.]

SALUTEM et amorem. Vobis narramus quod speramus auxilio Dei et vestro posse liberare progeniem Wallicanam de captivitate inimicorum nostrorum Anglicorum, qui oppresserunt nos et antecessores nostros a multo tempore jam elapso. Et sciatis ex sensu vestro proprio quod tempus illorum desinit, et triumphus vertit versus nos, secundum ordinacionem Dei a principio quod non

Ante mensem Julii: A.D. 1403.

refert alicui dubitare quin finis eveniet bona, nisi amittatur per desidiam et discordiam; et quod omnes progenies Wallicane est in dubio et periculo secundum subjectionem quam audivimus esse penes inimicos vestros predictos versus ipsos, secundum hoc vobis mandamus, et requirimus, et supplicamus quatenus satis parati venire in maxima fortitudine quam possitis ad nos, ad locum ubi audieritis quod sumus, comburentes opprimendo inimicos nostros itinerando; et hoc erit infra breve per auxilium divinum. Et hoc non omittatis sicut velitis habere libertatem vestram et honorem de cetero; et non admiramini quod non habuistis premonicionem primae surrectionis, nam ex nimio timore et periculo oportuit nos surgere non premonentes. Valete et Deus vos defendat a malo.

Per Yweyn ap Gruffuth,
Dominum de Glyn Dwfrdwy.

A noster trescher et
tressentierement bon
aime Henry Don.

LOUIS, DUC DE BOURBON A LE ROY DE CASTILLE ET LEON.

K 1482. B1. 11.

viie Juillet: A.D. 1404. TRES hault et très excellent prince et très cher sires et cousins, plaise à vous savoir que j'ay receu vos lettres que envoyées m'avez par vos ambaxeurs qui naguéres sont arrivez par deça, par lesquelles j'ay sceu le bon estat et santé de votre personne, de très hault et puissant princesse ma très chière dame et cousine la royne de Castelle et de Léon votre compaigne, et de ma très chière et très amée cousine la infanta votre fille, de mon très chier et très honoré cousin le duc de Penafil votre frére; dont j'ai esté très parfaitement joyeux, suis et seray toutes et quinte foiz que óir en pourray pareilles nouvelles, etc. Et l'estat de par deça si savoir vous plaist, Monseigneur le Roy, Madame la Royne, Monseigneur le Dolphin et les autres enfans de mon dit seigneur le Roy estoient sans et en bon point ou partir de ces lettres, et aussi estoit je, grâces à Dieu, etc. Plaise vous savoir que mon dit seigneur le Roy et les autres Messeigneurs de son sang ont oy vos diz ambaxeurs sur ce qu'ilz leur ont exposé de par vous, comme vous voulez envoyer à mon dit seigneur XL. nefs armées toutes prestes. De laquelle chose et du secours que vous lui presentés à présent il est moult content de vous et les a très agréables, car elles viennent en très bonne saison, mesmement pour ce qui mon dit seigneur le Roy a ordonné mon très cher et très amé cousin le comte de la Marche d'aller briefvement ès parties de Galles atout mil lances et v^c arbalestriers ; lequel se partira prouchainement pour monter en mer ès parties de Bretaigne et d'illec en Galles. Pourquoy je vous prie tant et si acertes comme je puis qui, en parsevérant en votre bon propos et continuant les bonnes alliances tous diz continuées sans enfranidre par vous et vos bons prédécesseurs avec mon dit seigneur le Roy et les siens, et pour le bien et avancement de ceste besoigne, il vous plaise envoyer et faire avancier les dictes xl nefs le plus brief et hastivement que bonnement faire se pourra, en maniere que elles puissent estre en Bretaigne dedens le xve jour d'aoust prouchain venant afin qui mon dit cousin de la Marche, qui en icellui temps sera ou dit païs de Bretaigne accompaignié comme dit est, s'en puist aider et les menner avecques lui es dites parties de Galles, ou il trouvera bonne entrée aide et secours pour envaïr, grever et dommaîgéer les Anglois noz ennemis. Et à ce ne vous plaise faillir.

Très hault et très excellent prince et très chier sires et cousins, se chose quelconque vous plaist par deça que pour vous faire puisse, mandez le moij féablement, et je le accomplirai à mon povoir de très bon cuer au plaisir de Dieu qui vous ait en sa sainte guarde et vous doint bonne vie et longue. Escript à Paris le viie jour de Juillet.

Loys, duc de Bourbonnais, conte de Fourez et seigneur de Beaujeu.

LOYS—DE BOR.

Au dos—A très hault et très excellent prince et mon chier sires et cousins le roy de Castielle et de Léon.

TENORES FOEDERIS TRIPARTITI.

[*Sloan MS.* 1776; *Reg. MS.* 13 *also printed in Ellis' Letters, Vol.* I., *p.* 27, 28, *Second Series*].

28• Feb: A.D. 1406

PRIMO quod iidem domini, Owinus, Comes, et Edmundus, erunt amodo ad invicem conjuncti, confoederati, uniti, et ligati vinculo veri foederis et verae amicitiae, certaeque et bonae unionis. Iterum quod quilibet ipsorum dominorum honorem et commodum alio volet et prosequetur, ac etiam procurabit dampnaque et gravamina quae ad unius ipsorum notitiam devenerit, per quoscumque alicui ipsorum inferenda, impedient bona fide. Quilibet quoque ipsorum apud alium aget et faciet ea omnia et singula quae per bonos, veros, et fidos amicos, bonis, veris, et fidis amicis agi et fieri debent et pertinent, fraude et dolo cessantibus quibuscumque. Item si et quotiens aliquis ipsorum dominorum sciverit vel cognoverit aliquid gravaminis sive dampni procurari sive ymaginari per quoscumque contra alium, ipse aliis, quam citius commode fieri poterit, ea significabit, et ipsos de et super hoc adjuvabit, ut adversus malicias hujusmodi, prout ei visum fuerit, sibi valeat providere. Solliciti quoque erunt quilibet ipsorum dominorum impedire dampna et gravamina praedicta bona fide. Item quilibet ipsorum dominorum in tempore necessitatis, prout decet, juxta posse, alium adjuvabit. Item si disponente Deo apparent praefatis Dominis ex processu temporis, quod ipsi sunt eaedem personae de quibus Propheta loquitur, inter quos regimen Britanniae Majoris dividi debeat et partiri, tunc ipsi laborabunt et quilibet ipsorum laborabit, juxta posse quod id ad effectum efficaciter perducatur. Quilibet quoque ipsorum contentus erit portione regni praedicti sibi ut infra scribitur limitata, absque ulteriori exactione seu superioritate quacunque, ymmo quilibet ipsorum in portione hujusmodi sibi limitata aequali libertate gaudebit. Item, inter eosdem Dominos unanimiter conventum et concordatum existit, quod praefatus Owinus et haeredes sui habeant totam Cambriam sive Walliam, sub finibus, limitibus, et bundis infrascriptis, a Loegrea quae vulgariter Angliam nuncupatur divisam ; videlicet, a mari Sabrino sicut flumen Sabrinum ducit de mari, descendendo usque ad borialem portam civitatis Wigorniae, et a porta illa directe usque ad arbores fraxineas in lingua Cambriensi sive Wallensi Onnene Margion vulgariter nuncupatas, quae in alta via de Brigenorth ad Kynvar ducente crescunt; deinde directe per altam viam, quae vetus sive antiqua via vulgariter nuncupatur, usque ad caput sive ortum fluminis de Trent, deinde, directe usque ad caput sive ortum fluminis Merse vulgariter nuncupati, deinde, sicut illud flumen ad mare ducit, descendendo infra fines, limites et bundas infrascriptas. Et praefatus Comes Northumbriae habeat sibi et haeredibus suis comitatus infrascriptas, videlicet, Northumbr., Westmoreland, Lancastr., Ebor., Lincolniam, Notyngam, Derb, Stafford, Leycestr, Northampton, Warwic, et Norffolch. Et dominus Edmundus habeat totum residuum tocius Angliae integre sibi et successoribus suis. Item quod pugna, riota, seu discordia inter duos dominorum ipsorum, quod absit, oriatur ,tunc tertius ipsorum dominorum convocato ad se bono et fideli consilio, discordiam riotam seu pugnam hujusmodi debite reformabit ; cujus laudo sive sententiae discordante hujusmodi obedire tenebuntur. Fideles quoque erunt ad defendendum regnum contra omnes homines, salvo juramento ex parte praefati domini Owini illustrissimo Principi domino Karolo Dei gratia Francorum Regi, in ligea et confederatione inter ipsos initis et factis praestito.

Et ut praedicta omnia et singula bene et fideliter observentur, ipsi domini Owinus, Comes, et Edmundus, ad sacrum corpus dominicum quod perseverant jam contemplans et ad sancta Dei Evangelia per eosdem corporaliter tacta jurarunt praemissa, omnia et singula, sicut posse eorum, inviolabiter observare, et sigilla sua alternatim praesentibus in testimonium apponi fecerunt.

JORNALE THESAURI A I^A^ JANUARII ANNO MCCCCXIIII USQUE AD ULTIMAM JUNII MCCCCXVIIII.[1]

Terminus inceptus j^a^ die Januarii anno mccccxiiii.

. . . . . .

. . . . . .

. . . . . .

Febrarius mccccxiiii.

. . . . . .

. . . . . .

22° Feb: A.D. 1414. 493. Veneris xxij. Dominus Griffin, episcopus de Bangor, et Philippus Haunier, scutifer, ambaxiatores apud regem, per ejus litteras datas iij die Decembris ultimo preteriti, sic signatas: *Par le Roy en son conseil, ou monseigneur le duc de Berry, vous, l'arcevesque de Bourges et autres estiez,* DERIAN, capiendis semel in thesauro, de denariis thesauri, pro supportandis expensis et aliis omnibus per eos passis et sustentis expectando responsum de Rege, c.l., valent iiij^xx.^ l.p., de eodem, xl. l.p., comp. per se et litteram suam datam viiij mensis.

[1] Bibliothèque de Rouen, Vol. III., fol. 211; Bibliotheque de l'Ecole des Chartes XLIX. 420

Translations.

OWEN TO THE KING OF SCOTLAND.

MOST high and mighty and redoubted lord and cousin, I commend me to your most high and royal majesty, humbly as it beseemeth me, with all honour and reverence. Most redoubted lord and right sovereign cousin, please it to you and your most high majesty to know that Brutus, your most noble ancestor and mine, was the first crowned king who dwelt in this realm of England, which of old times was called Great Britain. The which Brutus begat three sons, to wit: Albanact, Locrine, and Camber. From which same Albanact you are descended in direct line. And the issue of the same Camber reigned royally down to Cadwalladar, who was the last crowned king of my people, and from whom I, your simple cousin, am descended in direct line; and after whose decease I and my ancestors and all my said people have been, and are still, under the tyranny and bondage of mine and your mortal foes the Saxons; whereof you, most redoubted lord and right sovereign cousin, have good knowledge. And from this tyranny and bondage the prophecy saith that I shall be delivered by the aid and succour of your royal majesty. But, most redoubted lord and right sovereign cousin, I make grievous plaint to your royal majesty and right sovereign cousinship, that it faileth me much in men at arms. Wherefore, most redoubted lord and right sovereign cousin, I humbly beseech you, kneeling upon my knees, that it may please your royal majesty to send unto me a certain number of men-at-arms who may aid me, and may withstand, with God's help, mine and your foes aforesaid; having regard, most redoubted lord and right sovereign cousin, to the chastisement of this mischief and of all the many past mischiefs which I and my said ancestors of Wales have suffered at the hands of mine and your mortal foes aforesaid. Being well assured most redoubted lord and right sovereign cousin, that it shall be that, all the days of my life, I shall be bounden to do service and pleasure to your said royal majesty and repay you. And in that I cannot send unto you all my businesses in writing, I despatch these present bearers fully informed in all things, to whom may it please you to give faith and credence in what they shall say unto you by word of mouth. From my court. Most redoubted lord and right sovereign cousin, may the Almighty Lord have you in his keeping.

OWEN TO THE LORDS OF IRELAND.

Greeting and fullness of love, most dread lord and right trusty cousin. Be it known to you that a great discord or war hath arisen between us and our and your deadly foes, the Saxons: which war we have manfully waged now for nearly two years past, and which, too, we purport and hope henceforth to wage and to bring to a good and effectual end, by the grace of God our Saviour, and by your help and countenance. But seeing that it is commonly reported by the prophecy that, before we can have the upper hand in this behalf, you and yours, our well-beloved cousins in Ireland, must stretch forth hereto a helping hand; therefore, most dread lord and right trusty cousin, with heart and soul we pray you that of your horsemen and footmen, for the succour of us and of our people who now this long while are oppressed by our said foes and yours, as well as to oppose the treacherous and deceitful will of those same our foes, you do despatch unto us as many as you shall conveniently and honourably be able, saving in all things your honourable estate, as quickly as may seem good to you, bearing in mind our sore need. Delay not to do this by the love we bear you, and as we put our trust in you, although we be unknown to your dread person, seeing that, most dread lord and cousin, so long as we shall be able to wage manfully this war in our borders, as doubtless is clear unto you, you and all the other chieftains of your parts of Ireland will in the mean time have welcome peace and calm repose. And because, my lord cousin, the bearers of these presents shall make things known to you more fully by word of mouth, may it please you to give credence unto them in all things which they shall say unto you on our behalf, and, as it may be your will to confide in full trust unto them whatsoever, dread lord and cousin, we your poor cousin do. Dread lord and cousin, may the Almighty preserve your reverence and lordship in long life and good fortune. Written in North Wales, on the twenty-ninth day of November.

OWEN, LORD OF GLYNDYFRDWY, TO HENRY DON.

GREETING and love. We inform you that we hope to be able, by God's help and yours, to deliver the Welsh race from the captivity of our English enemies, who, for a long time now elapsed, have oppressed us and our ancestors. And you may know from your own perception that, now, their time draws to a close and [as] according to the ordinance of God from the beginning, success turns towards us, no one need doubt a good issue will result, unless it be lost through sloth or strife. And because all the Welsh race is in doubt and dread as to the subjection, which we have heard is within the intention of your enemies aforesaid against them, we command, require and entreat, that you will be sufficiently prepared to come to us with the greatest force possible, to the place, where you hear that we are, burning our enemies, by destroying them during the march, and this, by divine aid, shall take place shortly. And do not forget this, as you would wish to have your freedom and honour in the future. And be not surprised that you have not had warning of the first rising, because from great apprehension and danger, it behoved us to rise without fore-warnings. Farewell and God defend you from evil.

By Owen ap Griffith
Lord of Glyn Dyfrdwy.

To our very dear
and entirely well
beloved Henry Don.

LOUIS, DUKE OF BOURBON, TO HENRY III., KING OF CASTILE AND LEON.

MOST high and most excellent prince and dear sires and cousins, may it please you to know that I have received your letters which you sent me by your ambassadors, who have lately arrived here, from whom I have learnt of the good estate and health of your self, of the most high and puissant princess, my very dear lady and cousin, the Queen of Castile and Léon, your consort, and of my very dear and well-beloved cousin the Infanta, your daughter, of my very dear and very honoured cousin the Duke of Penafil, your brother; of which I am exceedingly glad, I am and shall be for all and the fifth time when I shall be able to hear the like news, &c. And of the state here, if it please you to know, Monseigneur the King, Madam the Queen, Monseigneur the Dauphin, and the other children of my said lord the King are in good health, at the moment of forwarding these letters, and I also, thanks be to God. May it please you to know that my said lord the King and the other lords of his race have heard your said ambassadors upon that question which they were to explain to them from you, that you will be pleased to send to my said lord forty ships all armed and swift. Concerning which purpose and assistance which you give him at present, he is very well content with you, and they are very acceptable, because they come at an opportune occasion, just now, for my said lord the king has ordered my very dear and well-beloved cousin, the Count of March, to proceed shortly to Wales with one thousand lances and five hundred crossbowmen; who will set out shortly to embark in Brittany, and from thence to Wales. I therefore pray you as earnestly as I can, that you persevere in your good purpose, and continue in the good alliances, all the said being continued, without breach by you and your predecessors with my said lord the king and his, and for the good and advancement of his needs, may it please you to send and despatch the said forty ships as quickly and as expeditiously as can be properly done, in such a way that they can arrive in Brittany about the fifteenth day of August next, in order that my said cousin de la Marche, who shall, at that time, be in the said country of Brittany, accompanied as explained, if it is possible to aid him and conduct them with him to the said parts of Wales, where he will find a good entry aided and assisted, in order to attack, harass, and injure the English, our enemies. And in this may you not fail us.

Most high and most excellent prince and very dear sires and cousins, whatever may please you here, that can be done for you, acquaint me with it faithfully, and I shall accomplish it according to my power and the good will and pleasure of God, and may He keep you in his holy care and grant you a good and a long life.

Written at Paris the seventh day of July (1404).

Louis, Duke of Bourbon, Count of Fourez and Seigneur de Beaujeu. *Louis, De Bor.*

Endorsement.—To the most high and most excellent most dear sire and cousin, the King of Castile and Léon.

TERMS OF THE TRIPARTITE TREATY.

In the first place that, the same lords, Owen, the Earl, and Edmund, shall henceforth be mutually joined, confederated, united and bound by a true league and true friendship and a sure and good union. Again that each one of the same lords shall and will pursue and also procure the honour and welfare of the other and shall in good faith, hinder any losses or damage which shall come to the knowledge of one of them, intended to be inflicted on either of them, by anyone whosoever. Each of them, also, shall act and do with one another, each and everything which pertains and ought to be done and suffered by good, true and faithful friends, to good, true and faithful friends, laying aside all deceit and fraud. Again, if at any time, any one of the said lords shall know or learn of any loss or injury intended or plotted against another by anyone whosoever, he shall notify it to the others, as speedily as possible, and shall assist them in that particular, so that each may be able to take such measures as may seem proper, against such malicious purposes. Also they shall be anxious, in good faith, to prevent any damage or injury aforesaid to any of the said lords, and each of the lords will help the other in time of necessity, as far as he can. Again, if according to God's arrangement, by the process of time, it should appear to the said lords, that they are the same persons of whom the Prophet speaks, between whom the government of Greater Britain ought to be divided and shared, then they shall labour, and each one of them shall labour to his utmost, that this more effectually may be brought to effect. Each one of them, also, shall be content with that portion of the aforesaid kingdom, defined as is written below, without further exaction or superiority whatsoever, indeed each of them shall enjoy equal liberty in such portion allotted to him. Again, between the same lords, it is unanimously covenanted and agreed, that the aforesaid Owen and his heirs shall have the whole of Cymru or Wales, within the borders, limits, and boundaries undermentioned, from Loegria, which is commonly called England; namely, from the Severn Sea, as the river Severn leads from the sea, going to the north gate of the city of Worcester, and from that gate directly to the Ash Tree, commonly called in the Cymric or Welsh language Onnen Margion, which grows on the high way leading from Bridgenorth to Kynvar; thence by the highway which is commonly called the old or ancient road, direct to the head or source of the Trent; thence to the head or source of the river, commonly called Mersey, thence, as that river leads to the sea in going down, within the borders, limits, and boundaries beforementioned. And the aforesaid Earl of Northumberland and his heirs shall have the counties written below, namely, Northumberland, Westmoreland, Lancashire, York, Lincoln, Nottingham, Derby, Stafford, Leicester, Northampton, Warwick, and Norfolk. And the lord Edmund shall have the remainder of the whole of England to him and to his successors. Again, should any battle, riot, or discord befall between two of the said lords, may it never be, then the third of the said lords, inviting to himself good and faithful counsel, shall duly correct such discord, riot, or battle, whose approval or sentence the parties quarrelling shall be held bound to obey. Also they shall be faithful to defend the kingdom against all men, saving the oath on the part of the aforesaid Owen, given to the most illustrious Prince, lord Charles, by the Grace of God, King of the French, in the league and covenant made and completed between them.

And that the aforesaid, all and singular, may be well and faithfully observed, the said lords, Owen, the Earl, and Edmund, have sworn, by the holy body of the Lord which they now stedfastly gaze upon, and the Holy Gospels by them now bodily touched, to observe the premises all and singular, inviolably, to their utmost, and have mutually caused their seals to be affixed to these presents.

TREASURER'S JOURNAL, FROM THE FIRST DAY OF JANUARY, 1414, TO THE LAST DAY OF JUNE, 1418.

Term commencing, first day of January, 1414.

. . . . . .

. . . . . .

. . . . . .

February, 1414.

. . . . . .

. . . . . .

493. Friday, xxij. The lord Griffith, Bishop of Bangor, and Philip Hanmer, esquire, ambassadors to the king, by his letters dated the 3rd day of December last past, thus decreed: *By the King in Council, where Monseigneur the Duke of Berry, you, the Archbishop of Bourges, and others, were present,* DERIAN, whereas there is to be taken, once only, from the treasury, of the monies of the treasury, for the discharge of their expenses, and everything else incurred and borne by them, awaiting the King's reply, one hundred livres, value eighty pounds parisian; from the same, forty pounds parisian, as agreed by his authority and his letter dated the ninth of this month.[1]

---

[1] Cf. note page 129.

SIGILLARIA.

I. THE SEAL OF LLYWELYN THE GREAT.

A round seal of about three inches in diameter, when entire. The fragment remaining is about one-third of the seal. (*cf.* Facsimile opp. p. 3).

Obverse, to the right of onlooker. A knight on horseback, in armour, shield seems slung over shoulder, but bears no device. The horse is galloping and has saddle, breast-band, and reins.

Inscription—

✠ Sigillum Leoli[ni principis Norwallie].

The wax is black, and the seal is fastened to the document by thongs under a double fold of the parchment. There is no impression on the reverse.

This seems to be an impression of the same matrix as that attached to a marriage agreement between John Le Scot, a nephew of Ranulf, Earl of Chester,[1] and Elen, Llywelyn's daughter (*circa* 1222), which Llywelyn witnessed (*Bibl Cott.* xxiv. 17).[2] It is No. 5547 in the British Museum Catalogue of Seals, which describes it thus :—

" Seal of Llywelyn ap Iorwerth.

" Obv : to the right. In armour, hauberk, surcoat, " round helmet, broad sword in right hand and scab- " bard at the waist, shield slung by a strap over the " shoulder. Horse galloping with saddle, breast-band, " and reins.

✠ Sig . . . . . . lie.

" Reverse. A small oval counterseal with mark of " handle, 1¼in. by 1in. Impression of an antique oval " intaglio gem. A lion passant to the right under a " tree.

---

[1] John the Scot was himself Earl of Chester from 1232–36, being the last to hold the dignity before it was escheated to the Crown. In 1222 he was Earl of Huntington.

[2] Cf. Owen Catalogue of Welsh Mss. at the British Museum, p. 526.

✠ Sigillum secretum lewlin.

" The wax is creamy white : fine, but very imperfect.
" About $3\frac{1}{4}$ inches when perfect."

II. THE SEALS OF OWEN GLYNDWR.

PRIVY SEAL.

A round seal about two inches in diameter.

Obverse. A quartered shield, on each quarter a lion rampant, surmounted by a crown and supported on the right by a dragon regardant, and on the left by a leopard regardant.

Inscription—

✠ Sig[illum Owenni] principis v[valliae].

This seal is attached to the commission issued by Owen to Griffith Yonge and John Hanmer (*cf.* Facsimile opp. p. 23), and is attached to it by thongs under a double fold of the document. The seal has also been impressed to the personal letter to Charles VI., which is written on paper. In both cases the wax is red.

THE GREAT SEAL.

A round seal about $3\frac{1}{2}$ inches in diameter, and about one-half inch thick. (*cf.* Frontispiece).

Obverse. Owen Glyndwr sitting on a throne under a Gothic canopy, bareheaded, with a sceptre in his right hand. The arms of the throne protrude on both sides, representing half the body of a wolf. The back-ground is a mantle semée of lions rampant, and held up by two angels. At his feet are two lambs.

Inscription—

✠ Owynus [Dei gracia] princeps Walliae.

Reverse, to the right of onlooker. A knight in full armour on horseback on a mount. The helmet has vizor closed, and is surmounted by a dragon crest. In his right hand is a broadsword and pendant from which is the long manche of the under robe. In his left hand a shield quarterly, with four lions rampant. The horse is galloping, and has saddle, bridle, reins, head-piece, and cloth, which last is semée of lions rampant. The horse's head-piece is surmounted by a similar dragon crest. The back-ground is diapered with pippin scrolls.

Inscription—

✠ Owenus dei gracia [princeps] Walliae.

The seal is attached to Owen's ratification of the treaty with Charles VI. of France (J623.96), and to the letter to the same promising obedience to Pope Benedict XIII. (J516.29). It is fastened to both documents by thongs under a double fold of the parchment. The wax of both seals is yellowish, and both are imperfect.

III. THE SEAL OF GRIFFITH YONGE.

A round seal about an inch in diameter.

On a shield within border dancetté a lion rampant.

Inscription—

✠ S. Griffi[ni Yon]ge decretorū doctoris.

The wax is red and the seal is fastened to the Treaty with Charles VI. (J623.96 *bis*) by thongs under a double fold of the parchment. There are three other seals attached to this treaty, this seal is placed in the centre. The two other seals are those of the French commissioners.

Stemma Aliciae, filiae et heredis Owenni Glyndowre.[1]

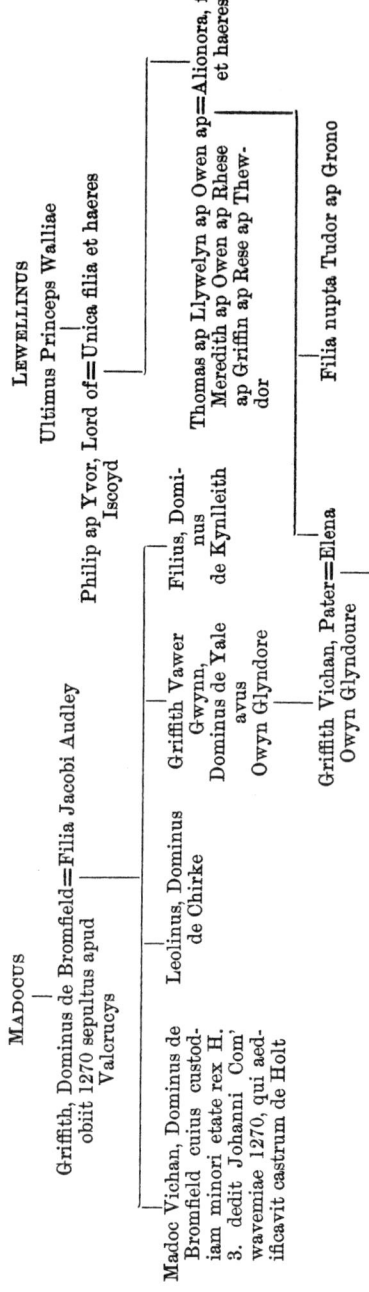

MADOCUS

Griffith, Dominus de Bromfield obiit 1270 sepultus apud Valcrucys = Filia Jacobi Audley

- Madoc Vichan, Dominus de Bromfield cuius custodiam minori etate rex H. 3. dedit Johanni Com' wavemiae 1270, qui aedificavit castrum de Holt
- Leolinus, Dominus de Chirke
- Griffith Vawer Gwynn, Dominus de Yale avus Owyn Glyndore
- Filius, Dominus de Kynlleith

LEWELLINUS
Ultimus Princeps Walliae

Philip ap Yvor, Lord of Iscoyd = Unica filia et haeres

Thomas ap Llywelyn ap Owen ap Meredith ap Owen ap Rhese ap Griffin ap Rese ap Thewdor = Alionora, filia et haeres

- Filia nupta Tudor ap Grono

Griffith Vichan, Pater Owyn Glyndoure = Elena

Owen Glyndoure, proditor Rg. H. 4

Johannes Skudemore, miles duxit Aliciam filiam et haeredem Oweni Glendoure, proditoris Regis H. 4 = Alicia, filia et haeres, nupta Scudamore

---

[1] Harleian, 807, 95

NOTES.

Richard le Carew.—Very little is known of this Bishop of St. Davids. He probably was a Pembrokeshire man, and took his name from the parish of Carew. He is referred to as the son of a clerk in minor orders, and was Canon of St. David's when elected bishop. His consecration (*Stubb's Registrum*) took place at Rome in 1256 at the request of the chapter. The only apparent reason for this course apparently would be a desire to maintain the independence of the see, by disregarding the Archbishop of Canterbury. In 1266 he was one of the arbitrators who drew up the Mise of Kenilworth. He was actively engaged in the work of building and repairing the Cathedral. In 1272 he built a chantry and endowed it out of the tithes of Llanafan Fawr; in 1275 he repaired the shrine of St. Davids. There still exists an interesting arbitration of a dispute between Richard ap John, Vicar of St. Peter's, and the Priory of St. John, Caermarthen, decided by Richard le Carew in 1278. The Vicar of St. Peter's complained that the stipend he received from the priory 'did not suffice to pay for his food and clothing.' The Bishop decided that the Priory of St. John was to pay the Vicar of St. Peter's in perpetuity (it is still paid as a charge on the farm of Wernddu) out of its endowment, ten marks per annum. The Vicar was also to have all the bequests made to him in the parish and the mass pence, but the latter were not to exceed one penny a day. The Priory also was to defray all the expenses connected with the church (Mr. T. E. Brigstocke's *Copy of Arbitration Settlement*). Bishop le Carew died in 1280, and was buried near the altar (Leland, *Collectanea* V. ii. 132). There seems to have been a dispute concerning his will, as on the 12th August, 1282, Archbishop Peckham requested Peter, Bishop of Exeter, to see that the provisions of his will were carried out (*Peckham Letters*).

Griffith Yonge.—The earliest reference to Griffith Yonge, 'Bachelor of the Canon and Civil Law,' which I have found occurs in the *Lateran Regesta*, XXVI. (4 Boniface IX.),[1] when

---

[1] Cf. also Bliss *Papal Registers*, IV., 445.

on the 17th October, 1393, on the petition of Queen Anne, the various dispensations on account of illegitimacy already granted to him were extended. From this dispensation it appears that he was the son of an 'unmarried man and woman.' The bar of illegitimacy was removed, and he was allowed the right to hold benefices, even without cures, and it is mentioned that he holds the canonry of Gertprynge,[1] in Abergwili, and Llanynys, in the diocese of Bangor. On April 1st, 1399 (*Lateran Regesta*, LXIX., f. 80),[2] he is granted the right to hold the highest appointments in the church, the bar of illegitimacy is now entirely removed and is not to be mentioned in future graces. He is given the right to hold with the canonry of Garthbrengy and the rectory of Llanynys, benefices of any number or nature, with or without cure. He is also granted the right to exchange any benefice or appointment of whatever nature as often as it would convenient for him and possible. This extension of former privileges was subsequent to his appointment to the prebend of "Brechrwyth,"[3] and the canonry of Lampeter, in Abergwili (*Lateran Regesta*). There seems to have been some difficulty concerning the preferments in the diocese of St. David's. They were already granted to a John Donne, of the diocese of Exeter. On the 16th December, 1399 (*Regesta* XCV., f. 107),[4] on an appeal, they were confirmed to Yonge. Their value is given as 20 marks, and that of Llanynys as 80 marks. However, on the appeal of John Bremor, canon of Chichester, Griffith Yonge, on August 24th, 1401 (*Lateran Regesta*, XCI., f. 291, 12 Boniface IX.), lost the canonry of Lampeter and the prebend of 'Bogheret,' but as Donne or Doneys was dead, Bremor was granted the preferments, value not exceeding 20 marks, and costs to the extent of 76 florins.

The first indication of the struggle in Wales is given in the *Lateran Regesta*, IX. (f. 221),[5] for on July 24th, 1402, an interesting decision is given on Yonge's petition, He is now referred to as Doctor of the Canon Law. The income of the church of Llanynys had never exceeded 100 marks. This was divided into 'claswriaithe,' which were allotted for the maintenance of twenty-four 'abbatathelaswyr.'[6] One of these portions is named that of 'David the priest,' and was the support of the vicar of the parish. On account of the pestilence and wars, the income of the parish had fallen to

---

[1] Garthbrengy, Breconshire, a Canonry of the old Collegiate Church of Abergwili. [2] Bliss *Papal Registers*, V., 239. [3] Boughrood, Radnorshire, One of the Llanddewi Brevi Prebends. [4] Bliss *Papal Registers*, IV., 445. [5] *Ibid.*, V., 412. [6] Cf. note, p. 130.

80 marks. The result of Yonge's petition was that these portions were consolidated, and it was decided that the perpetual vicariate should be in the appointment of the rector and his successors. On the 7th January, 1403, he was collated to the living of Llanbadarn Fawr (*Lateran Regesta*, CVI.).[1] This living was of the annual value of 300 marks. He was also appealing against the decision granting John Bremor the prebend of 'Brochwyth' and the canonry of Lampeter.

By this time he must have joined Owen, for on December 26th, 1403, he was granted the right to have a portable altar (*Regesta*, CXVIII., f. 185).[2] Probably, also, he was now Archdeacon of Meirionydd. On the 10th May, 1404, he was appointed one of Owen's ambassadors to France to discuss a treaty of alliance with Charles VI. He must have remained in France till about the end of the July of that year. Later in the year, when Richard Yong was translated from the see of Bangor to that of Rochester, Owen had him elected and consecrated, probably, by John Trevor, Bishop of Bangor. On the 10th of January, 1405, he witnessed Owen's pardon to a John ap Howel ap Ieuan Goch at Cefn Llanfair. His movements now are difficult to trace, but in the spring of this year he and John Trevor, Bishop of St. Asaph, were at the court of Scotland, as Owen's envoys. There is a probability that in May, 1408, he was with John Trevor as an envoy at Paris, and also that he visited Pope Benedict XIII., at Avignon. It is again clear that he is the Griffith, Bishop of Bangor, at Paris, who, with Philip Hanmer, were Owen's envoys to Charles VI. in 1415.

On the 27th August, 1414, he again appears in the *Lateran Regesta* (Vol. CLXXXV., f. 25*d*).[3] The reference is short, but to the point. Boniface IX. had appointed Lewis Bifort to the see of Bangor, but Owen had forestalled the Pope, and Lewis was 'despoiled.' 'Griffith Yonge, of the diocese of Litchfield,' a schismatic, being a follower of Peter de Luna, had already been consecrated Bishop of Bangor. The Pope, however, confirmed Lewis's appointment to the see.

We now come to a gap in his career, but on the 1st of March, 1418 (*Regesta*, CCCLIII., f. 87 sqq, 1 Martin V.),[4] Griffith, now Bishop of Ross and Finlay, in Scotland, is sent there as papal nuncio, to receive the submission of the adherents of Pope Benedict XIII, of Avignon. He is also given power to grant a limited number of dispensations for marriages within prohibited degrees, for granting absolution, for appointing

[1] Bliss *Papal Registers*, V., 521. [2] *Ibid.*, 621. [3] *Ibid.* VI., 502.
[4] *Ibid.*, VII., 6.

notaries, to remove illegitimacy, and given a safe conduct for two years. On the 14th of September he is given a grant of money to assist him till he obtains possession of his diocese (*Lateran Regesta*, CCII.).[1] On the 1st of February, 1423 (*Regesta*, CCXXXIII., f. 292),[2] he was appointed Bishop of Hippo. In February, 1424 (*Lateran Regesta*, Vol. CCXLVI., f. 163),[3] he is deprived of his appointment as commendatory prior of Benedictines at Aubigny and Landos. He, and Anne Troussier, a nun of St. George, near Rennes, also oppose Oliver de Brolio, a Benedictine, for the possession of the priories of Locmaria and Quimper, Anne Troussier claiming the gift of the same. Oliver had lost them on account of a certain offence, but having made submission was again allowed to obtain possession.

Probably further search may bring to light further details of the life of this remarkable man, but so far his public career seems closed with the above trial. It is a matter of regret that fuller particulars of one of Owen's most faithful supporters have not reached us.

The Bishops of St. Davids.—Cp. Giraldus Cambrensis' *Itinerarium*, Book II., Chapter i. Owen, however, does not, apparently, quote Gerald.

The descent from Brutus.—Owen probably refers to Geoffrey of Monmouth's *History*, Book II., Chapter i.

'*The Prophecy.*'—It is difficult for us to understand the influence which these 'prophecies' had in the middle ages. Generally Merlin is the 'prophet' referred to, the 'prophecy' referring to Scotland seems to be—

'Voci verisonae Merlini spem prope pone:
Scoti cum Britone sternunt Anglos in agone.
Flumina manabunt de sanguine, quos superabuntur,
Montes planabunt Britones, diadema levabunt.
Insula tunc uti, sic debet nomine Bruti
Cum Scoti vivunt, Angli quasi muti.'

The usual method of attempting an explanation of this strange jargon was to take the animals of the prophecy as representing the crests of the men referred to. A good example of this kind of prophecy is found in Geoffrey of Monmouth's *History*, Book VII., Chapter iii. Sackville's *Mirrour of Magistrates* can also be referred to as representing the animal symbolism of the prophecies of the period. Probably

[1] Bliss *Papal Registers*, VII., 19. [2] *Ibid.*, 288. [3] *Ibid.*, 374.

the comet of 1402 and the political and religious excitement of the time had the effect of increasing the influence of these 'brudwyr' (prophets). For the usual defence of Merlin and these 'prophets,' cf. Giraldus *Descriptio Kambriae*. Bk. I., 16. The prophecies of Merlin were exceedingly popular in Western Europe. French editions appeared in 1428 and 1528; English in 1528, 1533, and 1615 (in Edinburgh): 1641 (with Thomas Heywood's 'interpretation'); 1648 (London); in Italian in 1539 (Venice) and 1608 (Frankfort). There was also a German edition in 1608. In 1768 a 'Gweinidog o Eglwys Loegr' composed an imitation of the Merlin prophecies, which had great vogue, several editions being issued.

We need not, however, consider that Owen was more superstitious than his contemporaries in this respect. His great opponent, Henry IV., seems to have believed the 'prophecy' that he would recover Jerusalem for the Christians. In 1292, even the College of Cardinals succeeded in persuading the hermit, Peter Morrone, to accept the papal chair on the ground that it had been 'prophecied' by Merlin.

Owen Glyndwr.—The following extract from the *Lateran Registers* (Vol. XLV., f. 179*b*—8 Boniface IX.) is interesting as it throws some light on Owen's personal character. It occurs under the heading 'De plenaria remissione.' A plenary remission was again granted to Owen and his wife on 27th of October, 1403 (*Lateran Regesta*, Vol. CVIII., f. 217, 15 Boniface IX.).

'Bonifacio etc., dilecto filio nobili suo Oweno ap Gruffuth domnello, domino de Glyndyvyrdwy et dilecte marita filie nobilimissimum lien, maria verch david donelle sua uxori de sancte Assavensis diocesis salutem etc, procuravit. Data apud Sanctam Petram quarto kalendas Julij, anno ottavo de Benedicto.'

[Boniface etc., to his beloved and noble son, Owen ap Gruffydd, donsel, lord of Glyndyfrydwy and our beloved and most noble daughter, Mary (Margaret), daughter of David, damsel, his wife, of the diocese of St. Asaph, greeting, &c., has granted (plenary remission). Given at St. Peter's, 28th June, 1397.]

The Letter to Henry Don.—There can be but little doubt that this Henry Don was a member of the Kidwelly family of that name, and lived at Croesasgwrn, Llangyndeyrn (Alcwyn Evans Mss.). The letter has been ascribed to a Henry Don of Uckington, Cheshire, seemingly because Edward Lhuyd states, in his copy of the letter, that the original was found among the MSS. of Cefn-y-Garlleg, Denbighshire. The proximity of the two districts seems to be the only reason, for no Henry Don, of Cheshire, appears to have joined Owen, though many of that family fought for Henry Percy in the Battle of Shrewsbury. On the other hand, the circumstantial evidence indicating the Caermarthenshire man is supported by the internal evidence of the letter. Owen was in the Marches of Caermarthenshire early in 1401. That would be the former occasion spoken of in the letter.

Again, when Owen came the second time to the county, Henry Don was his leading supporter. He must have been one of the three leaders of 'Ystrad Tywi,' whom Iolo Goch refers to in the ode concerning the events in the South.[1] He seems to have been entrusted with the siege of Kidwelly, which commenced the 3rd of October, 1403. For it is probable that Owen went North after Percy's defeat at Shrewsbury (21st July, 1403). The leaders around Kidwelly were punished by confiscation of their property, among whom were Griffith ap Walter ap Ievan and William Gwyn ap Rees Lloide; a King's esquire, John Donne, Thomas Dyere of Kermerdyn, and others receiving their lands.[2] It seems impossible at present to trace Henry Don's career further than the 28th September, 1403 (*Rotulus Viagii,* 4 Henry IV.), when John Sely of Llanstephan was given licence "to have and to take away a ship lately seized in the port of Kermerdyn by Henry Don and William Gwyn, traitors." Whether the letter was written to the Caermarthenshire leader or not, it is clear that Owen's captain in that county was of considerable importance in the county, as is clear from the following pedigree:[3]—

Gryffydd Gethin ap Cydwgan—to Meurig, Brenin Dyfed

Gruffydh Dwn=Anne, d. Kydwgan ap Ieuan ap Philip o Rhydodin, Ynghaio

Henry Dwn=Annest, d. Ieuan Lloyd Vychan

Meredydd

Gruffydd	Owain=Catherine, d. & co-h. to Sir John Wogan of Picton, Kt.	Dafydd	Mabli=Gruffydd ap Nicholas of Dynevor	Alison	Gwladys=Gwilym ap Philip ap Syr Elidyr Ddu, of Cwrt-bryn-y-Beirdd

Henry Donne of Picton, Esq.=Margaret, d. to Sir H. Wogan of Wiston

Jane, d. and co-h.=1460, Sir Thomas Phillips of Kilsant, Kt.

[1] Iolo Goch, p. 206. *Corph*—'A welaist wŷr Cydweli?'
Enaid—'Gwiw olau stryd—gwelais Dri
Digon gennyf diegin,
Gweled o'r Tri Gwaladr Trin.'

[2] Patent Rolls, 5 H. 4, 1 Dec., 1403. [3] Lewis Dwnn, and the Pedigree Roll, Y Derwydd, Llandebie.

The Treasurers' Journal.—Derian is almost without a doubt the name of the notary, who drew up the letters patent referred to. The form 'Par le roy,' &c., is the usual form used in letters patent issued from the royal chancellery of France from the fourteenth century. The letters patent would contain the name of the person commanded, and that of the notary who was responsible for the issue of the letters. The object was both to fix any responsibility for any inaccuracy in the letters patent, and to enable the treasury to apportion the emoluments correctly between the several notaries or secretaries in the Chancellor's employ. The 'you' (*vous*), quoted from the letters patent, refers to the Chancellor.

It is difficult to indicate the method employed in counting money. The livre itself had a relative value, and was not the standard coin. It was worth 20 *sous*, and the *sou* worth twelve *deniers*. The real standard was the *denier*, consequently the value of the *sou* and *livre* varied with the *denier*. In France there was a great variety of *deniers*—parisian (*de parisis*), touraine (*tournois*), malgorian (*melgoriens*)—are the most common. The value varying according to the district in which they were used.

Owen Glyndwr's Pedigree.—The pedigree is almost contemporaneous, and seems to have been drawn up for the Scudamore family. It is not strictly in accord with others in the paternal line. Alicia alone of Owen's children is given in this pedigree. It is difficult to account for the others. Gryffydd was alive on the 21st March, 1411 (Nicholas' *Ord. Privy Council*, i. 304), as he and his father's secretary, Owen ap Griffith ap Richard, were ordered to be removed from Nottingham to the Tower on that date. Fordun (*Scotichronicon*, ii. 445) states he was captured at (?) Grosmont. It should be noted that the accounts of the Battles of Mynydd Pwll Melyn and Grosmont are difficult to reconcile. Nothing seems to be known of Madoc. Meredydd was alive in 1416 (cf. p. xxxix), and seems to have been regarded as his father's successor. Thomas and John are also so far unknown. Browne Willis states that some of them fled to Ireland and settled there. Isabel married a certain Adam ab Iorwerth Ddu. Alice is referred to in the pedigree. Janet married Sir John Croft, of Croft Castle. Margaret married Ralph Monnington, of Monnington, Hereford. Another, (?) Jane, married Edmund Mortimer (whence the connection with Hotspur); they had four children—a boy, Lionel, and three daughters. Early in 1409 she, her mother, and her children fell into Henry's hands on the re-capture of Harlech. Edmund Mortimer had died during the siege. Three of the children died shortly after being removed to London (1413 in *Dict. Nat. Biog.*). Gwenllian, another daughter, married Phylip ab Rhys, of Cenarth, Radnorshire (Lewis Glyn Cothi, ii. 400).

'Claswriaithe' and 'abatathelaswyr.' These two terms are reminiscent of a system peculiar to the Celtic church in these islands and also in Brittany. In the early period under the tribal system, the clergy of each church formed a 'college' or community to administer to the spiritual needs of the tribe. They had the 'parish' church and its 'capellae' to serve. The members of these colleges were of the kin of the founders, and succession was hereditary. It should however be pointed out that similar colleges existed, which were non-tribal, as, for instance, the cathedral corporations. Gerald refers to members of the tribal colleges as '*Glaswir*, id est, viri ecclesiastici' (*De Iure Menevensis.* Opera iii., 153). In his *Descriptio Kambrensis* (ii., 6), he states that the 'churches have almost as many parsons and sharers as there are principal men in the parish. The sons, after the decease of their fathers, succeed to the ecclesiastical benefices, not by election, but by hereditary right, possessing and polluting the sanctuary of God. And if a prelate should by chance presume to appoint or institute any other person, the people would certainly revenge the injury upon the institutor and instituted.'

It is therefore clear that the 'claswyr' were the ecclesiastics forming such a college (*clas*, an enclosure or a religious community; c.p. *clasdir*, *clasdy*, (cloister), the '*clas*' place-names, as in the parish of Llangyfelach, and Lat. *clausus*), and their superior would be called 'penclas,' which at a later period gave way to the term 'abat.' Hence 'claswreiddau' would be the designation of their shares or portions of the endowment. 'Abatathelaswyr' is clearly a scribal error for 'abatachelaswyr,' that is *abat a chelaswyr* (c.p. 'celaswyr' for 'claswyr,' with 'periodas' for 'priodas,' &c.). Even before Archbishop Peckham's visitation in 1284, these colleges had been to a large extent abolished, but his visitation must have hastened the process; for the hereditary principle was both out-of-date and obnoxious to the church. Gerald's opinion, already given, indicates its standpoint. The general method was to consolidate the shares (*portiones*) or 'claswriaithe' as they fell vacant. The system is to some extent illustrated in the *Taxatio* of 1291. The 'claswreiddyn' is termed 'porcio.' In the diocese of St. Davids, there are only two 'portiones,' which however may not be tribal (Deanery of Sub-Ayron. *Taxatio*, 272*a*).[1] It would appear that the system had disappeared in the diocese of Llandaff. In that of St. Asaph, there are twelve examples, of which the parish of Bettws Cadwaladr probably retains most of the original conditions (*Taxatio*, 286*b*.).

' Porcio Twyder ap Gwrgenen	£3	0	0
Porcio Lowelyn	£0	6	8
Porcio Eynon presbyteri	£0	6	8
Porcio Ewyn presbyteri	£0	10	0
Porcio Johannis presbyteri	£1	0	0
Porcio Emeystr'	£0	13	4

The introduction of a ' portion ' for a ' vicar ' seems to indicate a transitional stage, as in the case of Corwen (p. 286*b*.) and Llansannan (p. 287*a*.). Llansannan may be given as typical—

' Porcio Jorwerth Apadaf	£6	0	0
Porcio David ap Kenewr	£6	0	0
Vicaria	£4	3	4

The diocese of Bangor has eight, of which Aberdaron, Clynnog Fawr have not entered the transitional stage. ' Castro-Kyby ' (Holyhead) may also be under the Celtic system, especially if ' praepositura ' is given as an equivalent for the Cymric ' penclas.' It should, however, be remembered that the term ' porcio ' is loosely used in the *Taxatio*, and often refers to non-tribal conditions. In the case of Llanynys, it would appear that by 1291 the twenty-four ' claswreiddau ' had already been consolidated into two. For the value of the benefice is given as £10, and that of the ' portion of David the priest ' (*Porcio David, capellani in Ecclesia de Lan Evys*) as £4 6s. 8d. Hence in this case the mandate of Boniface XI. completed the transition from the Celtic to the Roman system.

Llanynys is no longer in the diocese of Bangor, for in 1859, the rural deanery of Dyffryn Clwyd was transferred to that of St. Asaph, in exchange for another.

---

[1] It is possible, however, that the ' ecclesiastic ' *gwele*, of the *Black Book of St. David's*, refers to the older ' claswreiddau.' Cf., *e.g.*, *Black Book of St. David's*, p. 207, under Blaenypennal. If so, the conclusions from the *Taxatio* would have to be modified.

INDEX.

SUBSCRIBERS.

The Right Honble. Lord Aberdare, 83 Eaton Square, London, S.W.
Professor E. Anwyl, M.A., Aberystwyth.
Messrs. Asher & Co., 13 Bedford Street, Covent Garden, W.C.
Messrs. E. G. Allen & Co., Ltd., 14 Grape Street, Shaftesbury Avenue, London, W.C.

J. W. Willis Bund, Esq., Shire Hall, Worcester.
Henry Blackwell, Esq., University Place, New York.
Dr. H. C. Bevan, Blaina, Mon. (per Mr. W. Larkin, Bookseller, Blaina.)

The Right Hon. Earl Cawdor, Stackpole Court, Pembroke.
Carmarthenshire Antiquarian Society (per Rev. George Eyre Evans, Ty Tringad, Aberystwyth).
COUNTY SCHOOLS—Headmaster, Lewis' School, Pengam (R. W. Jones, Esq., B.A.).

R. Gerald Davies, Esq., Iscoed, Landebie.
M. Pol Diverres (Tangwall), 144 Boulevarde Montparnasse, Paris.
Timothy Davies, Esq., M.P., J.P., 34 Onslow Gardens, London, S.W.
Chas. Morgan Davies, Esq., Architect, Merthyr Tydfil.
J. H. Davies, Esq., M.A., 20 North Parade, Aberystwyth.
H. R. Davies, Esq., J.P., Treborth, Bangor, North Wales.
Rev. Lloyd Davies, 47 Harold Street, Ammanford.

Rev. George Eyre Evans, Ty Tringad, Aberystwyth.
Evan Evans, Esq., Chemist, Ammanford.
Pepyat W. Evans, Esq., M.A., B.C.L., 6 King's Bench Walk, Temple, London, E.C.
Sir E. Vincent Evans, Esq., 64 Chancery Lane, London.
Isaac Evans, Esq., Builder, Treflys, Menai Bridge.
J. Gwenogvryn Evans, Esq., Litt.D., Tremvan, Llanbedrog, Pwllheli.

T. J. Evans, Esq., 13 Canonbury Park South, London, N.
J. Rosser Evans, Esq., Beethoven House, Resolven, Neath.

W. A. Foster, Esq., Glyn Menai, Bangor, North Wales.
Rev. J. Fisher, B.D., Cefn Rectory, St. Asaph.
Messrs. Hodges, Figgis, & Co., Ltd., 104 Grafton Street, Dublin.

A. Stepney Gulston, Esq., J.P., Y Derwydd, Llandebie (2 copies).
The Right Hon. D. Lloyd George, M.P., 11 Downing Street, Whitehall, London, S.W.
Rev. W. J. Gravell, St. Michael's College, Llandaff.
Miss F. W. Griffith, Tan-y-Bryn, Ffairfach, Llandilo.
Rev. Peter Hughes-Griffiths, Brynmorfa, Cross Hands, Llanelly

Sir Ifor Herbert, Bart., M.P., Llanarth Court, Raglan, Mon.
The Very Rev. Paul Hook, Ph.D., St. Mary's College, Holywell, North Wales.
The Hon. Augusta Herbert of Llanover, Llanover, Abergavenny, Mon.
Gabriel Hughes, Esq., 28 Vale Road, Rhyl.

E. D. Jones, Esq., J.P., 6 Addison Road, Kensington, London.
E. J. Jones, Esq., C.E., Fforest Legionis, Pont Neath Vaughan, Neath.
Lieut.-Gen. Sir James Hills-Johnes, V.C., G.C.B., Dolaucothy, Llanwrda, South Wales.
Sir D. Brynmor Jones, L.C.B., K.C., M.P., 27 Bryanstone Square, London, W.
C. H. James, Esq., J.P., 64 Park Place, Cardiff.
Major-Gen. R. Owen Jones, C.B., Bryn Tegid, Y Bala, North Wales.
Capt. John Jones, Gwernant, Llandebie.
J. Pritchard Jones, Esq., J.P., D.L., 76 Canfield Gardens, Hampstead, London.
Edward J. John, Esq., J.P., Llanidan Hall, Llanfair P.G.
Jenkin Jones, Esq., Council Schools, Brynamman.
Frank T. James, Esq., Penydarren House, Merthyr Tydfil.
Thomas Jones, Esq., M.A., Clunmore, Abergavenny.
J. Owen Jones, Esq., F.R. Met. Soc., F.I.S.E., Trigfa, Bigglesworth.
H. E. H. James, Esq., Springfield, Haverfordwest.
D. Jones, Esq., Lloyds Bank, Llandilo.
Ald. David Jones, J.P., Trosnant Lodge, Pontypool.
W. Garmon Jones, Esq., M.A., Elm House, Ashville Road, Birkenhead.

H. Meuric Lloyd, Esq., J.P., M.A. (Oxon), Delfryn, Llanwrda, Carmarthenshire.
Sir W. T. Lewis, Bart., The Mardy, Aberdare.
D. Rees Lewis, Esq., Plas Penydarren, Merthyr Tydfil.
Rev. H. Elvet Lewis, M.A., Bruse House, 37 Highbury Park, London, N.
Edward O. Vaughan Lewis, Esq., Rhaggat, Corwen, North Wales.
Rev. T. G. Lewis, Baptist College, Bangor.
Robert Lewis, Esq., 62 Green Street, Grosvenor Square, London.
Professor J. E. Lloyd, M.A., Gwaendeg, Bangor.
Sir John Llewelyn, Bart., Penllergaer, Swansea.
Gwilym Llewellyn, Esq., Gwernaffield, Near Mold.

LIBRARIES.

The National Library of Wales; per J. Ballinger, Esq., M.A., Librarian.
Cardiff Free Libraries; per the Librarian.
The Bodleian Library, Oxford; per the Librarian.
The University Library, Cambridge; per F. Jenkinson, Esq., Librarian.
British Museum, London; per M. Mayhew, Esq.
The Reference Library, Manchester; per C. W. Sutton, Esq., M.A.
The John Rylands Library, Manchester; per H. Guppy, Esq.
St. David's College, Lampeter; per the Librarian.
Newport (Mon.) Free Fibrary; per H. J. C. Brook, Esq Secretary.
Llanelly Public Library, per J. Boulton, Esq., Librarian.
The Meyrick Library, Jesus College, Oxford; per Ernest E. Genner, Esq., M.A.
University College, Cardiff; per the Registrar.
Trinity College Library, Dublin; per Alfred de Burgh, Esq.
The Swansea Free Library.
University College, Bangor; per Rev. J. Shankland.
The Resolven Reading Room; per W. T. Smith, Esq., 17 Railway Terrace.

Colonel Morris, Brynffin, Bettws, Ammanford.
D. Matthews, Esq., Rhymney.
Lieut.-Col. W. Llewellyn Morgan, Brynbriallu, Swansea.
Mrs. Mayhew, Aberglasney, Golden Grove.
Edward P. Martin, Esq., The Hill, Abergavenny.

John Morris, Esq., J.P., Lletty'r Eos, Llansannan, Near Abergele.
J. Miles, Esq., (*Y Tarianydd*), Highland Place, Aberdare.
Col. C. S. Mainwaring, Bwlch y Beudy, Cerrigydruidion, North Wales.
R. Matthews, Esq., Eryl, Llandebie.

The Hon. Mrs. Bulkeley Owen, Tedsmore, Oswestry.
Edward Owen, Esq., Secretary Royal Commission on Ancient Monuments in Wales and Monmouthsihre, 36 George Street, Westminster, W.
Henry Owen, Esq., M.A., D.C.L., F.S.A., Poyston, Haverfordwest.
Dr. Trafford Owen, St. Alban's Place, Blackburn.
O. Elian Owen, Esq., 16 Argyle Road, Anfield, Liverpool.

D. C. Parry, Esq., Llanelly.
Dafydd W. Prosser, Esq., Craig-y-Don, Neath Abbey.
A. Ivor Parry, Esq., 34 Penlan Street, Pwllheli.
L. J. Prichard, Esq., Menai Lodge, Chiswick, W.
Mrs. J. W. Prichard, The Priory, Cardigan.

D. M. Richards, Esq., F.J.I., (*Myfyr Dar*), Wenallt, Aberdare.
Miss E. J. Ross, M.A., County School, Llandilo.
L. J. Roberts, Esq., M.A., H.M.I., Tegfan, Rhyl.
The Hon. Lady Reade, Carreglwyd, The Valley, N. Wales.
Miss M. D. Roberts, B.A., Ynys, Abererch.
Llywarch Reynolds, Esq., B.A., Old Church Place, Merthyr Tydfil.
W. Rees, Esq., Post Office, Llandebie.
Evan J. Rees, Esq., 404 Goodwin Institute, Memphis Town, U.S.A.

Principal David Salmon, The Training College, Swansea.
D. Samuel, Esq., County School, Aberystwyth.
Miss Stepney, The Dell, Llanelly.

Geo. G. T. Treherne, Esq., M.A. (Oxon), 7 Bloomsbury Square, London, W.C.
Henry Thomas, Esq., London House, Llandebie.
Rev. J. Ll. Thomas, M.A., F.R.G.S., Vicar of Aberpergwm, Pont Neath Vaughan, Neath.
Miss F. A. Thomas, Gwynfan, Alan Road, Llandilo.
T. H. Thomas, Esq., A.R.C.A., 45 The Walk, Cardiff.
The Right Hon. Lord Tredegar, Tredegar Park, Newport, Mon.

D. A. Thomas, Esq., M.A., M.P., Llanwern, Mon.
Dewi Thomas, Esq., Secretary's Office, L.N.W.Ry., Euston Station, London, N.W.
Miss Talbot, Penrice Castle, Reynoldstone, S.O., Glam.
D. Lleufer Thomas, Esq., M.A., Stipendiary Magistrate, Pontypridd.
The Ven. Archdeacon Thomas, M.A., F.S.A., Llandrinio Rectory, Llanymynech.
D. E. Thomas, Esq., M.D., Llys-y-Graig, Ystrad Rhondda.
Abraham Thomas, Esq., J.P., Llansamlet, Glam.
Edward Thomas, Esq., (*Cochfarf*), 3 Windsor Place, Cardiff.
G. Caradoc Thomas, Esq., 88 Mosley Street, Manchester.
Llew Tegid, 239 High Street, Bangor.
Messrs. Kegan Paul, Trench, Trubner, & Co. Ltd., Dryden House, 43 Gerrard Street, London.
Rev. Jeffrey Thomas, 11 Pentwyn Road, Bettws.

M. Josiah Williams, Esq., Gelly, Llandebie.
R. E. Williams, Esq., Llanllawddog Council School, Carm.
Y Fonesig Mallt L. Williams, Gwyniondâl Dŷ, Llanarthne.
Sir John Williams, Bart., Plâs, Llanstephan, Carm.
Aneurin Williams, Esq., Menai View, Carnarvon.
Rev. Robert Williams, M.A., The Vicarage, Llandilo.
W. Llewellyn Williams, Esq., M.P., 135 Church Street, Chelsea, London.
T. M. J. Watkin, Esq. (' Portcullis '), M.A., F.S.A., H.M. College of Arms, London, E.C.
W. J. Williams, Esq., B.A., B.C.L., 42 Rutland Park Mansions, Willesden Green, London, S.W.
Dr. Horatio E. Walker, Corwen, North Wales.
D. Williams, Esq., M.A., Maesycwarre, Bettws, Ammanford.

Carmarthen: Printed by W. Spurrell & Son.